Science and the Stanislavsky Tradition of Acting

Science and the Stanislavsky Tradition of Acting offers new insight into the well-known tradition of Russian actor training. Rooted in practice, this is the first book to contextualise the Stanislavsky tradition with reference to parallel developments in science. It presents an alternative perspective based on philosophy, physics, Romantic science, psychology and theories of industrial management.

Working from practical sources, historical texts and unpublished archive materials, Jonathan Pitches traces an evolutionary journey of actor training from the roots of the Russian tradition, Konstantin Stanislavsky, to the contemporary Muscovite director Anatoly Vasiliev. The book explores two key developments that emerge from Stanislavsky's System, one linear, rational and empirical, while the other is fluid, organic and intuitive. The otherwise highly contrasting acting theories of Vsevolod Meyerhold (biomechanics) and Lee Strasberg (the Method) are dealt with under the banner of the rational or Newtonian paradigm; Michael Chekhov's acting technique and the little-known ideas of Anatoly Vasiliev form the centrepiece of the other Romantic, organic strain of practice.

Science and the Stanislavsky Tradition of Acting opens up the theatre laboratories of five major practitioners in the twentieth and twenty-first centuries and scrutinises their acting methodologies from a scientific perspective.

Jonathan Pitches is Principal Lecturer in Contemporary Arts at Manchester Metropolitan University, and the author of *Vsevolod Meyerhold* (Routledge, 2003).

Routledge advances in theatre and performance studies

Science and the Stanislavsky Tradition of Acting

Jonathan Pitches

Routledge
Taylor & Francis Group

LONDON AND NEW YORK

First published 2006
by Routledge
2 Park Square, Milton Park, Abingdon, Oxon OX14 4RN

Simultaneously published in the USA and Canada
by Routledge
270 Madison Ave, New York, NY 10016

Routledge is an imprint of the Taylor & Francis Group

Transferred to Digital Printing 2009

Typeset in Garamond by Wearset Ltd, Boldon, Tyne and Wear

British Library Cataloguing in Publication Data
A catalogue record for this book is available from the British Library

Library of Congress Cataloging in Publication Data
A catalog record for this book has been requested

ISBN10: 0–415–32907–8 (hbk)
ISBN10: 0–415–54403–3 (pbk)

ISBN13: 978–0–415–32907–1 (hbk)
ISBN13: 978–0–415–54403–0 (pbk)

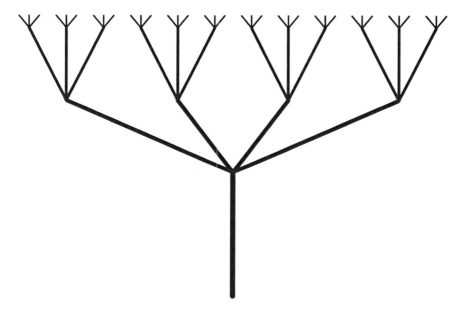

Frontispiece Systems Tree representing various levels of complexity (source: adapted from Capra 1983: 304).

I don't think I have invented anything in particular, in spite of the fact that the whole theory is a novelty. It is obvious that the top of the tree has changed but that its roots are still the same: of course my vain wish would be to change the roots, too. However, since I admire roots, and the roots of trees in particular, the new roots could only be an offshoot of the old.

(Anatoly Vasiliev 1992: 48)

Contents

Illustrations

Acknowledgements

First and foremost I am deeply indebted to Anthony Frost, whose critical insight and exceptional eye for detail as my PhD supervisor for seven years has made the task of rewriting this material as a book as painless as it could be. I am also grateful to George Savona and to University College Northampton for financial support to study and, specifically, for funding my first research trip to Russia in 1994. The Department of Contemporary Arts at Manchester Metropolitan University has also provided me with valuable time to transform my original PhD work and I am particularly grateful to Professor Robin Nelson for his enthusiasm and measured criticism at a late stage in this book's development. In addition, I would like to thank my colleagues at UCN, specifically Franc Chamberlain, Anthony Shrubsall and Bob Godfrey, for collaborating with me on a range of associated practical projects and for offering commentary and specialist insight on aspects of this work. Thanks must also go to Talia Rodgers, Joe Whiting and Terry Clague at Routledge, to the International Workshop Festival and Dick McCaw, to Martin Dewhirst, Rebecca Edgington and Annelis Kuhlmann, to Monika Koch and Richard Durham, to Angie St John Palmer and the Dartington Hall Trust Archive for permission to reproduce items from their Michael Chekhov holdings, to Robert Leach, Andrei Kirillov and to Gareth Edwards.

A huge debt of gratitude is owed to the practitioners with whom I have worked and who constitute a very significant part of this study: Sergei Desnitsky, Mark Rozofsky, Alexei Levinsky, Gennady Bogdanov, David Zinder and Anatoly Vasiliev.

Finally I would like to thank my wife, Ceri, and my children, Harri and George.

Introduction

Science and Stanislavsky – the evolution of a tradition

Stanislavsky on science

If you were to take Stanislavsky at his word, any search for a scientific root to the tradition of acting associated with his name would seem futile. His preface to *An Actor's Work on Himself* (1938) is unequivocal: 'Do not look for any scholarly or scientific derivations. We in the theatre have our own lexicon, our actors' jargon which has been wrought out of life' (Stanislavsky 1958: 35). In this revised version of his seminal text, published two years after the New York edition, *An Actor Prepares* (1936), Stanislavsky is eager to distance himself from any accusation of theoretical abstraction. Instead, he values a colloquial performance language based on experience and practice. True, the development of a 'jargon' for actors – that is a specialised terminology understood only by those who are part of a specific community – has its associations with scientific practice, especially if that terminology is derived from the practical study of life. But in principle it would seem that science and art are mutually incompatible in Stanislavsky's eyes.

Yet fourteen years earlier, in his autobiography, *My Life in Art* (1924), Stanislavsky had articulated a very different attitude to science. Recalling the period of work he undertook with Leopold Sulerzhitsky at the First Studio, he notes:

> We needed a new beginning. We needed new bases and foundations justified by knowledge and the laws of nature ... It will be asked: 'Can there exist a system for the creative process? Has it really got laws that have been established for all time?' In certain parts of the system, like the physiological and psychological, laws exist for all, forever, and in all creative processes. They are indubitable, completely conscious, tried by science and found true.
>
> (Stanislavsky 1980b: 483)

Rather than being opposed to any scientific connection with his System, here Stanislavsky appeals to science to validate his ideas. Both sides of his 'psycho-physical' acting theory (the internal, psychological side and the external, physiological side) are best expressed in universal 'laws', he argues. Nature (and specifically what Stanislavsky sees as the *natural* process of acting) is, in effect, legitimised by its associations with science.

Traditionally, this discrepancy is explained in one of two ways. Either he simply changed his mind, as we know Stanislavsky did throughout his career – fourteen years is, after all, a long time. Or, he wilfully shifted tack to suit his particular position at different points. As Sharon Carnicke puts it in *Stanislavsky in Focus*: 'Like any artist, Stanislavsky incorporates science only when it inspires his imagination' (1998: 87).

Carnicke cites Stanislavsky's own reluctance to meet with Soviet scientists late in his career and his professed ignorance of philosophy and psychology as further evidence for discounting any meaningful connection between his acting System and science.

But whilst there is clearly a case for seeing Stanislavsky as a pragmatist, adopting a positive attitude to science when it suited him and claiming ignorance when it didn't, there is still a need to pursue what lies beneath his selective appropriation of an interdisciplinary language. And, in particular, to question what his practice may have gained from his incessant pursuit of the natural 'laws' of acting.

For although there are inconsistencies in his own theoretical articulation of science, a careful analysis of Stanislavsky's *practice* reveals a startling continuity of ideas, a deep and consistent relationship between science and the System. What's more, when one turns to the practitioners who followed Stanislavsky, those figures who now delineate the Russian tradition of acting – Vsevolod Meyerhold, Richard Boleslavsky, Michael Chekhov and, later, Anatoly Vasiliev – this often unspoken relationship is maintained. Even in the United States, where Stanislavsky's ideas were transformed in very different cultural conditions, a scientific subtext to the work is detectable. From Lee Strasberg to Sanford Meisner, the otherwise sharply divergent interpretations of Stanislavskian practice in America can also be explored through the prism of science.

In the spirit of the early Stanislavskian 'table work', the aim of this book is to analyse this unspoken connection, to unpick the scientific subtext of the Russian tradition of acting, tracing a development from the 'root' of Stanislavsky (the System of systems,[1] if you will) to one of the more distant branches – Vasiliev's 'ludo' theatre.

The evolution of a tradition

Each one of the practitioners encountered in this book has a distinct and identifiable line back to Stanislavsky – their genetic inheritance, one might say, is clear. But each one of them has also sought to defy their theatrical genes and develop an alternative system of acting. Meyerhold focused more exclusively on physical form, Chekhov rejected emotion memory in favour of a responsive (and well-trained) imagination, Richard Boleslavsky exported

Stanislavsky's ideas to America and inflected the System accordingly, inspiring both Lee Strasberg and Sanford Meisner to take the ideas yet further away from their original source. And Vasiliev, working almost a hundred years after Stanislavsky's first formulations, has spent much of his career consciously 'reconstructing' the work of his mentor.

The story of the development of this tradition is, then, one of tension: between the linear evolution of an acting tradition and the contemporary forces that conspire to influence and affect that linearity. The former is identifiable thanks to one key characteristic of the Russian school: the master–pupil relationship. Since the early 1900s and Stanislavsky's first experiments with the System, the deep-seated connection between director and actor, teacher and student in Russia is striking. It is a connection that will be thoroughly exploited in the following pages. The latter, for the purposes of this book, will be confined to three areas: the political, the theatrical and the scientific.

Two strains of the System

For Stanislavsky and for Meyerhold, these three areas were enmeshed in the complex climate surrounding the Revolution. The orthodoxy imposed upon Stanislavsky's acting System, both near to and after his death, paralleled the orthodoxy imposed upon the scientific institutions by the then leader of the Soviet Union, Joseph Stalin. Both director and dictator will be shown here to construct a 'System for the World', pursuing their own versions of what science often calls a Grand Unifying Theory.

Meyerhold's response was much more calculated and aware than Stanislavsky's. He tapped directly into the scientific and industrial ideas of the time, transforming his actors into models of organisation and efficiency, the watchwords of the early Bolshevik era. But in the quicksand of post-revolutionary politics what was hot currency soon cooled in the eyes of Stalin's censors and Meyerhold's contemporaneity ultimately cost him his life.

Both practitioners in different ways exemplify one strain of the System's development, a strain identified here as fundamentally Newtonian, although it was equally responsive to the contemporary influences of Frederick Winslow Taylor, Alexei Gastev and Ivan Pavlov.

For Boleslavsky, his theatrical aspirations were most obviously caught up in the contrasting political landscape of 1920s America. Yet our understanding of his own theory of acting, documented before Stanislavsky's in *Acting: the First Six Lessons* (1933), is significantly enriched by attending to the key psychological conflict of the time: psychoanalysis versus behaviourism. The same is true of the second generation of Russian-inspired actor trainers in the US. Strasberg's psychoanalytical interpretation of Stanislavsky, drawing as it did on Boleslavsky's more measured balance of Ribot and Freud, may also be seen to reflect a strain of Newtonianism.

He, too, believed he was 'completing a project' and with his particular emphasis on emotion memory described a linear path back to the actor's emotional core that owes much to the model of the world propounded by Newton in the *Principia* (1687).

Whilst in other ways Stella Adler and Sanford Meisner's acting methods are in opposition to Strasberg's, they too may be grouped into this subset of the Stanislavsky tradition for their action-based, behaviourist approach can ultimately be traced back to a view of the world which is objectively measurable and material.

Michael Chekhov's legacy, his 'Technique of Acting', on the surface of things owes nothing to science. Driven from Russia in 1927, in part for his commitment to Rudolf Steiner's spiritualism, Chekhov sought a safer political environment in Europe to develop his ideas. He thought he had found it when he was enlisted by the Elmhirsts of Dartington to teach a three-year acting course on their estate but he was very soon moved on again, plagued once again by the spectre of conflict. His time at Dartington, however, was crucial in developing an alternative response to the Newtonian strain identified above – not Classical this time but Romantic, not mechanistic but organic, not Newtonian, in fact, but Goethean.

Anatoly Vasiliev's work will be discussed in the same terms. The only actual scientist amongst all the practitioners, Vasiliev, a trained chemist, has nevertheless distanced himself from his background and pursued a spiritual reformulation of Stanislavsky's System. His personal 'reconstruction' of Stanislavsky is to be viewed in the post-*perestroika* context of contemporary Russia but his debt to Plato as a philosophical base is a key factor in locating his particular laboratory work in an alternative paradigm to that of Meyerhold or Boleslavsky.

Thus, Stanislavsky's System, fluid and constantly evolving as it is, separates into two distinct paths – the material, Newtonian path and the Romantic path, associated here with Goethean science. This pattern is reflected in the structure of the book. Part I (and Chapter 1) focuses on the root of this scientific view of the Russian tradition, Stanislavsky himself, putting the case for a Newtonian view of his system whilst recognising that the tensions inherent in his own practice are in part responsible for the bifurcation which followed. Part II follows the Newtonian strain of development in Meyerhold's work (Chapter 2) and in the practice of Boleslavsky and Strasberg (Chapter 3). Part III looks at the counter-paradigm of Romantic science, focusing specifically on Michael Chekhov's anti-materialistic technique and Vasiliev's spiritual retreat into Dostoyevsky.

Focus

Where, then, does one find the definitive Stanislavsky? In a career spanning sixty years, from the formation of the Alexeyev Circle in 1877 to his death in 1938, several 'versions' of Stanislavsky are represented. Which one is the

most reliable? This question is further problematised by the range of published material written by practising ex-students, some of whom claim
independence from the System, others who are continuing to revise and
extend the work of the Russian director. Stanislavsky jealously obstructed
any dissemination of his System until very late in the day, a situation that
inevitably led to unauthorised leaks of the System and to a word-of-mouth
transmission of ideas.[2] The result of this resistance to make public his findings has been to divide his theory from his practice. As oral transmission
constituted the only method of studying the System in the 1920s and early
1930s, so the best forum for this communication was the practical workshop. Any analysis of Stanislavsky's work and of the tradition which followed needs to be sensitive to these different sources.

Where possible, the focus here will be on workshop-based material,
drawing on practical research undertaken in the theatre laboratories of
Stanislavsky teachers (Sergei Desnitsky and Mark Rozofsky), biomechanics
masters (Alexei Levinsky and Gennady Bogdanov), interpreters of the
Chekhov technique (David Zinder) and, finally, with the contemporary
'reconstructor' of the System, Anatoly Vasiliev.

But the theoretical writings of Stanislavsky and his disciples will offer an
important counterpoint to this examination of practice. All of the practitioners within the tradition have at some time theorised their practice, in
different formats and with different intentions and this book will bring
together these critical statements – some of them from unpublished sources
– to redress this division of theory from practice. Crucial to both sides of the
debate is the identification of 'when'. *When* was this particular inflection of
the system emerging? When was it being picked up, transformed or re-
appropriated by others?

For Stanislavsky, the principal centres of attention are the early and late
periods of the System: the early period (*c.*1909–1912) in order to pinpoint
the birth of an emotion-based, psychological pattern of thinking and to plot
its migration over the Atlantic to America; the late period (*c.*1935–1938) to
outline the impact of Stalin's governmental pressure on the System and to
facilitate a reading of Stanislavsky which illustrates his enduring commitment to causal thinking.

For Meyerhold's equally diverse career, the concern here relates to the
work he undertook immediately after the Revolution (1917–1922). At no
other time is the crossover between industry, Objective Psychology and the
theatre more tangible in Meyerhold's theatre practice than at this moment
in history, a moment which was the key catalyst in the development of his
system of biomechanics – the main practical focus for this chapter.

The book then shifts its attention to America, and to the sub-school of
Stanislavskian practice, which, for my purposes, I have divided into first-
generation (1920s–1930s) and second-generation (1950s onwards) practitioners. Concentrating on the former, via Boleslavsky, allows an analysis of
the beginnings of a particularly American reading of the System; the latter

enables an interrogation of the System's transformation in the hands of 'native' theatre directors (Strasberg, Adler, Meisner). Order is maintained by the dual focus of introspective and objective psychologies and their impact on the work of Strasberg and Meisner respectively.

Michael Chekhov's work is looked at through the lens of the Dartington Estate, in Devon (in the period 1935–1938). Dartington was the bolt-hole that saved Chekhov from the materialist pressures of the Soviet Union. It provided a sanctuary for the first assimilation of his teachings and continues to provide that function today. Its remarkable archive, full of the first fruits of his technique, was collated as a source for researchers by Deirdre Hurst du Prey in the late 1930s, a resource which when plundered reveals many insights into Chekhov's relationship with Romantic science.

Finally, the book concludes with a look at the post-*perestroika* output of Anatoly Vasiliev (specifically from 1991), a practitioner who is both resistant to and a follower of the tradition as outlined. Vasiliev's career began under Brezhnev, and has developed into a mysterious fusion of chemistry and metaphysics under Yeltsin and, finally, Putin. Emerging from the same Romantic sub-tradition as Michael Chekhov, his laboratory work, after Gorbachev's demise, will be of specific interest.

The paradigm in practice

Thomas Kuhn's compelling discussion of the paradigm, in *The Structure of Scientific Revolutions* (1970), has in recent years become a central reference point for theatre critics as well as for philosophers of science.[3] Kuhn's synchronic approach is detailed in his introduction: 'Rather than seeking the permanent contributions of an older science to our present vantage, [modern historians] attempt to display the historical integrity of that science in its own time' (1970: 3). Joseph Roach offers a convincing example of this paradigmatic cross-fertilisation of contemporaneous ideas in *The Player's Passion* when he cites William Harvey's 'radically revised explanation of the action of the heart' (Roach 1993: 61). Inspired by the very latest in pump technology at the time (as exploited by the miners and fire fighters of the day), Harvey was encouraged to see the workings of the heart in a new light and thus established the modern conception of blood circulation. To generalise from this specific example, the thesis of *The Structure of Scientific Revolutions* argues for a view of science that highlights formative moments of discovery stimulated by fortuitous collisions of ideas.

Kuhn's approach is not without its problems. At his own admission his use of the term 'paradigm' is ambiguous and has left itself open both to accidental and wilful misconception. Writing twenty-three years after the second edition of *Structure*, in a foreword to a critical synthesis of his work, Kuhn acknowledges the need for 'a considerable narrowing of focus' around the terms used in his book. The paradigmatic group is re-defined by Kuhn as: 'Language- or discourse-communities, sets of individuals bound together by the shared vocabulary which simultaneously makes professional communication possible and restricts that communication to the profession' (in Hoyningen-Huene 1993: xii). Language, then, is a crucial aspect in the formulation of groups, acting at one and the same time to facilitate communication within the group and as a vehicle for defining the boundaries of that group. Stanislavsky was appealing to the same logic in the preface to *An Actor's Work on Himself*, defining the community of System actors by their 'actors' jargon'. The difference is that Kuhn's definition allows for escalating specialisation, for ever-expanding coteries of like-talking scientists. Stanislavsky, by contrast, increasingly saw his performance language as a universal 'grammar of acting' and thus the 'specific' community addressed by his System constituted the entire acting profession, a point to which I will return in Chapter 1.

This book will follow Kuhn's lead in terms of identifying the concurrent points of contact between disciplines. It will, in common with other studies, extend Kuhn's umbrella of influence to include the interplay not just between the sciences but also between the sciences and the theatre, identifying specific moments of cross-fertilisation as evidence for this interplay. (The use of specific performance languages will play an important part in this analysis.)

But my aim is different from those who have sought to transform Kuhn's paradigm into another theoretical model.[4] I am not in this book trying to create more hybrid terms such as 'Quantum Theatre' or 'Chaotic Performance'. Instead, I am seeking to locate, with accuracy and definition, the measurable moments of paradigmatic exchange in the *practice* of Stanislavsky and his pupils. Where previously there has been an emphasis on the term 'paradigm' at a metaphorical level, allowing for wide-reaching connections between science and theatre, here I will interrogate the practical evidence for a scientific view of the Stanislavsky tradition of acting.

Part I

The roots of the tradition

1 A System for the world?

Newtonianism in Stanislavsky's science of acting

As if to stress his wavering attitude towards science, Stanislavsky concludes the second part of an *Actor's Work on Himself* (in English, *Building a Character*) by taking a different stance from the one he had adopted in the preface. Searching for a definition of what he calls 'the majesty of the searchings of science', he makes the following assertion: 'To me it is the urge to attain, with the help of a sensitive heart, the unattained. And it will be attained in time' (1979: 297). He goes on to define his own role in this process:

> In the expectation of these new triumphs of science I have felt there was nothing for me to do except to devote my labours and energy almost exclusively to the study of Creative Nature – not to learn to create in her stead, but to seek oblique, roundabout ways to approach her, not to study inspiration as such but only to find some paths leading to it. I have discovered only a few of them, I know that there are a great many more and that they will eventually be discovered by others. Nevertheless I have acquired a sum of experience in the course of long years of work and this is what I have sought to share with you.
>
> (Ibid.)

Here, in the chapter 'Some Conclusions on Acting', Stanislavsky casts himself in the role of scientist, planting in the mind of his reader a set of persuasive relationships between his System and the discipline of science. In doing so he is mining the conventional associations of science – rigour, clarity, objectivity, experimentation – and allying them with his own project.

He parallels the pursuit of science – 'the urge to attain . . . the unattained' – with his own quest: the search for 'roundabout ways' to the source of inspiration. He characterises his own practice in populist scientific terms, as a 'study of Creative Nature' and he himself as a 'discoverer', passing on the results of his 'deep study' to the next generation of experimenters. Above all, he allies the 'majesty' of the scientific method – the ability of science to proceed from premises without direct knowledge of the object in question – with his own approach. He may be focusing on other areas of enquiry, on 'genius, talent [and] the unconscious' (1979: 297), but he is nonetheless engaged in the same overarching search for truth.

In effect, Stanislavsky is revisiting the project he had begun at the Moscow Art Theatre three decades earlier. In a letter to the St Petersburg Imperial Theatre actress Vera Kotlyarevskaya, dated 5 May 1908, he explained the purpose of his System as he then saw it: 'I conduct experiments every day on myself and on others and often achieve highly interesting results. I am mostly busy with the rhythm of feelings, the discovery of affective memory and the psychophysiology of the creative process' (in Benedetti 1991: 265).

By the time he was writing the second part of *An Actor's Work on Himself*, thirty years later, he was able to look back at the intervening years and reflect upon his findings. By then, he was no longer interested in affective memory (although I will trace his early research into Ribot in Chapter 3). But he continued to be committed to the 'psychophysiology' of acting, right up until his death in 1938, constantly shifting the balance of the psychological and the physical within his System whilst remaining convinced of their interdependence.

In the passage above, from *Building a Character*, Stanislavsky is too self-effacing to claim any definitive discoveries on psycho-physical acting but he does intimate that one day this will happen – 'they will eventually be discovered by others', he argues. In other outlets he was less equivocal about the significance of his own findings and, specifically at the end of his career, began to view the System in curiously similar terms to his political leader, Joseph Stalin – as the orthodox acting approach for all the Soviet Union, if not the world. Anatoly Smeliansky, now Rector of the Moscow Art Theatre, sees this development as part of a religious mission for Stanislavsky: 'The theme of an endless coming to knowledge ... is perhaps the most fundamental theme in his artistic biography. Quite soon he began to feel he was the bearer of some sort of higher power, like a transformer, a medium' (Smeliansky 1991: 10).

But this 'endless coming to knowledge' may be viewed from another perspective, not as evidence of his religiosity but as a sign of his commitment to an altogether more material universalism. By focusing on his later work, specifically the period of the Method of Physical Actions (*Metod fizicheskikh deistvii*) and Active Analysis (*Deistvennyi analiz*), it is intended here to align Stanislavsky's discoveries not with an undisclosed higher power but with the definitive scientific paradigm begun by Isaac Newton.

In doing so, the aim is to reveal a consistency in Stanislavsky's approach that runs counter to the popular sense of him as 'shifting thinker'. There are, of course, tensions in his acting theory and a definite change of emphasis as he grew to mistrust the capricious nature of the emotions. But a scrutiny of the language he uses to describe the acting process betrays a subtextual scientific bias, both historical (in the case of Newton and René

Descartes) and contemporary (in the case of Frederick Winslow Taylor), which remains constant, underpinning both sides of his psycho-physical acting System.

In order to explain fully this kinship, some background will be needed of the Newtonian tradition, but before we can do this a reassessment of Stanislavsky's philosophical roots is required.

Stanislavsky and Aristotle

For a period of almost fifty years, many critics have been united on the issue of Stanislavsky's affinity with Aristotle (384–322 BC). Francis Fergusson, although lacking the evidence for a definitive view, suggests that Stanislavsky and Nemirovich-Danchenko 'rediscovered' (1949: 239) Aristotle's concept of action and Sharon Carnicke 'confirms' his suspicion with reference to the Russian edition of *An Actor Prepares*, citing a passage in which Stanislavsky traces the root of drama back to the Greek *dran*, 'to do' (1998: 201). The same point is made by Stanislavsky himself in *Creating a Role*: 'Life is action; that is why our lively art, which stems from life, is preponderantly active. It is not without reason that our word "drama" is derived from the Greek word which means "I do"' (Stanislavsky 1981: 48).

There is clearly some justification for a connection to be made between the two men for Stanislavsky's System does share significant common ground with Aristotle's thinking, specifically with *The Poetics* (*c.*330 BC). Both men, for example, stress the importance of logic in their work. For Aristotle this is to do with the organisation of the plot (*muthos*): 'Only by imagining events as clearly as if they were present in person can [the playwright] follow the logic of what is happening and avoid incongruity' (1999: 24). For Stanislavsky, the actor's organisation of the character's actions within the play (the Through Action or *skvosnoe deistvie*) must follow the laws of logic, ensuring that the development of the role is believable for an audience: 'all action in the theatre must have an inner justification', Tortsov tells his students early on in *An Actor Prepares*; it must 'be logical, coherent and real' (Stanislavsky 1980a: 46).

Both men, in their analysis of drama, seek a sense of order in the play itself. For Aristotle, this is articulated in famously clear terms: a *muthos* must have a beginning, middle and end and 'should not begin at random or end at random' (Aristotle 1999: 12). For Stanislavsky, order is to be found by a process of deep textual investigation, ensuring that the larger picture of the play can be organised into comprehensible parts.

Both men also advocate a theatre of feelings. For Aristotle, this was a direct rebuttal of the philosophy of his teacher, Plato (428–347 BC), whose utter rejection of emotion in the theatre (indeed of the theatre itself) will be fully investigated in relation to Anatoly Vasiliev in Chapter 5. 'The best kinds of *muthos* for tragedy', Aristotle states in *The Poetics*, 'are devised to represent incidents which arouse pity and terror' (1999: 17).

Stanislavsky is less emotionally prescriptive, but he still views the stimulation of feelings in the spectator as imperative, alongside the arousal of thought (*dianoia*). What does the spectator come for? 'To sense the emotions and discover the thoughts of the people participating in the play' (Stanislavsky 1980a: 197).

In *Actors and Onlookers*, Natalie Crohn-Schmitt goes further in uniting Aristotle and Stanislavsky. Focusing on the two men's attitude to Nature, Crohn-Schmitt identifies six areas of correlation between philosopher and director:

i   their view that nature is governed by universal laws and principles;
ii   their view of nature as linear and orderly;
iii   their belief that action is a series of obstacles to be overcome;
iv   their view of the determinate human being [Stanislavsky's superobjective and Aristotle's 'final cause'];
v   their view of nature as an ordered hierarchy from parts to wholes;
vi   their view that nature achieves the maximum with the minimum amount of effort.

(1990: 95–101)

Underpinning these six areas is one central point: that in their mutual commitment to *action*, Stanislavsky and Aristotle are philosophically united. Clearly, there is scope for developing such a thesis. Action (or *praxis*) for Aristotle is the primary constituent of tragedy through the active realisation of the *muthos*: 'Tragedy is the imitation of an action which is serious, complete and substantial ... It is drama [that is, it shows people performing actions] and not narration' (Aristotle 1999: 9; McLeish's text in square brackets).

And, likewise for Stanislavsky, action is at the core of the creative act. As he argues in *An Actor Prepares*: 'action, motion, is the basis of the art followed by the actor' (1980a: 36).

But to base the connections between Stanislavsky and Aristotle on the idea of action also has its problems, not least in the complex area of translation. Recent research has shown that Elizabeth Hapgood's English translations truncate Stanislavsky's methodical arguments and illustrations in the interest of brevity but at the expense of consistency and precision. Bella Merlin makes the point in *Konstantin Stanislavsky*:

Although the cuts may seem simple, some of them are particularly unhelpful. One crucial example concerns the Russian text of *An Actor Prepares*, which lists six important questions that all actors must ask of themselves ... *who, when, where, why, for what reason* and *how*. In the English translation, these six questions are given far less attention, with only four of them being summarised.

(2003: 40)

Elsewhere, the word 'object' is substituted for the more complex term 'objective' and the overall effect, Merlin argues, is that 'Stanislavsky's original intentions have become muddied' (2003: 41).[1] The terminology used by Stanislavsky, in the much fuller Russian versions of *An Actor's Work on Himself I and II*, is, by contrast, precise, consistent and, above all, simple.

Not only does this 'new' terminology resolve some of the confusions in Stanislavskian practice, particularly to do with the relationship of motivation to action, but it also reveals an alternative discourse to that associated with Aristotelianism, one which sits more comfortably with the cultural conditions of Stanislavsky's time. By considering each of the six proposed meeting points in turn it will be argued in this chapter that the 'natural' system of Stanislavsky is, in fact, far removed from the metaphysics of the fourth century BC. When focusing on the specific terminology for action in the Russian editions – in this case the relationship between the task (*zadacha*) and the action taken to realise that task (*deistvie*) – a particular discourse is revealed but it is not a discourse which owes any consistent debt to Aristotle. Instead, it is one bound up in the mechanistic thinking which grew out of Newton's *Principia* and which characterised much of the Western intellectual tradition, proving particularly popular in post-revolutionary Russia. To keep the scope of this chapter manageable Newton and Descartes will be used here as markers of the beginning of this tradition, Winslow Taylor, Henry Ford and Alexei Gastev as emblems of its final paradigmatic assertion.

The Newtonian paradigm: the seventeenth-century perspective

Newton

Isaac Newton's (1642–1727) talent lay as much in his ability to amalgamate the work of others as it did in his own scientific discoveries. Galileo, Kepler, Copernicus and Descartes all figure strongly in the thinking that gave birth to the *Principia* (1687) and the *Opticks* (1704), the two publications for which Newton is most celebrated and which contain his entire scientific methodology. His is the figure most prominent in the Scientific Revolution (begun by Copernicus's theory of heliocentrism) and the mechanistic worldview that developed from his theories has been widely influential both inside and outside scientific circles. Not only did he achieve a great synthesis of ideas but also a fundamental synthesis of *approach*, unifying the methods of induction and deduction, in what he called the method of 'analysis and synthesis'. In doing so Newton established what is still commonly known as the 'scientific method': theories are first derived from empirical observation (induction) and then used to predict other phenomena (deduction). He outlines the process in the *Opticks*:

> Analysis consists in making Experiments and Observations, and in drawing general conclusions from them by Induction ... [It] proceed[s] from Compounds to Ingredients, and from Motions to the Forces producing them; and in general from Effects to their Causes, and from particular Causes to more general ones, till the Argument end[s] in the most general.
>
> (1952: 404)

The method of synthesis then expands from these general causes – 'establish'd as Principles' (ibid.) – to suggest further explanations for other phenomena. Thus, Newton's method is geared to revealing the underlying causes of events in the empirical world, to working back from 'effect' (the observable results of the experiment), to 'cause' (the reasons behind such results), before generalising further to the level of principles.

Consider in the light of Newton's statement the famous passage in *My Life in Art* (1924) in which Stanislavsky observes the genius of the great tragedian Tommaso Salvini. Marvelling at the range Salvini displays playing the Moor, Stanislavsky offers a vivid description of his performance. Romanticised though it is (in keeping with the tone of much of the book), he illustrates a keen eye for detail, concluding with a statement and then a question:

> How simple, clear, beautiful, and tremendous was everything that Salvini did and showed! But why was it that when I saw Salvini I remembered Rossi and the great Russian actors whom I had seen? Why did I feel that all of them had something in common, something I seemed to know very well ... What was it?
>
> (1980b: 272–273)

The answer is provided a little later: the importance of a holistic preparation for the actor. Salvini not only put on the externals of Othello but 'prepared his soul in a like manner' arriving three hours early to indulge in what is rather awkwardly translated as 'some important preparatory toilet of his own' (274)! From this observed evidence, Stanislavsky goes on to abstract more general principles, first directly related to the example of Salvini and then to the wider sphere:

> Come, come, don't drag the wool over our eyes. Do you think we don't understand that there is no man in the world who can pass in five minutes from the sphere of restaurants and vulgar anecdotes into the empire of the superconscious. This requires a gradual, logical approach ... Creative nature has its laws.
>
> (1980b: 275)

The crux of Stanislavsky's own 'scientific method' may be seen in this example. First, he observes the effects, in this case the genius of Salvini's

Othello on stage; next he looks to what lies behind this effect – the seriousness with which Salvini prepares for a role (even if it is for the hundredth time); next he thinks beyond to other examples of acting greatness for a common link; finally, he generalises into a principle – the need for gradual and logical steps to access the elevated state of the superconscious. Significantly, the 'Argument end[s] in the most general' – the definitive conclusion that the laws of Creative nature will always prevail.

Interestingly, the approach initiated an *experimental* response in Stanislavsky. Salvini, in effect, launched the director on a lifelong investigatory journey. Aristotle's theories were based on very detailed observation of the natural world – both the *Poetics* and the *Physics* testify to that fact. But these observations were not supported further by interrogative experimentation, that is to say by dirtying one's hands in the natural world. The mutually supportive dynamic of experimentation and observation was, in fact, the contribution of modern scientists, led by Newton and his contemporaries. Stanislavsky, echoing the latter approach, performed 'experiments every day' and conducted his whole career in a similar vein. From the earliest days of objective self-criticism to the observation and criticism of his students in the 'experimental' context of the Opera-Dramatic Studio in the late 1930s, he was engaged in what he called 'laboratory' work, feeding back the results of his experiments into his fluid theory of acting – the System.

The three laws of motion

Newton's great contribution was to codify what he saw as the immutable laws of Nature in mathematics. His science is rooted in the study of motion, the science of mechanics. Accordingly, his quest was to explain the natural world in terms of motion – in three simple axioms or laws:

Law 1: Every body continues in its state of rest, or of uniform motion in a right [i.e. straight] line, unless it is compelled to change that state by forces impressed upon it.

Law 2: The change of motion is proportional to the motive force impressed; and is made in the direction of the right line in which that force is impressed.

Law 3: To every action there is always opposed an equal reaction.

(1966: 13)

The first law – known as the law of inertia – expressly states that the natural trajectory of a moving object is in a straight line. Newton modelled the world on geometric principles and a sense of him as the geometer of nature is clearly evoked by this axiom. Were it not for the force of inertia we would all continue on our linear paths forever. Aristotle reached a similar conclusion in his own thinking about motion but was so resistant to the idea that he denied even its possibility by ruling out the conditions needed for perpetual motion – that is, a perfect vacuum. Newton, on the other hand, saw motion in causal not in teleological terms. Things move not because they have to find their natural place, as Aristotle believed, but because they are forced to do so by other things.[2]

This view of causality is implicit in Newton's second law: changes in nature (effects) do not happen spontaneously; there is always a cause behind the change. It is what is often referred to as 'billiard-ball mechanics' – a metaphor designed to convey the linearity and predictability of the phenomena Newton is describing.

The third and most famous law conveys a similar sense of geometrical clarity – a perfectly symmetrical model of conflict. It is not a law that appeals to an intuitive understanding of the world. We do not think of a chair pushing up on us as much as we may be pushing down. But it is nevertheless the law that has best found its way into the non-specialist domain, explaining the underlying conflicting forces of everything from a boxer's punch to the manoeuvring of the space shuttle.

Determinism, causality and motion

Newton's description of motion gave birth to the scientific movement of determinism – the theory that the world is subject to causal laws. Determinism's ultimate aim is to reduce the world to a predictable mechanism – if we know what causes things to behave as they do then, given all the data available on the cause, we can predict the effect, before it happens. Newton's close associate, Edmond Halley, famously (and accurately) predicted in 1682 the return of the great comet seventy-six years later and in doing so lent considerable weight to such thinking. The technological explosion of clock-making at the same time, breaking down the day into equal parts and thus making the repetitive rhythms of life explicit, added to the growing confidence in predictive science. This development in technology (and chronology) almost inevitably led to an analogous vision of the universe in which a clockwork world ticks away forever. God was still ultimately responsible for setting this clock in motion – a throwback to an earlier medieval paradigm – but the new terminology signalled a rising tide of confidence in the measurable material world.

A measure of this confidence is afforded us by the title of Newton's last book (Book III) in the *Principia*: 'The System of the World'. Here, Newton applies his laws to the celestial realm and offers predictive models for lunar behaviour as well as explaining the forces behind tides. The project behind the final part of Newton's Principia is important in this context for it captures the overriding ambition of the scientific method. From its roots in the simplest of the axioms – the third law of motion – Newton succeeded in explaining the gravitational patterns of the solar system, mathematically systematising the furthest reaches of humankind's vision from observational data provided by Greenwich Observatory. Thus, for Newton, the local behaviour of an object in the laboratory could provide the principles for an understanding of the cosmos. The constant was motion:

> What was new [in the seventeenth century] was the concept of the universality of motion; not only that motion occurred everywhere, but it was the same kind of motion everywhere. Motion, it now seemed, was invariably subject to the same laws, from the scale of the sun through the scale of an apple to the scale of the least particles of matter.
>
> (Hall 1981: 37)

For over 200 years Newtonian theory succeeded in universalising motion, making it the 'primary science' (ibid.) and reversing the Aristotelian view that motion was purely a transition from one place to another in search of an overall natural state.

It was not until the birth of quantum theory in the early twentieth century that this universal theory of motion became problematic. After Einstein, Nils Bohr and Erwin Schrödinger, the scaling down of the laws of motion to include the behaviour of 'the least particles of matter' proved impossible. Far from subscribing to a billiard ball theory in which atoms would behave predictably and causally, quantum theory revealed the inner processes of the atom to be fundamentally uncertain.

To return to the context of the discussion, it should be clear that Crohn-Schmitt's first two points – Aristotelian universality and Aristotelian linearity – are in effect no proof of Aristotelianism at all. In fact, Newton's universal theory of nature was (unsurprisingly) far more developed than Aristotle's and his Laws and Principles were strongly underpinned by geometric orderliness and linearity. This is not to value Newtonian science above Aristotle's but to prioritise a Newtonian *reading* of Stanislavsky above an Aristotelian perspective on his work.

René Descartes

René Descartes (1596–1650) preceded Newton by some forty years. He shared Newton's desire to modernise science and break with the hegemony of Aristotelian natural philosophy and his own *Principia Philosophiae*, published in 1644, was still the main talking point when Newton arrived at Trinity College, Cambridge in 1660. It was subsequently found to be erroneous on every count.[3] Ironically, although his objective may have been to reject Aristotelianism, proposing a mechanical rather than a teleological model of the world, Descartes adopted the same anti-experimental stance as his Classical predecessor. This led him into the countless mistaken assumptions included in his *Principia* and to the emphatic anti-empirical standpoint that 'his own theories were correct and that in the experiments the necessary conditions could not be realized' (Bell 1961: 69). He was closer to Plato (and Galileo[4]) in his deep-seated belief in the power of theoretical mathematics to describe the world and shared the philosopher's belief that the senses are misleading:

> Various experiences have gradually ruined all the faith I had attached to my senses. For I have observed many times that towers, which from a distance seemed round, appeared at close quarters to be square, and that huge figures erected on the summits of these towers looked like small statues when viewed from below.
>
> (Descartes 1968: 154–155)

Irrespective of the inaccuracies of his science, the influence of Cartesian philosophy was considerable: first in creating the celebrated divide of Mind from Body; second for his atomistic approach to analysis; and third for the mechanistic model of nature he championed. These three points, raised in the *Discourse* (1637) and the *Meditations* (1641), are all interconnected.

The full implications of Descartes' separation of *res cogitans* (thinking thing) from *res extensa* (extended thing or body) are beyond the scope of this study, although the salient points can be considered here before their significance from a theatrical perspective is analysed. Separating the thinking side (or soul) of humankind from the material (and by extension soulless) side resulted in a view of nature that was mechanical. Humankind may be distinguished from the rest of nature in that it has a soul (the ghost) that drives the body (the machine) but the rest of nature's organisms are simply cogs in a great mechanistic system. In creating such a world-view Descartes was influenced by the great popularity of showpiece automata[5] at the time and looked to the self-governing machine to encapsulate his vision, not in metaphorical terms but as a literal facsimile of nature:

> We see clocks, artificial fountains, mills and other similar machines which, though merely man made, have nonetheless the power to move by themselves in several different ways ... I do not recognise the difference between machines made by craftsmen and the various bodies that nature alone composes.
>
> (in Capra 1983: 47)

Descartes' analogy in the *Meditations*, that a sick man is like a faulty clock and a well man like a properly functioning clock, extends the idea that his thinking was fundamentally linked with the technological explosion of the early seventeenth century. Indeed, the passage actually characterises the 'mindless' body as a kind of prototype robot:

> I consider man's body as being a machine so built and composed of bones, nerves, muscles, veins, blood and skin [that] although it had no mind in it, it would still move in all the same ways it does at present,

when it does not move by the direction of its will, or consequently, with the help of the mind, but only by the disposition of its organs.

(1968: 163)

If nature's organisms are mechanical, it follows they may be taken apart like machines, a corollary which we can see emerging in his compartmentalising of the body, above, and which was lent weight by Descartes' own mathematical reasoning. His method of analysis is articulated in the *Discourse on the Method of Properly Conducting One's Reason and of Seeking the Truth in the Sciences*, Chapter 2: 'To divide each of the difficulties that I was examining into as many parts as might be possible and necessary in order best to solve it' (1968: 41). Thus, for Descartes all the complexities of nature merely consisted of 'long chains of reasonings' (ibid.), which, if broken up and tackled in the right order, would yield up the truth. It is what is often referred to as a 'building-blocks' approach,[6] which assumes that the sum of the parts is equal to the whole and that the dismantling of something will not affect its overall health, providing it is reassembled correctly.

Stanislavsky and the Cartesian machine

The detail of Descartes' method of analysis and its implications for Stanislavsky's work will be dealt with in due course but it is helpful here to reflect more generally on Descartes' view of mind and body for, despite the 300-year gap, the Cartesian divide articulated in the *Discourse* is one which Stanislavsky was seriously contemplating when writing his acting journals in the 1930s. Whereas Descartes saw the two as completely distinct from one another – the mind being indivisible and the body divisible (Descartes 1968: 164) – Stanislavsky's whole system is predicated on the integration of mind and body. The actor is a psycho-physical being, whose work depends on both inner and outer training. These two sides to the actor's work are given consistent terms: *perezhivanie* and *voploscenie* respectively, and his acting volumes in both English and Russian reflect this duality. *An Actor Prepares* (*An Actor's Work on Himself Part 1*) deals with the inner work, while *Building a Character* (*An Actor's Work on Himself Part 2*) deals with the outer training. As has been well documented in the past, one of the key problems in the American tradition of Stanislavskian acting is the thirteen-year gap in the publication of *An Actor Prepares* (1936) and *Building a Character* (1949), and the resulting schism in the teaching of Stanislavsky's actor training.

Interestingly, this is the very same schism Descartes was creating with the *cogito ergo sum* debate, the annexation of 'thinking thing' from 'extended thing' – we might say of 'thinking actor' from 'external actor'. The dangers of such a division are treated very early on in *An Actor Prepares*, when Tortsov offers feedback on the first acting exercise of his course:

'As for you, Govorkov, you did not approach your role from its inner content, you neither lived nor represented it, but did something entirely different.'

'What was it'? . . .

'Mechanical acting . . . There can be no true art without living. It begins where feeling comes into its own.'

'And mechanical acting?' asked Grisha.

'That begins where creative art ends. In mechanical acting there can be no call for a living process, and it appears only accidentally . . . With the aid of his face, mimicry, voice and gestures, the mechanical actor offers the public nothing but the dead mask of non-existent feeling.'

(1980a: 23–24)

For Stanislavsky, the separation of mind from body is analogous with the division of feeling from technique.[7] Simple repetition of external behaviour learnt from actors of an earlier age (Stanislavsky's first flawed practice, in fact) does not produce creative art, irrespective of its dexterity. The result of such an approach, of Govorkov's soulless technique, is 'deadly theatre'. In the current context, Stanislavsky's concluding image of 'the dead mask', bereft of inner content, is strikingly comparable to the soulless automaton which Descartes describes in the *Meditations*. Both men see the outcome of dividing mind from body as 'mechanical'. For Stanislavsky, the term is deeply pejorative, superseded only by 'amateurish overacting' (1980a: 30) and systematic self-indulgence. For Descartes, it is simply a given of the superiority of mind over matter. Stanislavsky makes a claim for a holistic view of the actor – the psycho-physical performer – whilst Descartes severs the link between psychology and physiology. The tension between these two positions will be a common theme throughout this book.

Summary

The Cartesian model of the world was sharply divergent from Newton's in its accuracy and in its approach. It valued the power of deduction over experiment and distrusted the ability of the senses to measure objectively. But it shared important common ground with the Newtonian system. Both men revered geometry and used it in their explanations of natural phenomena. Both submitted nature to an analysis based on the discovery of laws and principles. Both aimed at an overall mechanical system, encompassing the world (the terrestrial realm) and the planets (the celestial realm). And both ascribed the design of their systems to a Higher Being – God, the ultimate designer. Natalie Crohn-Schmitt's fifth aspect of Aristotelianism – 'nature as an ordered hierarchy from parts to wholes' – may, therefore, be more closely aligned with the mechanistic paradigm than with the classical view of Aristotle for Descartes and Newton both relied on a 'building blocks' approach, viewing the scaling up of problems from small to large as an essential tool in the pursuit of truth. As we shift attention to the twentieth-century perspective, it will become clear that the sixth criterion – nature achieving 'the maximum with the minimum amount of effort' – must also be recontextualised.

The Newtonian paradigm: the twentieth-century perspective

Henry Ford and Frederick Winslow Taylor

If Newton's System of the World still relied on an omnipotent designer or 'driver', the early twentieth-century climate of systematisation, embodied in Henry Ford (1863–1947) and Frederick Winslow Taylor (1856–1915), more or less banished the place of a metaphysical being from the landscape – unless, of course, you focus on the boardroom which, through the development of Taylor's ideas particularly, became progressively isolated from the rest of the factory, housing a management which, if not actually godlike, was certainly all-powerful.

But whilst the place of God may have shifted in the intervening years, many other defining features of the Newtonian paradigm remained in the industrial thinking of the early twentieth century. The mechanistic model of the world retained its persuasive value but in the guise now of technological advances. Henry Ford's appropriately titled treatise 'Machinery, the New Messiah' gives a flavour of this phenomenon:

> Machinery is accomplishing in the world what man has failed to do by preaching, propaganda or the written word. The airplane and radio know no boundary. They pass over dotted lines on the map without heed or hindrance. They are binding the world together in a way no other systems can. The motion picture with its universal language, the airplane with its speed and the radio with its coming international programme – these will soon bring the whole world to a complete understanding. Thus we may vision a United States of the World. Ultimately, it will surely come.
>
> (1929: 18–19)

Notwithstanding the problems of this passage – the equating of universalism with 'understanding', as well as the imperial triumphalism implicit in the notion of a 'US of W' – there is a good deal here which accurately predicts our present state at the beginning of the twenty-first century. Ford's early identification of a fast-developing 'global village', bound together by advances in communication technology, is a case in point. At the same time, his rhetoric speaks very clearly to the conditions of his time, just a few years before the depression in the US. Most significant, here, is the unquestioned confidence in the machine age – a literal deification of machines, which, in keeping with religion's function of old, is seen as a universalising force, capable of crossing geographical boundaries and delivering world prosperity.

Ford's belief in 'the universal', in a system (or systems), which could be applied in many contexts, was not unique. In many ways his ideas were an extension of the Enlightenment tradition and of eighteenth- and nineteenth-century scientific rationalism. But they spoke to a twentieth-century context too. Within industry, the move to discover universal laws in management theory and in the emergent science of ergonomics was being directed by Taylor and his associate Frank Gilbreth (1868–1924). Taylor, like Ford, shared an evangelical belief in the power of systematisation, ranking the development of an organised system of management above the people within that system. 'In the past Man has been first, in the future the System will be first',[8] he argued, and through the publication of his own 'principia', *The Principles of Scientific Management* (1911), he set out to address the unsystematic basis of his industry. Sharing Ford's drive for efficiency, Taylor identified a need for rigid organisational structures in business, defining his approach with five key precepts:

> Science, not rule of thumb.
> Harmony not discord.
> Cooperation, not individualism.
> Maximum output, in place of restricted output.
> The development of each man to his greatest efficiency and prosperity.
>
> (1947: 140)

Ostensibly, the basic tenets of Taylorism depend on a harmonious and cooperative workforce, operating to the peak of their efficiency and reaping the rewards. But whilst this list of polarities suggests that collectivity is at the heart of his system, Taylor's discourse belies the underlying intention of his system. In introducing his management practice into the workplace, Taylor's objective was, in fact, in direct opposition to the harmonious union of workers he romanticised in *Principles*. He incentivised the work by offering 'differential piece rates' to those who worked faster. Thus, he explicitly divided rather than united his workforce. He is surprisingly candid about the objectives behind such a system in *Shop Management*:

> When men throughout an establishment are paid varying rates of day-work wages according to their individual worth, some being above and some below the average, it cannot be for the interest of those receiving high pay to join a union with the cheap men.
>
> (1947: 183)

It is no surprise, then, that the implementation of Scientific Management was not always as smooth as Taylor may have suggested.[9]

Although the workers were distinguished from each other in their pay packets, the work itself was standardised. Ford's production line took the large problem of assembling a motor car and broke it down into separate parts, giving each worker on the line one simple task. As the car proceeded down the conveyor belt each worker made a small contribution to the ultimate problem of constructing an automobile. As the tasks were repetitive and did not require valuable time for thought, Ford's production soared whilst his car prices dropped bringing the prospect of car ownership to millions of ordinary people. The key to this success was in the layout of the factory. Efficiency targets were met, as Peter Ling puts it, 'by arranging the hardware of manufacturing in a progressive sequence' (1990: 134).

Ford eliminated the inefficiencies of the past by creating a linear sequence of clearly delineated tasks. When these tasks were carried out in the right order and to time, the result was the rapid production of a car. Shifting from a situation where tools were spread around the factory and used by multi-skilled workers, to one in which the car itself was central, imposed a logic on the operation that had hitherto been absent. Thus, the story of the Model T unfolded along the conveyor-belt 'plot' of Ford's production line.

Bringing the Newtonian fascination for clocks into a modern industrial context, Taylor timed each individual task to ascertain the fastest completion times. In doing so, he developed huge and complex chains of micro-actions, which, when looked at in their entirety, constituted the macro-problem for the manager. In *Shop Management*, for example, Taylor reproduces a worksheet for 'hand work on machine tools' (1947: 166–167), dividing the work up into forty-nine separate tasks. For each of these tasks he stipulates a preferred completion time (the fastest possible) and an actual completion time. Such a detailed analysis, according to Taylor, ultimately allows for predictions to be made:

> No system of time study can be looked upon as a success unless it enables the time observer, after a reasonable amount of study, to predict with accuracy how long it should take a good man to do almost any job in [any] particular trade.
>
> (1947: 167)

The Newtonian credentials of Fordism and Taylorism thus become clearer. Not only is the system designed, after detailed observations, to rationalise the behaviour of the worker, it is also a predictive science which can anticipate the performance of any 'good man ... [in] almost any job'. At the same time, the analytical technique adopted by Taylor has its roots firmly in the Cartesian school, viewing the complex problem of car-production (or lathe work) as a systematic series of steps – a Cartesian 'long chain' of sub-problems to be solved separately.

Ford and Taylor's systems were, in effect, systems of control, designed to mechanise the person as well as the job and thus ensuring their employees' 'cooperation' whilst denying their 'individuality'. His ideas were popular across Europe and, surprisingly, in post-revolutionary Russia, where the need for productivity superseded the ideological problems of introducing a starkly capitalist system to a proto-communist state. The main vehicle for the dissemination of Taylorism in the Soviet Union was Alexei Gastev (1882–1941).

Alexei Gastev

Scientific Management (or NOT as it is abbreviated in Russian[10]) impacted on Russia remarkably quickly. As early as 1912, Gastev, who was later to found the Central Institute of Labour (CIT), had come into contact with the principles of Taylor and by 1919 he was preaching a synthetic vision of industry which saw no contradiction in American capitalism coming to the Soviet Union. Compare his declaration in the Proletkult journal with Ford's quoted earlier:

> The metallurgy of this new world, the motor car and aeroplanes of America, and finally the arms industry of the whole world – here are the new, gigantic laboratories where the psychology of the proletariat is being created, where the culture of the proletariat is being manufactured. And whether we live in an age of super-imperialism or of world socialism, the structure of the new industry will, in essence, be one and the same.
>
> (in Bailes 1977: 377)

The shift to a focus on the proletariat is clear but the rest of what Gastev is saying is tellingly close to Ford's vision: a world order united by the dominant industries of car and aeroplane manufacture. That the precise politics behind the development of this world order is of little significance for Gastev is striking evidence of his priorities, although clearly what appeals to him in both socialism and 'super-imperialism' is their mutual ambition for world domination: both, in fact, offered him a system of the world.[11]

The encroachment of Taylorism into Russia was steady. In April 1918 'it was decided to introduce piece-work and set production norms for each worker' (Johansson 1983: 104). By 1921 a conference was organised on Scientific Management by Trotsky, the arrangements of which made clear the growing association of Scientific Management with Objective Psychology – the science which had developed independently in America and Russia through J. B. Watson's Behaviourism (in the US) and Ivan Sechenov's early Reflexology (in Russia). The conference gathered together eminent scientists and practitioners under specific themes: the biological line included Vladimir Bekhterev, contemporary of Pavlov, and the professional line incorporated Gastev's Institute of Labour, for which Gastev gave a paper, 'How to Work'. In this paper Gastev made implicit reference to Pavlovian thinking, describing the need to inculcate a 'culture of severity', to bring about what he called, 'a postponement of immediate satisfaction which may be called conditioning for work' (in Bailes 1977: 384).

In stating as much, Gastev was unifying Taylor's belief that workers naturally 'soldier' (that is waste time) with the Pavlovian ethic of conditioned reflexes. The new proletarian psychology, he argued, must divest itself of any proclivity for 'loafing' (Johansson 1983: 110) and be encouraged (or conditioned), to work efficiently using a military-style discipline.

The key to productivity for Gastev was in the workers' physical responsiveness. Describing a training for the worker that had strong similarities with Meyerhold's actor training, as we shall see, Gastev preached that the body must be reactive, functional and precise. In searching for a metaphor to describe such a body, he aligned himself strongly with the mechanistic paradigm we have thus far outlined. The language he uses is redolent both of Descartes and of Taylor, although he takes both perspectives to an extreme:

> Our first task consists in working with that magnificent machine that is so close to us – the human organism. This machine possesses a sophisticated mechanics, including automatism and a swift transmission. Should we not study it? The human organism has a motor, 'gears', shock absorbers, sophisticated brakes, delicate regulators, even manometers.
>
> (in Johansson 1983: 113)

Quite what Gastev had in mind for the bodily equivalent of a pressure gauge remains to be seen but his demonstrable belief in industrial mechanics could not be more strongly communicated. Whilst this aspect of his thinking clearly owes a debt to the Cartesian view of the body or 'extended thing', Descartes' 'thinking thing' is conspicuous in its absence; 'automatism' is stressed, recalling the mechanical puppets which so inspired the French philosopher, but no mention is made of the soul or ghost which inhabits the machine.

This is not simply an oversight on Gastev's part but a fundamental aspect of his thinking. *Res cogitans* is the individual aspect of humankind – without it humanity is homogenised. Gastev actively sought such an outcome, which fitted his grand plans for universalising the workforce and which accorded with his view of proletarian psychology: 'whose work was completely standardized and devoid of any subjective element' (in Bailes 1977: 377).

Whilst Gastev may, therefore, have embraced an American-inspired industrial model, his psychological paradigm was defiantly Soviet, part of a general thrust towards collectivism that René Fulop-Miller called 'mass man'. He quotes the folk bard Demian Bednyi to illustrate his point:

> Million footed: a body. The pavement cracks
> A million mass: one heart, one will, one tread!
> Keeping step, keeping step.
>
> (Fulop-Miller 1927: 6)

The Soviet 'mass man' walked in perfect step with a million others of his kind, organised by a rigidly militaristic system of control. For Meyerhold, this sense of the collective man inspired a deep-seated belief in the ensemble and this theatricalising of Gastevian thinking will be the subject of Chapter 2. For Stanislavsky, the impact of a Taylor-inspired working method is more difficult to trace but is nevertheless evident in the subtext of his training.

Summary

What, then, emerges from this survey of early twentieth-century industrial practice in Russia and America?

First, there is the strong bilateral belief in the machine as 'saviour'. This late flourishing of the Newtonian paradigm is characterised by a parallel movement of Scientific Management in both countries, which promoted the positive qualities of the machine: productivity, efficiency, precision, longevity. In America, this movement was linked with major industrial giants such as Henry Ford. In Russia, it was promoted by the Gastev Institute and, while Gastev's views remained popular, extended to all fields of life, including the arts. Natalie Crohn-Schmitt's contention that nature's efficiency is a sign of Aristotelianism needs reassessing in such a context, for those who were most vigorously pursuing the aim of efficiency in the twentieth century, contemporaries of Stanislavsky all, were demonstrably part of a mechanistic not a teleological project.

Second, there is the emphasis found in both Taylor's and Gastev's work on analysis – the Cartesian approach of breaking problems down into their constituent parts is reflected both in Taylor's systematic analysis of industrial tasks and in Gastev's attitude to the body, defining each limb's most efficient purpose. Indeed, the Gastev Institute was engaged in the very same research, or 'motion study', as Taylor's colleague Frank Gilbreth, with both men using photography to slow down and analyse physical actions.[12]

Third, and more generally, there is the conviction both countries shared of the power of systematisation and its promise of creating a universal understanding. Common ground is to be found between these otherwise divergent superpowers in their joint Modernist project to determine a 'system for the world'.

The mechanics of Stanislavsky's System: *perezhivanie*

Recognising that his notes on theatre, culled from an already wide range of experiences as an actor and director, 'had been thrown in willy-nilly [with] no system' (Benedetti 1990a: 162), Stanislavsky began a wholesale rationalisation of his work, which impacted on his future teaching, acting and writing. His antidote to the disorder in which he found his theatrical memoirs in 1906 was to organise his work into a systematic analysis of the process of acting. It was an undertaking that engaged Stanislavsky's energies for the next thirty-two years. 'My lifelong concern', he said in 1938 in *An Actor's Work on Himself Part 2*, 'has been how to get closer to the so-called System' (Carnicke 2000: 33).

Almost all of the written material on the System comes from the end of Stanislavsky's career. The earliest document, *My Life in Art*, (1924) has very little practical evidence. *An Actor Prepares*, *Building a Character* and *Creating A Role* all hail from a period of writing after 1936, although they do contain material which had been gathered many years before. The other key references, culled from the eye-witness accounts of Vasily Toporkov, Maria Knebel and Irina Novitskaya,[13] are from workshops conducted by Stanislavsky in the last days of his life. There is evidence, though, that much of the terminology and the working practices described by Stanislavsky in these writings were in place much earlier than this. By 1911 – the very same year Taylor was publishing his *Scientific Management* – Stanislavsky's System was sufficiently formalised for it to be taught by Sulerzhitsky at the Moscow Art Theatre School and the next year saw the foundation of the First Studio in which much of the work was tested out in a laboratory context. Pavel Markov records that in this studio Stanislavsky was already talking of 'the right selection of tasks, their composition, the right pattern, the execution of every task' (Carnicke 1998: 151) – a terminology that he used right up until his death. Just as Taylor and Ford, in America, and Gastev, closer to home, were striving for the most efficient and systematic, task-based approach in industry, Stanislavsky was proposing an organised system for the actor based on the same foundations.

Taylorism is more frequently associated with, Stanislavsky's colleague, Vsevolod Meyerhold, not least because of Meyerhold's explicit citation of Taylor in his theoretical pronouncements on biomechanics (see Chapter 2). But what has not been recognised by critics is the interplay between Taylor's industrial efficiency drives and the practice of Stanislavsky, an interplay which is disguised by Hapgood's translations of key terms but which comes into sharp relief when analysing the simple terminology first proposed by Stanislavsky. Let us return to the concept of action to see where this is most evident.

From the macro-level to the micro-level

Stanislavsky approached the macro-problem facing the actor – how to access the 'creative state' – in much the same way as he dealt with the specific details of play analysis: 'If [the creative state] cannot be mastered all at once, can it not be achieved bit by bit, that is to say, by constructing the whole from its parts?' (in Benedetti 1989: 30). Stanislavsky's rhetorical question reveals an underlying thought process that will be familiar in the current context. His likening of the acting process to building or construction is indicative of his developmental approach, which 'bit by bit' sets the actor on the road to inspiration. Indeed, the whole of his system is predicated upon the belief that if one follows the constituent parts of the psycho-technique a favourable set of conditions will be established to stimulate unconscious creativity. In this way the actor's behaviour on stage appears second nature, spontaneous and real.

At the local level of textual analysis Stanislavsky is committed to the same atomistic approach. Using a rather awkward metaphor, Tortsov, Stanislavsky's alter ego, explains:

> 'Imagine this is not a turkey but a five-act play, *The Inspector General*. Can you do away with it in a mouthful? No, you can't make a single mouthful of a whole turkey or a five-act play. Therefore you must carve it, first, into large pieces, like this...' (cutting off the legs, wings [etc.]) ... 'But you cannot swallow even such chunks. Therefore you must cut them up into smaller pieces ... There's a big piece for you. That's the first scene.'
>
> (Stanislavsky 1980a: 111–112)

The play is carved up to make its analysis by the actors more manageable – a rehearsal device used to help solve the larger problem presented by the entire play text. In the manner of Cartesian analysis Stanislavsky breaks the play down into its constituent parts in order to reconstruct it, fully understood.

Bits and tasks

Hapgood translates these parts as 'units' each of which has an attendant objective, best expressed in a verb. Stanislavsky actually uses the more colloquial term 'bit' (*kusok*), as in bits of meat (Benedetti 1998: 151), which may explain his choice of metaphor. Thus, where Hapgood creates a more scientific sounding term – results are measured in units – Stanislavsky, true to his word about the practical bent of his System, uses a simple everyday word.

Each of these chunks includes both an objective or, more accurately, 'task' (*zadacha*) and an action to satisfy the task (*deistvie*). The distinction is significant. Where Hapgood's 'objectives' fuse the motivation for the action and the action itself (an error repeated in Crohn-Schmitt's reading of action[14]), Stanislavsky's terminology distinguishes clearly between the two. The task or 'mathematical problem' – *zadacha* has both meanings in Russian – is the stumbling block for the performer which has to be solved in action to continue the forward momentum of the play. This action is stimulated by what Stanislavsky calls the 'Inner Motive Forces' (reason, will and feeling) – the 'triumvirate' of energies that combine to motivate the actor (Stanislavsky 1980a: 247). It is an approach to text, which makes specific demands on an actor: to think forward, purposefully and actively.

But whilst all these stimuli conspire to provide forward momentum, the performer is at the same time impeded by the problems inscribed within the play and by the actions of others. Embedded in the task is a problem to be solved. Thus, the Stanislavskian actor is dynamised by the tension between action and resistance: reason, will and feeling provide the 'force' to set the actor's 'creative apparatus . . . in motion' (1980a: 244), while the problematic task holds them back.

Superficially speaking Stanislavsky avoids a scientific terminology with this more colloquial performance language, but a closer reading suggests something different. Not only does he consistently refer to the process of acting as 'motion' and to the actor as 'apparatus' but the central dynamic tension in the play is the performative equivalent of Newton's first law – the law of inertia. The actor/apparatus is a body in motion, initiated by a force (the motivation), and subject to contrary forces of inertia (the problems of the play). For each new performance the actor must readdress these tasks, must seek to *re*-solve the problems. By focusing on the task (rather than on the product of the task) the performer engages afresh with the creative process, avoiding clichés and the temptation to 'play the result'.

It should be clear from this that Stanislavsky's view of action as a series of obstacles to be overcome, far from owing a debt to Aristotle is essentially a Newtonian perspective, a point that is given further weight by the mechanistic language used by Stanislavsky in his journals. Jean Benedetti elucidates: 'One of the most frequent terms I had to translate for the actor's body was *apparat* (motor apparatus). All the time it was coming up: *apparat, apparat, apparat*.'[15]

Stanislavsky's 'task management'

Whilst the Newtonian sense of the body/apparatus comes through in both Hapgood's and Benedetti's translations, the significance of the stress on tasks is lost in the American version of *An Actor Prepares*. When focusing on the Russian term, *zadacha*, the contemporary context in which Stanislavsky was working is highlighted. A task is compact, well defined and unquestionably connected with action. Objectives on the other hand tend to have a longer lifespan and connote a more cerebral approach. Frederick Taylor's scientific or 'task' management was founded on this relationship between action and task setting. The key to his system is in reducing the individual mental input of a worker, to eradicate the counter-productive faculties of 'initiative and incentive'. Instead, the worker is set explicit tasks to be completed physically. There are simple activities (most famously the loading of pig-iron) and more complex ones (the multiple variables attached to lathe work) but all of these activities can be scientifically analysed and rationalised according to laws. In doing so, Taylor's aim was to eliminate the chance factor in the work pattern of employees:

> The first great advantage which scientific management has over the management of initiative and incentive is that under scientific

management the initiative of the workmen – that is their hard work . . . is obtained practically with absolute regularity while under the best of the older type of management this initiative is only obtained spasmodically.

(Taylor 1947: 39)

Stanislavsky's aim in terms of theatrical work was similar: to discover the physiological and psychological laws of behaviour and to systematise the performance process so that those who are not blessed with the intuitive genius of Salvini can regularly create the necessary conditions for truthful acting. Leaving behind the hit-and-miss approach that characterised his earliest performances at the Society of Art and Literature, he developed a System that offered all actors a rationalised and coherent performance language.

Given the place of Taylorism in Russia at the time, it is enlightening to discover that an analogous language, based on the establishing of discrete tasks combined to form a larger whole, is adopted by Stanislavsky. We may not, however, be too surprised by Stanislavsky's affinity with Taylorism. He was, after all, an industrialist himself and continued to play a role in the family textile business whilst he was formulating his System. His very upbringing juxtaposed the industrial with the artistic as his factory was situated alongside the family mansion and he used the considerable wealth generated by his business to subsidise his theatrical endeavours – before, that is, the Revolution levelled the playing field. He was, moreover, 'familiar with the theory of Taylorism' (Benedetti 1990a: 164) although no consistent analysis has yet been made of the significance of this familiarity.

The through-line of action

Having broken the play up into bits, each with an attendant task or problem, the actor then considers the relationship of these constituent parts to each other. They must not exist independently but blend seamlessly together in what Stanislavsky called the through-line of action (*skvosnoe deistvie*). Each 'bit' of action is created by the last 'bit' of action and flows logically into the next, forming what Tortsov calls the life-giving 'backbone' of the play (Stanislavsky 1980a: 276–277). Further weight is given to this biological model of the actor in the later translations of his work. In *An Actor's Work on the Role* Stanislavsky refers to the role as a 'skeleton', the play as an 'anatomy' and the substrata of the role as having 'arteries, nerves' and a 'pulse' (Carnicke 1998: 159).

But running counter to the organic language is a mechanistic methodology. Stanislavsky is, in effect, asking his performers to construct a causal structure to their roles, one that he illustrates diagrammatically in *An Actor Prepares*:

— — — — — — — ——→ The super-objective
The through-line of action

(1980a: 276)

The actor pieces together a developmental structure of problems and solves them in action. A new action is born out of the previous action as the role evolves along a clearly defined causal line. It is impressed upon his students how essential it is to keep this chain intact. It may be broken by extraneous details or by a director imposing a concept on the play but if this should happen the production is inevitably 'deformed ... [and] cannot live' (ibid.: 277).

Indeed, for Stanislavsky this chain of action is synonymous with life:

> On the stage, if the inner life is broken an actor no longer understands what is being said or done and he ceases to have any desires or emotions. The actor and the part, humanly speaking, live by these unbroken lines. That is what gives life and movement to what is being enacted. Let those lines be interrupted and life stops.
>
> (Ibid.: 254)

The actor's life force, 'humanly speaking', is inseparable from these unbroken lines. Vitality is defined by its linearity.

Stanislavskian time

If Stanislavsky's model of thinking is so explicitly linear it follows that the success of his actors can be measured by their ability to *delineate* character – to plot a life for themselves looking back to the past and anticipating the future. The causal model above fits into a wider pattern, an image of time which again has its roots in the Newtonian vision of the world: in this instance Newton's notion of absolute time which, 'flows equably without regard to anything external' (1966: 6). From *Creating a Role*:

> There can be no present ... without a past. The present flows naturally out of the past. The past is the roots from which the present grew; the present without any past wilts like a plant with its roots cut off. An actor must always feel that he has the past of his role behind him ... Neither is there a present without a prospect of the future, dreams of it, guesses and hints about it.
>
> (Stanislavsky 1981: 16)

There is an undertone of the deterministic world created by Newtonian causality here, in the relationship of past to present and of both to the future. Whilst Stanislavsky's thinking is a long way from the arch-Newtonian Pierre Simon de Laplace, and his belief that the entire universe's future may be predicted, Stanislavsky's work on text is predicated upon the same general belief that past and future are determinable. His 'Plan of Work' in *Creating a Role* says as much: 'Act out improvisations dealing with the past and future (the present occurs on stage): Where did I come from, where am I going, what happened between the times I was on the stage?' (1981: 253). It is, of course, the actor's imagination that has to be called upon to help construct this temporal backbone, for even the most naturalistic of playwrights can only hint at the life of the character beyond the action of their play. Imagination functions as the 'welding' agent (1980a: 257), binding together the fragments of a role and ensuring overall temporal integrity, even when the text might resist such treatment.

Sergei Desnitsky, a Moscow Art Theatre actor for twenty-seven years, now acting at the Nikitska Gate Theatre (*Theatr u Nikitski vorot*) in Moscow, illustrates this idea in practice. Working in a masterclass on the following extract from Act One of Anton Chekhov's *The Three Sisters* (1901), Desnitsky provides a memorable example of the linear mode of thinking:

CHEBUTYKIN [*laughs.*]: You know, I've never done a thing and that's a fact. Since I left the university I haven't lifted a finger, I've never even read a book . . . [*There is a banging on the floor from below.*] Aha! They want me down there, someone must have come to see me. I'll be with you in a moment. Just a second. [*Hurries out combing his beard.*]

IRINA: He's up to something.

TUZENBAKH: That's right. He went out looking terribly solemn, he's obviously going to bring you a present.

(Chekhov 1980: 175)

A few moments later Chebutykin does indeed return with a present for Irina – an ill-judged gift of a silver samovar.

Occupying Desnitsky was the same question Stanislavsky asks in *Creating a Role* – what happens in between? Why does Chebutykin exit after the knock on the floor and what prompts Tuzenbakh to prophesy that he will be back with a gift for Irina? This inconsequential action (characteristic of Chekhov's style, and particularly in *The Three Sisters*) needed sequencing. He knew of course that in Chekhov's text the doctor lives downstairs as a lodger – an index of the territorial pressure the sisters are already under even before Natasha asserts her influence. But what, if any, connection there was between the subterranean call to his quarters and the offering of the present remained elusive. Sitting at breakfast, Desnitsky found the answer:

As I was staring at this stained teaspoon it dawned on me: Chebutykin has asked for the samovar to be polished in his rooms downstairs whilst he enjoys Irina's party. When the polishing is finished his servant makes the agreed sign, banging on the ceiling [the Prozorov's floor], to alert the doctor and to call him to pick up the shining samovar.[16]

In making these decisions Desnitsky is clearly engaging imaginatively with the play's given circumstances. At the same time he is looking to find order beneath the text, to make connections where Chekhov deliberately leaves gaps. Put another way, he is seeking to establish linearity where, for Chekhov, there is discontinuity. It may well be the latter quality of Chekhovian drama that has led to his renaissance on the post-modern stage but for those following Stanislavsky's classical system the problems posed by the gaps in the narrative are there to be solved, through reason and improvisation.

That Stanislavsky cut his directorial teeth on texts such as *The Three Sisters* is not insignificant. Whilst he was formulating his very first thoughts on the psycho-technique he was practically engaged with producing Chekhov. His belief in the ordering role of the imagination may well be seen as part of a developing strategy to deal with the particularities of the Chekhovian text. For Chekhov's drama is notably resilient when probed from the imaginative angle Stanislavsky suggests. His plays do lend themselves to the conjectural approach taken by Desnitsky and they consistently yield more and more 'evidence' to substantiate such hypothesising. Why is Chebutykin's present so badly received, we might ask? Because it flouts the tradition behind the offering of a samovar: to celebrate a wedding anniversary not a birthday. Chebutykin is, in fact, remembering the sisters' mother with whom he is clearly still in love. This, in turn, complicates our understanding of his intimate relationship with Irina. She may well be the product of Chebutykin's historic liaison with Mrs Prozorov, which, given the leitmotif of infidelity in the play – from Masha and Vershinin to Natasha and Protopopov – would hardly be out of the ordinary.

Of course, other explanations are possible. Indeed you might resist looking for answers in the first place. But Desnitsky's response to the problems Chekhov poses does offer a measure of the particular mindset in which he is operating. It is a mindset which models the text as if its narrative occupies an absolute space which can (and should) be filled both by the creative decisions of actor and director and by the audience's imaginary input – a three-dimensional and geometrical model of performance. The audience is drawn into this model by a similar desire for order, subconsciously completing the Euclidean space, assisted by the indices of language, setting, movement and (surprisingly frequently) sound.

The supertask

As Stanislavsky indicates in his causal diagram of the 'through line', it is the super-objective, or more accurately the super-task (*zverkhzadacha*) which provides the ordering influence, the strength of which pulls all the constituent problems into line: 'the greater the literary work, the greater the pull of its superobjective'. Again, Stanislavsky appeals to the organic sciences when looking for a simile to help him explain to his students: 'If it is human and directed towards the accomplishment of the basic purpose of the play it will be like a main artery, providing nourishment and life to both it and the actors' (1980a: 271). Yet when Stanislavsky elaborates it becomes clear that the relationship between characters' supertasks is modelled more closely on classical physics than on biology. In addition to the smaller tasks with which the actor is concerned at a local level, each character has an overall drive or motivation – the supertask. Again this is expressed in active terms and its function is to bring into focus all the individual actions of a character. For Stanislavsky, echoing dramaturgical practice since the great flowering in classical Greece, drama emerges from conflict, specifically in the conflict between these supertasks.

There is nothing surprising in this conflict-based model of drama. If Stanislavsky does owe something to an Aristotelian model of drama, in his focus on 'doing', then so too might the ancient roots of dramatic structure – rising action leading to crisis brought about by the clash of characters – be seen to be reflected in his thinking.

What is revealing, however, is the language he chooses to express such conflict:

> Every *action* meets with a *reaction* which in turn intensifies the first. In every play, beside the main *action* we find its opposite *counteraction*. This is fortunate because its inevitable result is more action. We need that clash of purposes, and all the problems to solve that grow out of them. They cause activity which is the basis of our art.
>
> (1980a: 278)

The very foundation of Stanislavsky's art is rooted not in an Aristotelian 'final cause' but in mechanics – in Newton's third law of motion, here emphasised by Stanislavsky himself. Each character progresses through the play via a series of clashes with the other characters. These clashes are mutually productive, providing renewed impetus for the performer until the next conflict occurs. Again, it is 'action' that is the product of this formula, sustaining the impetus of the play. Stanislavsky deviates from Newton in the balance of action (*deistvie*) and reaction (*kontrdeistvie*). It is not an equal or symmetrical arrangement for him, rather the opposite, in fact: it is a cumulative and ever-intensifying process. But the central dynamic of action and reaction is explicit. Crohn-Schmitt's bold assertion that: 'Stanislavsky's "superobjective" is the same as Aristotle's "final cause"' (1990: 96) does not take into account this conflicting dynamic. Instead, she unites the two men's philosophies around the notion of 'spirit': 'Like Aristotle he [Stanislavsky] meant not physical activity but a movement of the spirit' (1990: 96). Such an interpretation obfuscates the role of the actor, distancing it from what Stanislavsky saw as the material bedrock of the actor's craft – action – and describing it instead as an intangible, mysterious process. The translation 'superobjective' partly contributes to this preference for Aristotelian teleology, connoting something more distantly purposeful than the simple, functional 'supertask'.

Models of conflict

Stanislavsky's insistence that the supertasks of the characters *clash* is what aligns him with Newton. Where this conflicting model is not immediately apparent in the play it has to be found. This is evident even early on in Stanislavsky's career, in the promptbook for his 1901 production of Chekhov's *Three Sisters*. M. N. Stroeva tells us that: 'the clash of two hostile forces constitutes the dramatic pivot in the director's prompt book' (1967: 122) and, in *My Life in Art*, Stanislavsky himself declares that it is the sisters' active 'surge to overcome' (1980b: 372) the enervating forces of their society which underpins the dramatic content.

For Stanislavsky, conflict is the lifeblood of the play, establishing a motive force for the sisters to combat the inertia of their circumstances. In one sense this is due simply to the optimistic vision Stanislavsky had at the beginning of a new century. Nemirovich-Danchenko's 1940 production, by contrast, showed Irina, Masha and Olga as pawns in a chess game, unable to determine their fate in any way (Gottlieb 1984: 47). But in the current context, it is further evidence of Stanislavsky's particular view of nature. The 'life' of a play is found when it is arranged in accordance with Newtonian law, when the individual actions of each character are organised in a causal line and when the overall motivation behind the role reacts with others in a series of dramatic clashes.

This thinking is not confined either to Naturalism or to a specific period in Stanislavsky's life. In his work on Molière's *Tartuffe* (from 1938), there is the same fundamental pattern of action and reaction underpinning his structural analysis. In the preparatory process for the production Stanislavsky asked his actors to narrate the simple circumstances of the play using clear and accurate verbs: 'By this means, the through-line-of-action and counter-action were established. After this was done, it was possible to recognize the factions which were fighting and ask each actor: "where do you stand in this struggle?"' (Toporkov 1979: 164). Almost four decades on from his production of *The Three Sisters*, Stanislavsky's approach to textual analysis has changed very little. Still he looks to find the struggles within the play and still those struggles constitute the point and counter-point of the play's dynamic. A little later, feeding back on the scene between Cléante and Orgon, in which the latter sings the praises of the hypocrite Tartuffe, Stanislavsky offers the following commentary:

> We must play this scene every time as if for the first time ... Otherwise, your playing becomes stereotyped instead of what I ask you for: live organic action each time. Just remember your tasks: Each person in the scene is convinced that he is right and wishes by any means to

immediately bring the other to terms; each one wants that passionately. So solve this task today, right here, right now.

(in Toporkov 1979: 192)

In saying as much Stanislavsky was drawing upon an intellectual tradition stretching from the seventeenth to the twentieth centuries. From the former, and from Newton himself, he takes the conflict-based clash of forces, while from the latter, from Taylor, he takes the immediate solving of 'tasks' – here translated as such well before Carnicke and Benedetti raised questions around Hapgood's translation of *zadacha*.[17]

Active analysis at the Nikitska Gate Theatre, Moscow

This emphasis on clashing tasks remains central to the contemporary practice of Sergei Desnitsky. Workshopping Act Four of *Uncle Vanya*, at the Nikitska Gate, Desnitsky's simple credo was: 'find a different physical action for each different thought'.[18] Recorded below is a plan of these actions, developed as Desnitsky directed the scene in which Vanya and Astrov dispute the whereabouts of the doctor's morphine. First, observe the actions themselves, separate from the text:

> *Enter Vanya gesticulating quickly. Astrov follows slowly and pauses in the doorway, looking directly at Vanya. Vanya sits at a table abruptly, looking away. Astrov goes further into the room standing opposite his friend. Vanya continues to look away. Astrov sits slowly and begins to polish his glasses. Vanya looks across the table. Astrov takes out his medical case and begins to tidy it. Vanya and Astrov make eye contact for the first time. Vanya grabs Astrov's hand and squeezes it. Astrov leans back on his chair away from Vanya. Vanya points to his heart. Astrov leans forward on his chair towards Vanya. Astrov goes behind Vanya's chair and whispers in his ear. Vanya looks ahead. Astrov returns to his place and opens up his medical case.*

Even for readers with no knowledge of the text a few things should nevertheless be clear from this 'score of actions' (*partitura deistvii*):

1 Vanya is in a state of excitement and Astrov is calm.
2 Vanya is keen to enter the space whereas Astrov appears reluctant.
3 Vanya's actions, in the main, initiate responses from Astrov.
4 They share a significant moment of contact over the table, which leads to a fluctuating pattern of intimacy and distance.
5 Astrov's medical case is in some way important.

Viewed thus, as a kind of 'silent étude', it is clear that Vanya and Astrov are in constant conflict with one another both rhythmically and spatially. The score of actions created by Desnitsky thus complements the subtext of the scene: the tensions between two old friends, both of whom are in love with one woman – Yelena.

Now consider the text alongside the score of actions:

VOYNITSKY: [*Enter Vanya gesticulating quickly.*] Let me alone!

ASTROV: [*Astrov follows slowly and pauses in the doorway, looking directly at Vanya.*] I should be delighted to. I ought to have gone away ages ago, but I repeat I won't go till you give back what you took from me.

VOYNITSKY: [*Vanya sits at a table abruptly, looking away.*] I did not take anything from you.

ASTROV: [*Astrov goes further into the room standing opposite his friend.*] I am speaking in earnest, don't detain me. I ought to have gone long ago.

VOYNITSKY: [*Vanya continues to look away.*] I took nothing from you.

ASTROV: [*Astrov sits slowly and begins to polish his glasses.*] Oh! I'll wait a little longer and then, excuse me, I must resort to force. We shall have to tie your hands and search you. I am speaking quite seriously.

VOYNITSKY: As you please. [*Vanya looks across the table.*] To have made such a fool of myself: to have fired twice and missed him! I shall never forgive myself for that.

ASTROV: [*Astrov takes out his medical case and begins to tidy it.*] If you wanted to be playing with firearms, you would have done better to take a pop at yourself . . .

VOYNITSKY: I saw you kissing her! I saw! [*Vanya and Astrov make eye contact for the first time.*]

ASTROV: Yes, I did kiss her, and that's more than you ever have! . . .

VOYNITSKY: [*Vanya grabs Astrov's hand and squeezes it.*] Give me something! Oh my God! I am forty-seven. If I live to be sixty, I have another thirteen years. It's a long time! How am I to get through those thirteen years? What shall I do? How am I to fill them up? [*Astrov leans back on his chair away from Vanya.*] . . . Give me something. I have a scalding pain here. [*Vanya points to his heart.*] . . .

ASTROV: There is only one hope for you and me. [*Astrov leans forward on his chair towards Vanya.*] The hope that when we are asleep in our graves we may, perhaps, be visited by pleasant visions. Yes, old man, in the whole district there were only two decent, well-educated men: you and I. And in some ten years the common round of the trivial life here has swamped us, and has poisoned our life with its putrid vapours . . . [*Astrov goes behind Vanya's chair and whispers in his ear.*] But don't try to put me off: give me back what you took from me.

VOYNITSKY: [*Vanya looks ahead.*] I took nothing from you.

ASTROV: You took a bottle of morphia out of my travelling medicine-chest. [*Astrov returns to his place and opens up his medical case.*] Look here, if you insist on making an end of yourself, go into the forest and shoot yourself. But give me back the morphia or else there will be talk and conjecture.

(Chekhov 1994: 178–179)

There is nothing remarkable, showy, or overtly theatrical about this directorial score. Desnitsky is merely shaping the externals of the scene to communicate the 'inner monologue' of the characters.[19] He is setting an external tempo-rhythm for each character – Vanya fast, Astrov slow – which complements both characters' internal tempo-rhythm: Vanya has just attempted the murder of Serebryakov, and Astrov, having decided he must leave, is nevertheless tarrying, perhaps to realise another encounter with Yelena. Desnitsky is simply physicalising the two men's shared agenda over Yelena and shaping the ebb and flow of their relationship in the movement patterns around the table.

Most important to this score is the underlying premise upon which Desnitsky bases his choices. He is establishing the conditions for a simple and tangible *battle*, in this instance over the bottle of morphine. Indeed, the extract is an almost ideal example of the function of oppositional conflict in the creation of a dramatic scene. Chekhov's own mastery of this pattern of behaviour is crystallised in this extract for he defines the clashing objectives of Astrov and Vanya with clarity and simplicity at the very beginning of their scene: Vanya's 'Let me alone' versus Astrov's 'Give me back what you took from me.' Astrov's task throughout the scene is very simple – he wishes to retrieve his bottle of morphia. Whilst, during the course of the scene, Astrov is deflected from this overarching action, he returns to it at the conclusion of the extract, spelling out explicitly what he wants. Thus, the task keeps him 'on line' through the scene. Vanya's task is as simple: to keep the bottle from Astrov. His agenda is, of course, more complex: to keep his friend and rival from leaving and thus to seek an outlet for his melancholy. But, as the director of the Nikitska Gate, Mark Rozofsky, argued: 'all that is psychology, you cannot play psychology'.[20] These emotional subtleties emerge as the scene progresses. They are the by-product of playing the simple and opposing actions surrounding the ownership of the bottle.

Desnitsky does not attribute his thinking to any particular aspect of Stanislavsky's training, but it is not difficult to see the roots of his approach: the Method of Physical Actions (*Metod fizicheskikh deistvii*). Just as Stanislavsky looked to physicalise the characters' psychological battles in *Tartuffe*, so Desnitsky is exploiting a psycho-physical link between external behaviour and internal motivation, through Vanya and Astrov's conflicting scores of action. Bella Merlin puts it clearly in her definition of the Method of Physical Actions:

> Physical Actions were small achievable tasks that were directed towards the other actors on stage ... actors found that [these] small achievable tasks could encapsulate great psychological complexities ... At the same time, they were so simple and direct that actors could accomplish them without any emotional strain whatsoever.
>
> (2003: 29)

The step-change from the playing of simple tasks, at a local level, to the discovery of 'great psychological complexities' may remind us of the 'building blocks' approach outlined earlier. At the same time, there is an emotional economy to this process, a deliverable efficiency, which has strong associations with the Taylorist formula for work: break things down to achievable tasks, take the strain out of the work by rationalising how it is delivered, and above all strive for simplicity.

The mechanics of Stanislavsky's System: *voploscenie*

The psycho-physical actor

Thus far the focus has been on the first part of Stanislavsky's *An Actor's Work on Himself*, that is the 'experience' or 'living through' of the role (*perezhivanie*). It is clear already that the process described in this volume owes a debt both to Newton's geometrical and mechanistic analogue of the world and to the particular materialist context in which Stanislavsky was operating, exemplified in Taylor's Scientific Management. A less exhaustive survey, focusing on *voploscenie* from Stanislavsky's second volume (in English, *Building a Character*) will serve to consolidate and extend this reading.

The physical apparatus of the performer – the actor's mechanism as Stanislavsky often calls it – must be developed in tune with his/her internal faculties. Of all of his teachings this principle of psycho-physical integration is the most fundamental. It is evident in Desnitsky's work, in his setting of physical actions to coax out the inner content of a scene, and it is evident in a number of contexts in Stanislavsky's own writing.

At the end of *Building a Character*, in the chapter 'Patterns of Accomplishment', Stanislavsky engages in a rather drawn-out exposition of the two sides of the System, incorporating a description that is nailed up to the studio wall in a series of banners by his students: 'Now we have the fundamentals all lined up for both sections of this wall ... To the left let us put Psycho-technique, and to the right External Technique' (1979: 271). Once the work is complete Tortsov claims a success: 'Wonderful ... It's clear and pictorial. Even a stupid person would get the idea' (273).

But without the same kind of visual aid in the book it is arguable that the System's complex internal relationships are in fact clear. Benedetti alleviates this problem by offering a version of this chapter in diagrammatic form in his *Stanislavsky: an Introduction* (1989: 61). Here, the individual elements of both outer and inner technique, roughly corresponding to the chapters of *An Actor Prepares* and *Building a Character*, are arranged according to the parallelism suggested by Stanislavsky on his studio wall. What *is* clear, however, is the illustrative choice made by Stanislavsky to communicate the nature of his System. The diagram originally drawn by Stanislavsky, published in Volume 4 of the Russian edition of his works and upon which Benedetti's table is partly based, is in fact charged with a telling symbolism (see Figure 1.1).

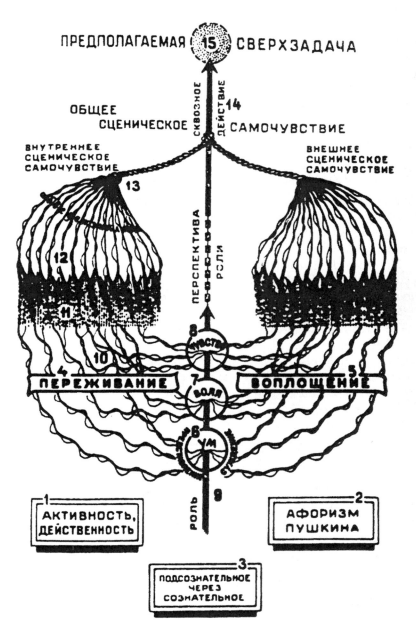

Figure 1.1 Stanislavsky's diagram of the System, 1938 (source: Carnicke 1998: 99).

The interdependence of mind and body is still made explicit in this Russian version and follows the arrangement described in *Building a Character*: on the left of the diagram is *perezhivanie* with an allusion to the elements contributing to the internal theatrical state, and on the right is situated the external theatrical state (*voploscenie*). Bisecting these two halves in a straight line leading to the supertask is the 'perspective of the role' and the actor's 'through-line' and located along this line but towards the bottom are the inner motive forces of 'reason', 'will' and 'feeling'.

Whilst it fulfils the function of displaying the balance of outer- and inner-training in the System, the form of the diagram also speaks to the central tension already identified in Stanislavsky's thinking. On the one hand, it appears to be a biological life-study, evoking the organic, natural process of creative acting. *Perezhivanie* and *voploscenie* take the form of two lungs that connect to the central spine[21] by means of a braided artery and streams of nerves appear to be emanating from the triumvirate of motive forces.

On the other hand, we can clearly see the linearity of the system. The central spine does not on closer inspection have vertebrae but rectangular blocks of material (presumably signifying the constituent actions of the role). These are given direction by arrows emerging from the forces of reason, will and feeling. The arrow motif is repeated at the top of the central line and points directly to the supertask, highlighting the ordering influence of the *sverkhzadacha*.

Indeed, if one focuses anew on the diagram as a whole, it is easy to review its network of lines not as nerves but as charged electrical wiring feeding into the System's main cabling. Viewed as such, Stanislavsky's chosen diagram perhaps unconsciously captures the mixed messages in the System – the fusion of the organic and the mechanistic.

Evidence for the latter point of view as it appears in the second volume of actor training follows.

The actor's motor apparatus

In the chapter in *Building a Character* entitled 'Plasticity of Motion' Stanislavsky provides a model for his students: 'You do not have to be so much of an actor as an engineer or mechanic to comprehend and fully appreciate the action of our motor apparatus' (1981: 52). He goes on to describe the human body in terms of a Pullman carriage, the legs as the under-structure and shock absorbers, the hips, knees and ankles all contributing to the forward motion of the machine: 'This body, again like a railway carriage, will move as smoothly as possible on a horizontal line with few vertical ups and downs' (ibid.: 53).

Later in the book, whilst he is summarising the whole System, he continues this reading:

> All the parts which contribute to your external, physical technique are now flexible, receptive, expressive, sensitive, responsive, mobile – like a well oiled and regulated machine in which all the wheels, rollers and cogs work in absolute co-ordination with each other.
>
> (1981: 281–282)

For his actors to appreciate fully the workings of their bodies, Stanislavsky looks to mechanical metaphors to make his point. The train has all the qualities of purpose and linearity that appealed to him so greatly. It offers a model of efficiency, of fluidity, and, by extension, of beauty. The engineer, for their part, has control over the machine, s/he is sensitive to its complex workings and, as such, is able to derive maximum output from it. By analogy, the actor must aspire to this level of control over his/her physical apparatus. This will entail learning anew how to walk, to see, to act. It will require a fresh and objective analysis of the most fundamental aspects of behaviour – in short, a Taylorisation of the body:

> The movements and action of a character being portrayed gain immeasurably in significance and attraction when they are not clouded over with superfluous, irrelevant, purely theatrical gesticulation ... There is also this to be said against this excess motion. It absorbs a great deal of energy which could better be used.
>
> (Stanislavsky 1981: 75)

In the light of such commentary it is little wonder that, in this final period of their work, he and Meyerhold were beginning to be seen as a 'convergent movement' and that the traditional 'dividing lines' between their theatres had 'become confused' (Rudnitsky 1988: 190). The reduction of superfluity in the behaviour of the actor is a centrepiece of Meyerhold's practice (as we shall see in the coming chapter) and his appropriation of Taylorist theory is far more explicit. But we have already seen that in the subtext of Stanislavsky's psycho-technique (the subject of *An Actor Prepares*) there is a strong affinity with Taylor's industrial management theory and here, in the accompanying volume *Building a Character*, there appears as keen an emphasis on efficiency as there is in the system of his erstwhile colleague.

At the same time, the words used by Stanislavsky are unmistakably redolent of Alexei Gastev's machine-inspired rhetoric. Of course, for Stanislavsky any emphasis on the actor's external 'motor apparatus' must always be viewed in the light of his/her inner emotional work, whereas for Gastev feelings were simply to be distrusted as counter-efficient. But it is interesting to surmise what image America may have had of Stanislavsky had the problematic timetable of publication for the two acting volumes been reversed.

Plasticity of motion

The chapters in *Building a Character*, devoted to training the body are given a distinctly mechanistic slant, with the metronome substituting for Gastev's (and Taylor's) favoured instrument of control: the stopwatch. Asking his students to raise their arms to the count of four, Tortsov divides up the movements needed to perform the overall action into separate sub-actions, correlating with the joints of the arm: from shoulder to elbow, from elbow to wrist, from wrist to fingers and finally the fingers themselves. By slowly increasing the counts within the steady beat of the metronome the jerkiness of the movement is reduced, beginning with:

> 'One, two, three, four...' Tortsov now barked the count abruptly, like a military command ... Our arms moved in jerks like a cart lumbering across deep ruts.

and accelerating to:

> One-one-one-one-one-one-one-one-two-two-two-two-two-two-two-two-three-three-three-three-three-three-three-three-four-four-four-four-four-four-four-four.

'At this top speed', Kostya then informs us:

> My arm moved without a break and very slowly because the beat of the metronome was still set at ten. The result was a marvellous smoothness.
> (Stanislavsky 1979: 66–67)

Thus, a staccato, robotic movement slowly develops into an organic, fluid one – like the neck of a swan unfurling, as Stanislavsky puts it (1979: 65). By increasing the number of 'building blocks' in the overall movement, the transitions between them become progressively seamless – no less than a Cartesian breakdown of bodily movement.

Coupled with the tempo-rhythm work that plays such an important part in *Building a Character* as well as the mechanical bodily metaphors that punctuate the whole volume, Stanislavsky's book, like Gastev, appropriates the positive connotations of the machine. One can only wonder how significant the impact of this book, dedicated to *voploscenie*, would have been had it emerged thirteen years earlier than the psycho-technique of *An Actor Prepares*. How strong would have been the following around Lee Strasberg's introspective school of acting in a climate of external rather than internal actor training?

By the time *An Actor's Work on Himself Part 2* was published in Russia, Gastev's particularly extreme mechanising of humanity ceased to reflect the particular concerns of the State. His science of labour, it was thought, subordinated the worker to the strict functionality of the machine, returning him/her ironically to the pre-revolutionary condition of 'victim' in an exploitative industry.[22] Gastev was arrested that year (1938) and died in custody three years later.

Stanislavsky managed to avoid any such overt political harassment but his affinity with the language of Gastev does indicate a desire on his behalf to respond to the new age. It is, at the same time, consistent with the reading we are proposing here – that Stanislavsky's industrial background was more influential than has previously been acknowledged. Indeed, this feeling is strengthened if one considers in more detail the 'marvellous smoothness' to which Stanislavsky's second self, Kostya, refers. For 'smoothness' is a constant benchmark of efficiency for Stanislavsky in *Building a Character*. Consider his exemplary model of movement in the chapter entitled 'Plasticity of Motion' – a garrison of soldiers: 'They did not appear to be walking at all but rolling along on skates or skis over an absolutely smooth surface. One had the sense of their gliding, there was no abrupt stepping up and down' (1979: 53).

Both Gastev, in Russia, and Frank and Lillian Gilbreth, in America, were coming to the same conclusions in their industrial researches into movement: the smoother the movement, the more efficient it was. Gastev in his article 'How to Work' (1921) defines the ideal smooth arc for the worker's arm in the process of hammering (Johansson 1983: 158) and pioneered the use of photography in movement analysis. The Gilbreths developed similar 'efficiency movement' research in the United States, breaking behaviour down into its constituent parts, also with the aid of slowed down film footage; this they considered to be more accurate than the stopwatch. Their purpose was to produce models of action that would eliminate energy-wasting movement. Smooth and continuous motion was found to be the most productive, along with simultaneous and rhythmic actions (Gordon 1995: 88). These models of actions, fashioned out of wire, were named 'therbligs' (roughly 'Gilbreth' backwards) and were used first to analyse and then to choreograph the movements of workers engaged in repetitive tasks. Whilst the parallels with Meyerhold's work will become clear in the next chapter, particularly in respect of his biomechanical études, Stanislavsky's analysis of the physical work of the actor may also be seen as part of this zeitgeist. He, like Meyerhold, aspired to the condition of the highly trained and proficient worker, whose movements were both rhythmic and fluid.

Summary

The Gilbreths' work in 'motion study' and Stanislavsky's metaphor of the Pullman carriage return us to the Newtonian context of this chapter. For although in the late 1930s Stanislavsky's extolling of the train may be seen as a little dated (Alexei Gastev, in his guise as a poet, was mining its hyperbolic possibilities as early as 1916 in *Express*), it is fully integrated with his thinking. His System is fundamentally a System *in* motion and *of* motion, a fact that is no better expressed than in his approach as director to the appropriately entitled *The Armoured Train* (1928): 'As always for him . . . it was the dynamic, the forward drive of the play as a whole which mattered' (Benedetti 1990a: 298). Whilst Stanislavsky always extended and developed his work, the methodology underpinning his findings remained constant. From the pre-System Chekhov productions to the posthumously produced work of the late 1930s, the forward momentum of the actor is always central.

In trying to explain this constant fluidity, Stanislavsky regularly referred back to Nature for guidance. 'There is no System', he states in *An Actor's Work on Himself Part 2*. 'There is only Nature' (in Hodge 2000: 33). In the American version of the same book, *Building a Character*, he articulates the same belief, contrasting his own ignorance with the omnipotent understanding of 'the great artist Nature' (Stanislavsky 1979: 300). In saying as much, he was expressing a deep-seated belief that the natural world has laws that are binding for all, that Nature holds all the secrets, so to speak.

Such statements appear to distance him from any profound connection with science, allowing him instead to hide behind the mysteries of Nature. But both the practical and the theoretical evidence cited here suggest something different. Rather than there being an opposition between creative Nature and science in the System, there is a consistently stable union between the two. It is not so much that his mechanical methodology is in conflict with a natural view of life, but that for Stanislavsky in an Enlightenment tradition stretching back to Newton, Nature is most commonly thought of in mechanical terms. His appeal to the universal laws of nature is as much an appeal to the Newtonian 'System of the World', which succeeded in at first uncovering and then rationalising these natural laws in a remarkable and universal synthesis.

This underlying and typically Modernist universalism is reflected in the aspirations of many of the key thinkers of this chapter: Ford and Taylor saw their systematic visions extending across the world and Taylor's colleague, Frank Gilbreth, viewed his therbligs as 'fundamental elements of hand motion', clearing the ground for what he called 'The One Best Way To Do Work' (Haber 1964: 40–41). Gilbreth's concept is reflected almost exactly in Gastev's aforementioned treatise 'How to Work', and Gastev's own methodology, extreme though it was, had the same universalising mechanics as its keystone. By way of conclusion let us consider now how far Stanislavsky shared such a conviction in the universalising capacity of the System.

A System of (and for) the world

The name most conspicuous in its absence from the list above is Joseph Stalin's. Stalin was, as David Joravsky colourfully characterises him, the '*coryphaeus* of thinkers' (1978: 108), orchestrating a hugely complex govern-mental machine and restricting independent thought through a culture of terror.[23]

Indeed, the State and scholarly activity were progressively seen as insep-arable, as Ernst Kolman indicated in a speech to mathematicians in 1930: 'Now it is clear to everyone that all efforts to think of any theory, of any scholarly discipline, as autonomous, as an independent discipline, objec-tively signify opposition to the Party's general line' (Joravsky 1978: 109). This was as true for the artistic disciplines as it was for those practising science and, in Stanislavsky's case, it meant that his System was adopted to the general cause of Socialist Realism as defined by Andrei Zhdanov and Stanislavsky's erstwhile colleague, Maxim Gorky. Zhdanov's famous speech to the First All-Union Congress of Soviet Writers in 1934 drew on Stalin's definition of the artist, 'the engineer of the human soul', enquiring: 'what does this mean?' The answer to his own question is revealing:

> The truthfulness and historical exactitude of the artistic image must be linked with the task of ideological transformation, of the education of the working people in the spirit of socialism ... Yes, our Soviet liter-ature is tendentious and we are proud of it, for our tendentiousness is to free the working people – and the whole of mankind – from the yoke of capitalist slavery.
>
> (Zhdanov 1950: 15)

Gorky followed this speech with his own declaration, one informed by a similar vision of a unifying literature of the proletariat, a literature that could 'unite the whole world of the working people that capitalism has torn asunder' (Zhdanov *et al.* 1935: 59). Where, almost contemporaneously with these statements, Ford in America saw capitalism (and its concomitant technological advances) as a global homogeniser, Zhdanov and Gorky viewed it as a destructive force, tearing apart the 'whole of mankind'. Either way, each side considered they had the answer – world unification.

Given Zhdanov's definition, it is easy to see why Stanislavsky and Nemirovich's Moscow Art Theatre was embraced by the Party machine. With a past record and international reputation for 'historical exactitude', as well as an acting System whose central pursuit was for 'truth', the MAT was a natural target for Stalin's project of 'soul engineering'. Stanislavsky also had a long-term working relationship with Gorky, who returned to the USSR in 1931, 'honored by Stalin ... as a symbol of reconciliation' (Fitz-patrick 1992: 245).

Gorky not only took the lead on the 'literary front' of the cultural revolu-tion but also acted as a mediator between the sciences and the arts, establish-ing a group of favoured individuals whose respective disciplines became the accepted orthodoxy. Joravsky notes that in October 1932, Gorky brought together in his house a group of prominent Pavlovian scientists to discuss matters of interest with Stalin. Shortly after, he organised a similar meeting, this time with writers. Emerging from these dialogues was a Stalin-backed policy for the manipulation of the people's psyche: 'on the medical level [the psyche would be cared for] by physiologists "above all Pavlov's school", on the spiritual level . . . by imaginative writers' (Joravsky 1978: 127).

As the figure of theatrical legitimacy under Stalin, as well as Gorky's friend, it is more than possible that Stanislavsky would have been at this meeting but even so, the synthesising of science and art in Stalin's mind is notable.[24] By the 1960s, the association of materialist psychology with artistic activity led to tendentious Marxist analyses pointing up the Pavlovian aspects of Stanislavsky's Method of Physical Actions. Pavel Simonov, for example, claims in *The Method of K. S. Stanislavsky and the Physiology of Emotion* (1962) that 'the determinism of the Stanislavsky system is a direct reflection of the theory of Sechenov and Pavlov' (1962: 36). Interestingly, at the same time, he highlights the universality of the System which, he claims, operates on laws that are equally obligatory 'for all theatrical creators without exception' (ibid.: 35).

But the effects of Stalin's backing did not take as long as the 1960s to impact on Stanislavsky. There are clear Pavlovian references in *An Actor Prepares* (set against the more 'dangerously' mystical sources) and more attention will be paid to these in Chapter 3. More importantly in this context is the evidence that, as Stalin began to see the MAT as the progenitor of a universal acting System for the whole of the USSR, so too did Stanislavsky. In his last days, a victim of Stalin's policy to 'isolate and preserve', he spent his time in his apartment imagining the extent to which his writings might be disseminated. The System, according to Anatoly Smeliansky, ceased at this time to be simply an actor's book but instead '[It] was addressed to the nation, to the world, because it discussed how to preserve oneself in the joy of creation' (1991: 13).

It is a view which is substantiated by Stanislavsky's own writings: 'My system is for all nations', he claims in the collection of writings entitled *An Actor's Handbook*. 'All peoples possess the same human nature' (1990: 160). It was also a view that informed his textual choices at the end of his career – better to work on *Tartuffe* than on Chekhov, he reasoned, if one is to illustrate the universal efficacy of the System.[25]

Clearly the kind of zealotry evident in this universalism owes something to the climate Stalin had created for him. He was isolated, ageing and, naturally, reflecting on the worth of his fifty-year theatrical career. The governmental sanctioning of his System, although it had given him problems in the expression of some of his ideas – chiefly the more mystical aspects such as the 'magic if' and the 'life of the spirit' (Carnicke 1998: 81) – had brought about the wholesale dissemination of his systematic practice.

But his last-gasp commitment to a universal theory of acting speaks more to the Newtonian context in which he has been situated in this chapter, than it does to the pressures of Stalinism. It is, in fact, the logical outcome of a search for the 'natural laws' of acting. For when Stanislavsky stated in *My Life in Art* that the laws of creativity 'exist for all, for ever, and in all creative processes' (1980b: 483), he was committing himself to a Newtonian project as early as 1924, a project which sought to systematise the world. His conclusion, that these laws have been 'tried by science and found true' (1980b: 483) may, then, be read as tacit confirmation of this.

Stanislavsky is doing much more than simply cashing in on popular contemporary support for a mechanical world-view. He shares with Newton an overarching ambition to unpick the subtext of the natural world.

Part II
The Newtonian branch

2 The theatricality reflex

The place of Pavlov and Taylor in Meyerhold's biomechanics

Whilst it may have been necessary to probe the subtext of Stanislavsky's System for evidence of its scientific leanings, Meyerhold's work draws explicitly on the industrial and scientific thinking of his time. Speaking publicly in 1922, in a lecture entitled 'The Actor of the Future and Biomechanics', Meyerhold made his case: 'Art should be based on scientific principles; the entire act should be a conscious process. The art of the actor consists in organizing his material; that is, in his capacity to utilize correctly his body's means of expression' (1991: 198).

There is something strangely fitting about these two attitudes to science – Stanislavsky's subtextual affiliation with Taylor and Newton and Meyerhold's open appropriation of the current technological and industrial thinking. For in many ways these stylistic differences are echoed in their acting systems, developed in parallel around the Revolution in 1917, but sharply divergent in their response to the momentous events of that year.

Meyerhold's emphasis is clearly on the physical craft of the actor, what he viewed as the material, manageable side of the actor's psycho-physical arsenal. He did not ignore the inner, emotional aspects of performance but was eager to find a way in which they could be controlled, understood, in physical and objective terms. This pursuit led him to the contentious statement he made in 1922, that Art should be 'based on scientific principles'. He even went as far as expressing this belief in an algebraic 'formula of acting' and was vilified by many of his theatrical colleagues for his claims. But which scientific principles did he mean and what did he think they might offer an actor in his theatre? These are two key issues for this chapter.

The other implicit reference in Meyerhold's statement is to the contemporary art movement of Constructivism. Where Meyerhold was seeking to define the actor's work in terms of its efficacy and utility, the movement of Constructivism was eschewing aestheticism with the same goals in mind. Alexei Gan, one of the movement's key theorists, remarked that: 'The socio-political system conditioned by the new economic structure gives rise to new forms and means of expression. The emergent culture of labour and intellect will be expressed by intellectual material production' (in Bann 1974: 37). For Meyerhold, the productive energies of 'labour and intellect' were combined in his system of 'biomechanics', a consciously contemporary term designed to affirm the scientific and industrial foundations of his physical actor training. Before the Revolution, his system of training involved a rich mixture of popular forms: circus, *commedia*, pantomime and improvised études. After 1917, these influences were subsumed under the banner of biomechanics, a banner that was waved by Meyerhold and his students in a range of public meetings in the early 1920s.

Of course, Meyerhold's influences before the Revolution did not simply disappear in the post-revolutionary system of biomechanics – popular theatre forms continued to inform his practice, as did many aspects of the Oriental theatre. But the training system he taught from 1921 in Moscow had a distinctly different method of *articulation* – one that drew explicitly on industrial management theory and on contemporary ideas of Objective Psychology.

It is this 'scientific' basis of biomechanical practice that needs to be evaluated in this chapter, not just in its own context but with reference to the tradition of biomechanics which emerged after Meyerhold's death and which is continued today in the work of two key practitioners: Alexei Levinsky and Gennady Bogdanov. The aims of this chapter are, then, twofold: first, to examine the theoretical case for a scientific reading of Meyerhold's biomechanics and, second, to evaluate how far this may have penetrated the actual training.

The context

Biomechanics, Constructivism and the machine

Meyerhold shared with the Constructivists a utilitarian focus and for the director that meant shaping the principal material resource of the theatre – the actor's body. This mutual celebration of productivity was reflected in a collective passion for the working machine, so much so that collaborations between Meyerhold's theatre and prominent Constructivists were common in the first years of the 1920s. Liubov Popova, described by Camilla Gray as 'one of the most enthusiastic believers in production-art' (1986: 204), worked on Meyerhold's production of *The Magnanimous Cuckold* in 1922, transforming his stage into a moving machine, with the actors cast as workers in a theatre factory. Later that year, Popova's Constructivist colleague Varvara Stepanova designed Meyerhold's set for *The Death of Tarelkin*, again basing the staging on the workings of a machine but this time with a huge meat-mincer centre stage. Such designs paralleled one of the key philosophical principles of Meyerhold's acting system: 'the body is a machine, and the person working it is a machine-operator' (in Leach and Borovsky 1999: 310).

There is much to remind us here of Stanislavsky and the declarations he made in *Building a Character* on the bodily training of the actor's physical 'apparatus', and progressively it will become clear that both men share a common, Newtonian root to much of their acting theory. But it is also important to note how differently Stanislavsky and Meyerhold responded to the shifting political landscape of the early revolutionary years.

Reactions to the revolution

In the three weeks that followed the 1917 October Revolution Stanislavsky's Moscow Art theatre remained closed in what Edward Braun calls a state of 'artistic paralysis' (1995: 152). In the same period, Meyerhold declared his emphatic support for the new order and had already attended a meeting called by Lunacharsky to discuss the reorganisation of the arts in the new Soviet Union.[1] After a torrid period in the south, during which time he was arrested and almost executed by the White guard, Meyerhold returned to Moscow in September 1920 and was made head of the Theatre Department of *Narkompros* by Lunacharsky. Although his elevated position in the political hierarchy of Lunacharsky's Commissariat of Education did not last – he resigned in the following February – Meyerhold's conscious manoeuvring in officialdom as well as his creative relationship with the contemporary art world must be distinguished from Stanislavsky's altogether more passive approach in these first years after the Revolution.

Donald Rayfield, Chekhov's biographer, sums up the position of the Art Theatre in uncompromising terms:

> For all that it did in the first 25 years of its existence to show the world how Chekhov can be performed and interpreted, [the Moscow Art Theatre] spent the next 25 years as Stalin's favourite theatre, fossilising itself on the lines of the old system, which Chekhov so detested, of 'serfs and master, directors and mistresses' and for political survival, throwing to the wolves fresh talent that would not conform.
>
> (1998: 24)

This may be overstressing the point and the ironic contrast between Stanislavsky's naive pragmatism in his relationships with Stalin and Meyerhold's overt (and ultimately fatal) stance does not need any further discussion here. But the relative distances between the two directors and their immediate cultural surroundings are of importance not least because they may explain, in part, the implicit presence of industrial theory in Stanislavsky's System and the much more overt appropriation of Taylorism in Meyerhold's pronouncements on his own acting system. Stanislavsky absorbed the mechanistic and industrial influences of the age over time; Meyerhold was onto them in a flash.

Meyerhold and Taylor

Witness Meyerhold's declaration in the lecture he gave at the Moscow Conservatoire in June 1922: 'The methods of Taylorism may be applied to the work of the actor in the same way as they are to any form of work with the aim of maximum productivity' (1991: 198–199).

And, from another source of the period:

> Biomechanics strives to create a man who has studied the mechanism of his construction, and is capable of mastering it in the ideal and of improving it. Modern man living under conditions of mechanization cannot but mechanize the motive elements of his organism. Biomechanics establishes the principles of precise analytical execution of each motion, establishes the differentiation of each motion for purposes of maximum precision, demonstrativeness – visual Taylorism of motion.
>
> (Rudnitsky 1981: 294)

Evident in both these statements is a rhetorical force that is clearly distinguishable from the writings of Stanislavsky. Where almost all of Stanislavsky's acting theories are communicated through a series of staged dialogues with fictional and obliging students, Meyerhold's theories come down to us in a more fragmented fashion – transcripts of speeches and lectures, articles written for immediate publication, journal contributions. As such, they are often imbued with the persuasive vigour needed to communicate a message quickly and efficiently.

The latter source recalls the overarching ambition we have seen in the writings of Ford, Taylor and Gilbreth, whose theories were always thought (by themselves, at least) to be applicable beyond their specific fields. Biomechanics, we are told, is not simply a training for actors but a programme for 'Modern man', responding to the mechanical zeitgeist of post-revolutionary Russia. Its project is to establish the fundamental principles behind 'each motion', enabling the human organism to move with perfect precision. Indeed, the actual focus of the training – the actor – seems relatively downgraded in this passage, appearing almost as a footnote to a far more universal project.

This style of expression, coupled with the tendency Meyerhold had of keying into the culturally buoyant ideas of the time, has led critics to question the validity of his influences. Edward Braun, for example, sees Meyerhold's claims for a scientific system as 'specious':

> Initially, Meyerhold advanced biomechanics as the theatrical equivalent of time-and-motion study and compared it to the experiments in the scientific organization of labour by the American Frederick Winslow Taylor and his Russian follower Gastev. However, the resemblance was superficial

and was exaggerated by Meyerhold in order to show that his system was devised in response to the demands of the new mechanized age, as opposed to those of Stanislavsky and Tairov, which were unscientific.

(in Meyerhold 1991: 183)

Braun has a point when he identifies the over-emphasis placed on the relationship between Taylorism and biomechanics – indeed we shall see later that some aspects of Meyerhold's system are demonstrably in opposition to Taylor – but the natural predilection Meyerhold had for 'talking up' his subject and for locating his ideas in the new socio-political climate, does not invalidate the connection entirely. The focus here will be on the practical evidence, looking beyond the persuasive rhetoric of his writings on biomechanics to the étude work itself – the fulcrum of biomechanical training.

Meyerhold and Pavlov

In addition to Taylor's Scientific Management, Meyerhold's writings also indicate an interest in another prominent scientific theory of the time: Objective Psychology or Reflexology. Defined, by Ivan Pavlov (1849–1936), as the detailed study of 'the physiology of the higher parts of the central nervous system' (Pavlov 1955: 245), Reflexology was an attempt by Pavlov and his disciples (including Vladimir Bekhterev, 1857–1927) to base an understanding of behaviour on physiological *reflexes*. As such it was an 'anti-psychological' movement, in the sense that it viewed psychological phenomena strictly in physical terms.

Meyerhold's own position was similarly materialistic. He too was suspicious of the inner psyche, viewing it as an uncontrollable, immeasurable quicksand. 'A theatre based on psychological foundations', he states in his biomechanics lecture of 1922, 'Is as certain to collapse as a house built on sand. On the other hand, a theatre which relies on *physical elements* is at the very least assured of clarity' (1991: 199). It was Pavlov's explicit preference for the material side of psychic research, coupled with a stress on practical experimentation (as opposed to abstract theorising), which proved popular in the Marxist-Leninist political arena of the 1920s. Pavlov's work was at the other end of the scale to the science of particle physics, a largely unpopular (if not heretical) discipline, viewed, that is, from a strictly Soviet perspective. As far as the Bolsheviks were concerned, Pavlov's experiments were appropriately rooted in the real world. Where Erwin Schrödinger and his colleagues in Europe mused on thought experiments and alive/dead cats, Pavlov was in the far safer domain of the laboratory with salivating dogs.

What worried the authorities most about the new physics, including Einstein's Relativity theories, was the threat to the determinist world-view. Graham Loren elucidates:

The suspicions of the Soviet critics of quantum mechanics and relativity physics were heightened when several prominent West European philosophers and scientists concluded that the probabilistic approach of quantum mechanics meant the end of determinism as a world view, while the equivalence of matter and energy postulated by relativity theory marked the end of materialism. Several of them concluded that relativity physics and quantum mechanics destroyed the basis of Marxist materialism.

(1993: 146–147)

In such a climate the Newtonian tradition of experimental practice offered a model of 'healthy materialism' (ibid.: 148) – a reading that was later imposed on Stanislavsky's work by Marxist critics such as Pavel Simonov (1962). Indeed, Lenin appealed to Newton directly in notes published after his death, stretching his point to reveal what he considered to be the dialectical basis of all the sciences:

In mathematics: $+$ and $-$
In mechanics: Action and Reaction
In physics: Positive and negative electricity
In chemistry: Association and dissociation of atoms
In social science: The class-war.

(in Fulop-Miller 1927: 66–67)

From a Bolshevik point of view, Newton's materialism and, specifically here, his third law of motion raised his status above the modern challengers to the throne. Accordingly, the prominent scientists of the period were those who aligned themselves with Lenin's bold synthesis, with a determinist world-view built on an action–reaction dialectic. Writing eight years after Lenin's death, Pavlov made his own case in the *Psychological Review*:

The theory of reflex activity finds its support in three fundamental principles of scientific investigation: in the first place, the principle of *determinism*, i.e., an impulse, appropriate conditions, or a cause for every given action or effect; secondly, the principle of *analysis and synthesis*, i.e., the initial decomposition of the whole into its parts or units, and then the gradual reconstruction of the whole from these units or elements; finally, in the third place, the principle of *structure*, i.e., the distribution of the activity of force in space, the adaptation of function to structure.

(1932: 102)

Pavlov's own Newtonian credentials come into sharp relief here: his belief in causal determinism and the centrality of the 'scientific method' provide persuasive evidence of his debt to Newton. At the same time, his methodology

– the 'decomposition of the whole into its parts' – clearly has its roots in Cartesian thought.

But his statement also offers a helpful starting point to analyse the relationship between Pavlov's Reflexology and Meyerhold's biomechanics, particularly with regard to the formal principles of the études, for Meyerhold devised the études to explore the same Cartesian-derived principles of composition and decomposition, developing in his actors what he transparently called a capacity for 'reflex excitability' (1991: 199) and encouraging them to concentrate first on matters of form.

At the same time, Meyerhold looked to the Soviet champion of Time and Motion studies, Alexei Gastev, consciously allying himself with the industrial movement in biomechanics.

Meyerhold and Gastev

For certain contemporary critics Meyerhold's liberal use of Pavlovian buzzwords was evidence of the superficiality of his understanding. By making his theoretical basis explicit, Meyerhold, in effect, left himself open to criticism. Ippolit Sokolov, responding to a demonstration staged by Meyerhold's students, was particularly suspicious:

> Meyerhold's system doesn't establish and doesn't advance a single elementary law of genuine Biomechanics. And even more, it ignores the laws of biology and mechanics. It is clear that Meyerhold is attempting to use at any cost the great ideological and mnemonic power of the promising term 'Biomechanics'. Meyerhold's understanding of the term is extremely general, amorphous and hazy.
>
> (in Law and Gordon 1996: 145)

According to Sokolov, Meyerhold's scientific understanding amounted to nothing more than a series of 'chaotic, unrelated aphorisms [read] by one of his pupils at GVTM' (in Law and Gordon 1996: 145). In saying as much, Sokolov was raising an important question concerning Meyerhold's motivation. Was the very term 'biomechanics' coined simply for its 'great ideological ... power' – a lure for those (younger) actors searching for a performance training which reflected the new age?

Stanislavsky baulked at such a strategy, claiming to use a language which spoke directly to actors and which avoided fashionable scientific terminology. But much of his work nevertheless owes an intuitive debt to science and his own term for the System, the *psycho-technique*, actually referred to the branch of industrial psychology called 'psychotechnics', a discipline which rose to great heights in the Soviet Union in the late 1920s and early 1930s. Psychotechnics was taught in Alexei Gastev's Institute of Work (CIT) and was the branch of science dedicated to pursuing 'the application of physiology and psychology to problems of industry, the military and the like'

(Joravsky 1978: 118).[2] Stanislavsky simply extended this definition to encompass the arts.

Biomechanics, similarly, was not a term of Meyerhold's invention and it too has its associations with Gastev. At the same time as Meyerhold was giving public lectures on the subject, Gastev had set up a laboratory for the study of biomechanics. Here, he worked with one of Meyerhold's acting students, Ilia Shlepianov, calling for 'a system of precise exercises' to explore what he called 'motorial culture' (Johansson 1983: 112).[3] The favour was returned when Meyerhold cited Gastev by name in the 'Laboratory' section in his *Programme of Biomechanics*, attributing to him the idea of the 'new, high-velocity man' (Hoover 1974: 314). Gastev's work was seen as a vital contribution to the general industrial development of the country and, like Pavlov's research, it was well supported. But the popularity of the term and of the research itself may explain Sokolov's cynicism concerning Meyerhold's ambitions; an actor training which is demonstrably part of a wider, state-supported research programme is surely going to attract attention, irrespective of the strength of its theoretical grounding.

The veracity of Meyerhold's theoretical references must be tested with these cautionary words in mind, examining whether his own inspirational rhetoric also engages the actor at a performative level.

Reflexology and Taylorism in the theory of biomechanics

There can be little doubt that on one level Meyerhold's appropriation of Pavlovian theory was a calculated step to emphasise his place as a contemporary thinker and practitioner. In broad terms he had nothing to lose from the association of his own 'laboratory' researches with those of Pavlov's school and could only benefit in the climate of the time from stressing a common scientific project. Both he and Pavlov (the associative logic implies) were actively investigating the universal laws underlying behaviour; Meyerhold's experiments, conducted in the laboratories of GITIS and GVYRM, were simply restricted to the theatre.[4]

But Meyerhold found more in Pavlov's work than mere reflected cachet, as his collaborator Alexander Gladkov explains:

> Individual scientific problems interested him ... He carefully followed the experiments and work of Ivan Pavlov, and after the scientist's death, he maintained connections with his followers. He believed that Pavlov's work could at some stage of its development help in the creation of a genuinely scientific theory of the art of acting.
>
> (Gladkov 1997: 72)

For Nikolai Kustov, one of Meyerhold's teachers in the 1920s and eventually the man responsible for passing on the work to Alexei Levinsky and Gennady Bogdanov, the theoretical root back to Pavlov was also significant.

Lee Strasberg's notes, taken at one of Kustov's lectures in 1934, make this clear: 'Since we demand as much from the actor it was necessary to create some theory for his training – and Meyerhold took Pavlov's reflex system' (Strasberg 2002: 52). Later, Strasberg records the other key influence for Meyerhold: 'Taylorism is taken as a basis for work', Kustov lectured. 'In this school we try to find the mechanical movements which should educate the actor' (ibid.).

Mikhail Korenev, Meyerhold's collaborator on *The Government Inspector* (1926), and one of the men charged with defining the scientific basis of bio-mechanics, spoke in similar terms: 'absolute economy is essential', he states in *Principles of Biomechanics*, 'a total Taylorism' (Law and Gordon 1996: 138).

For at least three of his theatrical collaborators, therefore, Meyerhold's interest in Pavlov and Taylor was significant – enough for Kustov to cite Taylor as 'the basis' of biomechanics and for Gladkov to see Pavlovian theory as the key to a 'genuine' science of acting. Speaking sixty years on from these historical sources, Alexei Levinsky also acknowledged the significance of Pavlov in the genesis of biomechanics, betraying his own theoretical scepti-cism at the same time: 'Pavlov *was* significant for Meyerhold', he asserted, 'but that was his business!'[5]

Chains of reflexes

Pavlov's concept of reflex activity, drawing as it did on Sechenov's *Reflexes of the Brain* (1863), saw animal behaviour as a series of chain reactions (or reflexes).[6] He gradually rejected any 'psychical' explanation of behaviour in favour of a materialistic and physiological basis of understanding. Indeed, for him the psychical was only distinguished from the physiological in terms of its complexity. He explains his view in colourful terms:

> Are not the movements of plants towards the light and the seeking of truth through mathematical analysis essentially phenomena of one and the same order? Are they not the last links of an almost endless chain of adaptation taking place throughout the living world?
>
> (in Vucinich 1970: 306)

Both Pavlov's determinism and his Cartesian 'building blocks' approach are encapsulated in this statement. He ambitiously connects the rudi-mentary reflexivity of plants (specifically their heliotropism) to the pursuit of mathematical truth along a progressively complex causal chain of adaptations. The sophistication of mathematical reasoning, he argues, may only be distinguished from the movement of plants by its greater complexity.

Compare Pavlov's statement with Meyerhold's own set of notes in the ter-minologically heavy *Programme of Biomechanics*. Under the subheading of 'The Actor', Meyerhold lists the following characteristics:

1   a   The human organism as an auto motive mechanism.

     b   Doubly automatic actions.

     c   Mimetism and its biological significance (Bekhterev).

2   d   Motor action of the human being

       1   muscles, turning of the eyes, mimetic movement of the head, arms, legs and single groups of muscles.

       2   Complex of movements of the whole organism or chain of movements, movements of the whole organism: walking, running, acts of reading, writing, transporting loads, the most complex movements in work of one kind or another, acts of doing . . .

3   i   Psychic phenomena, simple physico-chemical reactions in the form of tropisms, taxis,[7] or purely physiological reflexes.

       j   Reflex Instinct.

       k   Reflexes, their connection, sequence, mutual dependence.

       l   Mechanization, subconsciously habitual acts.

(in Hoover 1974: 312)

Where Pavlov steps up from the tropic movement of plants to the development of mathematical thinking in humankind, Meyerhold (less ambitiously) sees the complex actions of the actor – what he calls their 'work of one kind or another' – as a chain of physical responses to external stimuli. Later on in the *Programme* he goes on to define what kind of external stimulus an actor might be responding to in the context of his theatre – not 'light' but 'sound stimuli' (ibid.), an equally Pavlovian concept. This might be the shout of an actor at a key moment or more generally the construction of movements in relation to a musical score, the disciplining of the actor's work through 'meter and rhythm' (ibid.).

For Frederick Winslow Taylor behaviour was also best understood in terms of chains of action. As recounted in Chapter 1, Taylor reduced the complexity of industrial work down to a series of connected sub-actions or tasks, allowing a specific time for each of these tasks to be completed. These 'work cycles' together made up relatively complex overall projects and became the definitive work structure for the employee in the factory. They exemplified the Taylorist watchwords of productivity, organisation and efficiency.

Drawing on both contemporary sources, Meyerhold brought Taylorism and reflexology together in his development of the biomechanical études. From Taylor's 'work cycle' Meyerhold took the idea of a smoothly executed, rhythmically efficient action, punctuated with rest periods or pauses. From Pavlov, he borrowed the idea of a chain of reflex responses, described in *Conditioned Reflexes* as 'the foundation of the nervous activities of both men and of animals' (Pavlov 1927: 11). Together, they formed Meyerhold's notion of the 'acting cycle': 'The Taylorization of the theatre will make it possible to perform in one hour that which requires four at the present. For this the actor must possess: 1) *the innate capacity for reflex excitability* ... 2) "physical competence"' (Meyerhold 1991: 199). Jumping from one source of inspiration in his opening sentence to another in the next, Meyerhold seamlessly fuses Taylor and Pavlov together. In doing so, he was arguing that the revolutionising of the theatre, based on industrially economic principles, can only be delivered by a Pavlovian actor – one who possesses an ability to *excite* rather than emote.

As with Pavlov's theory of psychic activity, this excitation emerges from an external cause, in this case from finding the correct 'sequence of physical positions' (Meyerhold 1991: 199). Only then may the biomechanical actor complete the process and infuse the audience with the same quality of excitation.

The volitional reflex

To suggest such a root to Meyerhold's biomechanics is not without its problems. One could argue that the Taylorised worker, unquestioningly carrying out the tasks set by the management, or the Pavlovian dog, instinctively salivating, are the very antithesis of the Meyerholdian actor. 'Nothing is automatic', Gennady Bogdanov (1999) repeats throughout his workshops and yet his biomechanical practice is indebted to a theoretical viewpoint that sees humanity as 'non-conscious'.

On the one hand, Meyerhold tells us, all art should consciously conform to objective scientific principles. On the other, the artist must utilise his/her expressive body: which, understood through Pavlov and Bekhterev, is a reflexive 'auto-motor'. Reflexes, according to Pavlov, are 'like the driving belts of machines' (1927: 8), entirely without consciousness.

Meyerhold chose to crystallise this tension between the instinctive and the conscious responses of the actor in formulaic terms: '$N = A_1 + A_2$. Where N = the actor; A_1 = the artist who conceives the idea and issues instructions necessary for its execution; A_2 = the executant who executes the conception of A_1' (1991: 198). The artistic conception (A_1) constitutes the thinking part of the acting divide. The execution of those ideas by the 'other half' of the actor (A_2) must then be performed instantaneously. Where Stanislavsky proposed a *grammar* of acting, Meyerhold advanced an *algebra*, indicating the latter's enthusiasm to be seen embracing the new scientific age in Soviet Russia. Whilst open to criticism from those such as Sokolov, for its spurious form of mathematical expression – Joseph Roach calls it pretentious (1993: 203) – this formula does clearly indicate the perennial paradox of acting: of being both sculptor and clay, canvas and artist at once.

For Meyerhold, it also expresses a dialectical tension in his own thinking. Taylor and Pavlov offer Meyerhold a model of performance based on spontaneous efficiency. But it is one that is stripped of awareness. From a political perspective, Meyerhold had to reconcile this reflexivity with the need for an actor's ongoing consciousness of the performance itself, as it is realised on stage and as it impacts on an audience. Thus, the instantaneous response in biomechanics, the conditioned reflex of the actor (A_2), is held in constant tension with the actor's self-knowledge of the stimulus and self-regulation of that response as the performance continues (A_1). The biomechanical actor (N) is, therefore, both experimenter and subject, simultaneously determining the stimulus, responding to it and measuring its effects. Meyerhold's own term for this fusion of opposites is paradoxical in itself: the 'volitional reflex' – an instinctive motor reaction subject to wilful control. Put another way, Meyerhold wanted Pavlov's dog to decide whether or not to salivate!

Whilst there is, then, clear evidence of a consistent theoretical basis to Meyerhold's thinking, the question remains as to how this indebtedness to reflexology and Scientific Management impacts on the practice of biomechanics. Should Pavlov be dismissed, in the way Levinsky does, as Meyerhold's personal baggage, or does his particular contribution to the movement of Objective Psychology shed new light on any of the processes within biomechanical training today?

The focus of this study must, then, shift, from the historical documents produced by Meyerhold and his colleagues in the 1920s to the biomechanical work done in the laboratory today.

Reflexology and Taylorism in the practice of biomechanics

Tracing the living link: from Kustov to Levinsky and Bogdanov

Whilst Gennady Bogdanov's work may be better known than Alexei Levinsky's, both men offer us a 'pure' line back to the work of Meyerhold. They began their training in biomechanics with Meyerhold's co-teacher, Nikolai Kustov, in 1972, as part of a small class of eight students run in association with Valentin Pluchek's Theatre of Satire. Developing their careers in the Soviet Union in the 1980s, the onset of a more 'open' governmental approach under Gorbachev led to them both accepting teaching projects outside Moscow in the 1990s – principally in America and Germany. In 1995 both men brought their biomechanical training to Britain under the aegis of the Centre for Performance Research and now Bogdanov, in particular, is a common face in the UK, working regularly with at least one contemporary theatre company in England.[8]

Bogdanov also teaches biomechanics at the Russian Academy of Theatrical Art (formerly GITIS) as well as at the Mime Centrum in Berlin. Levinsky, for his part, runs his own experimental theatre company in Moscow, having formerly been the principal director at the Yermelova International Theatre Centre.

That Valentin Pluchek should invite Kustov to work with his actors at the Theatre of Satire was hardly surprising. Pluchek had made his debut in Meyerhold's famous production of *The Government Inspector* (1926). As part of the highly theatrical officers' scene, in which the Governor's wife, Anna, was energetically serenaded by a fantastic garrison of adoring soldiers, Pluchek's crowning piece was to leap out of a hatbox brandishing a bouquet of flowers. Years later, as the director of the Theatre of Satire and in a climate of secrecy, he persuaded his associate Kustov to teach biomechanics on a part-time basis, alongside the theatre's other activities. Kustov, then in his sixties, had originally been one of Meyerhold's teachers, instructing students in biomechanics alongside Valery Inkizhinov (a specialist in Oriental theatre) and Mikhail Korenev (later the co-adaptor of *The Government Inspector* with Meyerhold). Kustov taught his class at Pluchek's theatre for three and a half years, right up until his death in 1975. In doing so, he managed to sustain a living link with the biomechanical training of the past, a link that might otherwise have died with him. Even so, his condition during these years had a profound impact on his teaching methods: 'No longer able to sustain the pace of the physical work, Kustov sat most of the time, chain smoking, observing the students closely, only getting up to show the form of the exercises, the nuances and the subtleties' (Baldwin 1995: 182). Thus, the outlawed system of biomechanics, suppressed for over thirty years, was reborn at Pluchek's Theatre of Satire.[9] Kustov bequeathed to his students the physical record of five *études*, devised by Meyerhold and his collaborators in the 1920s. These were the solo études, Throwing the Stone and Shooting the Bow, and the pair études, the Slap, the Stab with the Dagger and the Leap to the Chest.

The evolution of the études

Borrowing from the musical term for a short solo composition devised to develop technical virtuosity, the études are physical studies, drawn from different sources and comprising a series of repeatable actions. They often take the form of a simple narrative, sub-divided into discrete actions, and were underscored by the common tripartite rhythm: *i (and), ras (one), dva (two)*. Thus, not only do they share the aim of a musical étude (honing a performer's technical skill) but they are also structured musically with the *i* preparing the actor for the main action just as the upbeat of a conductor prepares a musician before the rhythmical count begins proper.

In 1922 there were twenty-two different études, listed by Béatrice Picon-Vallin from evidence in the Meyerhold archive (1990: 111). Many of them were documented in prose and pictorial form and ranged from simple pair work (Jumping on your Partner's Back) to complex, narrative-led studies such as Shooting the Bow. By the time Bogdanov and Levinsky began sharing their methods, this wide range of material had been reduced to the five essential biomechanical études listed above.

In the years between the birth of Socialist Realism in the mid-1930s and Kustov's classes at Pluchek's theatre, these études had been forgotten. Even Igor Ilinsky, Meyerhold's virtuoso actor-collaborator and one of the best placed to disseminate the practice of biomechanics, had remained silent, 'still traumatized by years of enforced silence' (Law and Gordon 1996: 7).

It is well documented why Ilinsky was so disturbed. After his execution in 1940, Meyerhold's own name had been erased from Russian theatre history and his face from theatre portraits. All that remained of his system for those in the West were the reports of contemporary enthusiasts, privileged to have seen (but generally not practised) biomechanics at work: Huntly Carter, Lee Strasberg, André van Gyseghem, John Martin, Joseph Macleod, Harold Clurman, Norris Houghton.[10] Stalin's eradication of biomechanics was so chillingly successful because it silenced the practitioners, those who were able to pass on the physical record of the work. Once Meyerhold's acting system was reduced to a collection of descriptions and divorced from its cultural and theatrical context, it could only wither on the vine.

There were attempts to reconstruct Meyerhold's études in the West using these descriptions. But translating the static documents of an essentially dynamic style of theatre training back into a living form led, perhaps inevitably, to problems and misunderstandings. Mel Gordon's article 'Reconstructing the Russians' crystallises the issue:

> The Living Theatre held a workshop in Meyerhold's Biomechanics [in May 1975]. Watching their demonstrations with a large and curious audience, I felt something between horror and amusement: Almost everything I had written was misunderstood. While the poses the actors had copied from the photographs in my article were correct, all the transitions and body rhythms were wrong.
>
> (1984: 13)

Such complications are a function of the particular mode of interpretation forced upon the company in the absence of any other material. The Living Theatre company was working from photographs and amalgamated descriptions published in Mel Gordon's 1974 article: 'Meyerhold's Biomechanics'. But without documentary evidence designed to capture the movement *between* the actions of an étude, the rhythmic and dynamic aspects of the work were bound to be misconceived. More recently such documents have been published in the form of video archives (Levinsky 1997 and Bogdanov 1999) and in written form (Pitches 2003), and the following examination of biomechanical practice is based on this 'living' material as well as on direct experience of the practitioners' work in the studio.[11]

Two approaches to biomechanics

Unlike Kustov, whose state of health prevented him from illustrating the études himself, both Levinsky and Bogdanov use their physical dexterity in the studio as an example of the benefits of a biomechanical training. In this sense they have adopted the same approach as Meyerhold himself, who was always willing to amaze his students with feats of theatricality, inspiring them to embrace the principles of the training. Erast Garin describes such a moment in his memoirs, *With Meyerhold*:

> When Meyerhold decided to introduce students to the complicated étude called 'the Dagger Attack' [the Stab with the Dagger] he would do it for them first himself . . . He acted out a pantomime of creeping up on the student and leaping upon his shoulders with his right knee resting on the student's ribcage . . . It always produced a tremendous effect upon the students. Vsevolod Meyerhold at that time was my father's age, and although my father was a hunter, I could never imagine him making such a leap.
>
> (in Schmidt 1996: 39)

In the studio workshop Levinsky uses the demonstration of his own skill in a calculated manner – to train the eyes of his participants to develop a deeper perception of biomechanics. Thus, in my own work with him, he performed the entire étude Throwing the Stone as an introduction to the first session but only demonstrated individual actions of the étude during the rest of the classes. Finally, at the end of the programme, he was ready to perform the étude again and to watch his students show their completed work.

The shift in perception brought about by this approach is notable. As someone newly familiar with the principles underlying the études, one reviews the material with a developed eye for detail – a fundamental aspect of the biomechanical approach. Questions concerning which foot is leading, where the actor's weight is situated at a particular moment and what rhythmic changes there are within the tripartite pattern become evident. In short, the eye becomes trained to see the artistry in the étude performance. As a consequence, the skill base from which Levinsky is working becomes demystified and a clear language between actor and director can be shared.

Speaking in public in 1995, at the Meyerhold symposium in Aberystwyth, Levinsky made the same point, comparing his work with actors who are schooled in biomechanics with those who are not: 'It is not possible to say that it is easier to work with actors who have experience of biomechanics. But, for those who have, there is an open language, more trust, less trickery' (1997). This belief, in a kind of 'streamlined' communication for those in the specialised community of biomechanics practitioners, recalls Thomas Kuhn's definition of the term paradigm, in which the boundaries of a group are delineated by the particular vocabulary adopted by that group (Hoyningen-Huene 1993: xii). For Levinsky, working outside his native Russia, this language is chiefly physical although, as we shall see, there are key verbal commands in his teaching which together form a rudimentary lexicon for the biomechanical actor.

Gennady Bogdanov, whose approach is far more theorised, extends this specialised language, making explicit a lot of what remains implicit in his associate's work. Where Levinsky actively resists his participants' attempts to intellectualise the process, only talking at the end of a class, Bogdanov's sessions are punctuated consistently by detailed theoretical reflections. His demonstrations function differently from Levinsky's in that they do not simply illustrate an étude but highlight the implications of étude work for other activities. As such his exercises are more varied than the three distinct areas of focus taught by Levinsky (foot work, stick work and étude work). Bogdanov includes acrobatics, skipping, juggling and a military-style physical training of the body in his sessions, all of which are underpinned by the biomechanical principles of precision, efficiency, musicality, balance and coordination. Unlike his counterpart, Bogdanov is prepared to allow a measure of improvisation around the form of the études, encouraging his students to absorb the tripartite rhythm and to apply it to more general movement work, informed (but not prescribed) by the content of the étude. In doing so, Bogdanov is stating clearly what Levinsky leaves unsaid: the rhythm of biomechanics influences all the actor's actions on stage.

The difference in the two mens' approach to biomechanics is as evident in their performance as it is in their pedagogy. Levinsky's work, unconsciously perhaps, prioritises the aspect of 'play' referred to in Meyerhold's *Programme*. He has a deliberate Chaplinesque quality. He infuses the études with lightness and humour and adopts a soft muscularity throughout. Even when there are definite contrasts in body tensions within an action, Levinsky's hands and wrists are relaxed. The lines of the étude are thus imbued with a subtle roundness. The same is true of his work with objects, particularly with sticks. Levinsky uses his twirling skills in a dance-like manner and the stick he manipulates is often used as a kind of quotation of Chaplin's dexterity with his cane.

Bogdanov on the other hand, even when performing the same étude as Levinsky, creates a wholly different aesthetic. He resembles a Socialist Realist painting rather than a comic mime, embodying a sense of the machine more than the aspect of play. The lines of the study are highly defined and his physical strength dominates the aesthetic impact of the étude. The extremities of the body are kept taut, which does not compromise the fluidity of the transitions between actions, but does create an overall sense of power rather than lightness. In class work, he shares with Levinsky a natural predisposition to comic improvisation but generally takes the high status in such work as opposed to Levinsky's beguiling, low status game-play.

Inner soul versus outer form

These variations in interpretation are consonant with the purpose of biomechanics as Meyerhold conceived it. The études, Levinsky explains,

Were created so that there would be no ideal interpretation of them. The ideal way for an actor to interpret them is that he or she completely frees their body and uses their own speed and resonance . . . Everything depends on the individual concrete performance . . . As with the theatre, each role depends on the actor who is playing it.

(Levinsky 1997)

Whilst the work in biomechanics should encourage a sense of humility in the individual, then, it should not be revered to the extent that the actor's creativity is compromised. Biomechanics must not make the performer feel 'second best', but galvanise his or her physical and mental resources in the pursuit of excellence. The result is not slavish mimesis but, Levinsky contends, a kind of 'co-authorship': 'What [Kustov] taught us wasn't just the science of it, he taught us his individuality. It was the biomechanics of Meyerhold *through* Kustov. They were co-authors as he added his own soul to the work' (Levinsky 1995).

Such a dialogic reading of the process of biomechanical training directly challenges the popular view of Meyerhold as director-dictator, shaping the actions of his actors to fit a preordained pattern. David Allen is one critic who sees Meyerhold in this light:

The style of the performance [Chekhov's *The Proposal*] was created by the director, and imposed on the actors . . . The production in some ways demonstrated the limitations of Meyerhold's approach to acting . . . In his enthusiasm for theatrical truth, Meyerhold did away with emotional truth.

(2000: 83)

Allen's view does not, however, give credit to the function of Meyerhold's physically exacting directorial approach and as a consequence misplaces emotion in the overall process. It is not that a clear and predetermined formal vision of a scene eliminates its emotional truth, but that 'theatrical' form precedes emotional content in Meyerhold's thinking. Form gives shape to emotion and allows it to be rigorously and consciously controlled by the actor, a point to which we will return.

Nor is it necessarily true to say that in clearly defining the physical score of his actors Meyerhold was 'imposing' his vision on them – a term connoting a lack of co-operation between director and actor. If this were true then the biomechanical études would be the very quintessence of Meyerholdian regimentation – a two-minute physical pattern of action, shaped by the teacher to fit an 'ur-form' first established in the 1920s. Yet, both Levinsky and Bogdanov, who do 'impose' the form of the étude on their students with an exacting eye for detail, challenge this perception of biomechanical training and performance. Instead, they stress the importance of *personalising* the étude work, not to change its archetypal form but to imbue the externals of the étude with an inner character and rhythm – one might say 'truth'.

The same must be true of an actor in performance: the director may offer a very precise vision of a scene's physical shape, as Norris Houghton's description of Meyerhold's direction of *The Proposal* indicates (1975: 108–113), but it remains the actor's task to transmit this vision to the audience, employing his or her own technique.

For the training in étude-work, this process of individualising is crucial. It means that the living link with the first teachers of biomechanics, forged over eighty years, remains alive as each practitioner imbues the work with their own individuality, not simply aping a shape from a bygone age. The latter results in a slow diminution of the formal quality of the étude; the former in a continual revivifying of the étude each time it is passed on. Viewed thus, biomechanics is not, as Allen might have it, a one-directional imposition of style, but a shared means of discovery – a far more dynamic and organic creative process.

What is remarkable in this process is the persistent integrity of the external form of the étude. Levinsky's version of Shooting the Bow, whilst unmistakably exemplifying the characteristics of his own work, outlined above, follows the shape of Kustov's Bow (captured by a stills camera in the 1930s) to a very close degree.[12] There clearly have been changes since the first versions of these études were created but for the last sixty years the evolution of the études has been markedly limited.

At the very core of biomechanical training then, is a creative dichotomy. On the one hand, the participant is learning an external form, 'preserved' in the physical frames of biomechanics enthusiasts since Meyerhold launched his laboratory work directly after the Revolution. On the other hand, as a trainee or a performer, one's individual 'soul', as Levinsky puts it, must resonate within.

The latter point is important in the light of René Fulop-Miller's charge in *The Mind and Face of Bolshevism* that the effect of Bolshevik mechanisation was to 'de-soul' (1927: 152) art. Certainly this was true for some key areas of artistic practice, for the lunatic exercise of writing 'conflictless' drama, for example. But biomechanics in *practice*, irrespective of its trumpeted associations with Pavlov and Gastev, is neither mechanical nor materialistic in the terms Fulop-Miller advances. Its study does not 'de-soul' the art to which it is being applied but instead keeps alive a 'flower' of individuality and imagination within a universal form.

Biomechanics and Japanese Noh Theatre

Close affinities might be discerned here with the discipline of Noh Theatre, an influence which Meyerhold cites in his own curriculum for second-year students at the Meyerhold Workshop (Hoover 1974: 318) and which has been pointed out by other critics such as Robert Leach. Leach stresses the rhythmic and gestural debt Meyerhold owed to the Oriental theatre (1989: 56) but what is interesting in this context is the concept of 'novelty within structure'. Where Levinsky talks of an inner soul within a brilliantly mastered external form, Zeami, the fifteenth-century Japanese playwright and performer of Noh, uses the analogy of the flower.

Emerging from the seeds of a lifetime's training, a truly beautiful performance, Zeami argues, is one that keeps its novelty, its individuality, within the strict parameters of the Noh dance language: 'The flower blooms from the imagination; the seed represents merely the various skills of our art' (Zeami 1984: 30). Such tensions between external discipline and inner freedom are typical of Meyerhold's practice. They are indicative of an attitude to creative work that sought not to smooth out problems or to resolve paradoxes but to let them resonate within the minds of his performers and his audiences. This is particularly clear when attention is paid to the relationship between Meyerhold's scientific sources and his biomechanical practice.

There are five key interconnected areas:

- The acting cycle
- Neutrality
- Rhythm
- Reflexivity
- Resistance

The acting cycle

Each étude devised by Meyerhold and his collaborators is made up of a series of actions. Each constituent action has a title, which in a workshop context may be called out by the leader to help the group locate themselves within the study. The titles of the actions for Throwing the Stone, taken from Alexei Levinsky's own 1997 commentary on his presentations, are as follows:

1 Dactyl
2 Leap to the Stance
3 Preparation to Run (followed by the first run)
4 Seeing the Stone
5 Falling on to the Stone
6 Lifting of the Stone to the Foot
7 Transition of the Stone to the Knee
8 Refusal (before the second run)
9 Spinning/Winding up the Stone
10 Taking Aim (followed by the third run)
11 Refusal (before the throw)
12 Throwing the Stone

13   Abstract Gesture (Ducking)[13]
14   Strike! *Papal*
15   Turn
16   Dactyl

Following points 3, 8 and 10 the performer executes a short circular run in an exaggerated, vaudeville style. These runs serve a range of purposes. They change the rhythm and quality of the étude, breaking its concentrated focus and establishing a wider circle of operation. As a consequence, the tone of the étude is transformed too, as the extended, comic style of the running brings a sense of levity and fun. The rigour of the exercise remains, however: the leap must be from the left foot which for most performers is unnatural and hence provokes conscious reflection; the increased tempo makes it difficult to keep the overall shape of the run, demanding that the performer pay specific attention to form; and the abrupt return to a static position at the end of the run forces the actor to bring the action back under control with balance and precision.

The breaking of an action down to a series of smaller, fluently linked sub-actions, imbued with forward momentum, has something in common with the atomistic approach to play analysis we have seen in Stanislavsky's work. But where Stanislavsky's analysis takes a large problem and reduces it down to smaller, solvable 'bits' (that is *reducing* complexity), Meyerhold takes a simple action and, in the process of dividing it up, *increases* the complexity of the action tenfold. Throwing the Stone and to a larger extent Shooting the Bow are 'melodramas in themselves' (1991: 202), as Meyerhold put it, stretching the simple narratives defined by the études' titles to near-impossible lengths. Take the constituent actions for Levinsky's Shooting the Bow (1997), which has five more actions than the photo-record documented by Gordon (1995: 94–95):

 1   Dactyl
 2   Shift to the Stance
 3   i   Indicating the Bow: pointing up
 3   ii   Indicating the Bow: pointing down
 4   Falling on to the Bow
 5   Lifting the Bow
 6   Transition of the Bow to the Knee
 7   Shifting the Bow to Eye Level
 8   Checking
 9   1st Refusal (before the shooting)
10   2nd Refusal (before the shooting)
11   Hand on Hip
12   Taking the Arrow
13   Checking
14   Preparation to Shoot

15   i   Aiming: in front
15   ii   Aiming: to the side
15   iii   Aiming: below
16   Checking
17   Preparation to Release the Arrow
18   Shooting the Bow
19   Throwing away the Bow
20   Dactyl

It is clear from these listings, that both études have a common narrative: both represent picking up a weapon, aiming it, discharging it and reacting to its impact; both begin and conclude with a dactyl (an extended double handclap incorporating the whole of the actor's body); both include a shift in perspective (*racours*) from front- to side-on; and both involve a fall to the floor, which delays the action still further.

In sum, both études *prolong* the narrative structure with unforeseen actions; at each step the audience's expectations are frustrated. When we expect the stone to be thrown, it is spun round in circles. When we anticipate the bow will be fired, a further elaborate series of checks are performed. All the time the action is being elongated, amplified and problematised – the very opposite of a Taylorised work cycle in fact. Indeed, Meyerhold's acting cycles expressly resist his own Taylor-inspired demand for a shortened or rationalised theatre event designed to fit into the workers' busy productive schedule.

The études are perhaps better viewed through the Russian Formalist Victor Shklovsky, and specifically with reference to his seminal essay *Art as Technique* (1917). There is, of course, nothing new in this connection. Metatheatrically speaking, Shklovsky's notion of *ostranenie* or 'making strange' fits very comfortably alongside the Meyerholdian project. But in this particular context, Shklovsky's stark declaration that 'habitualization devours work' and his subsequent plea that art should 'exist to make one feel things, to make the stone *stony*' (Shklovsky 1965: 12) are especially resonant. Shklovsky, effectively turns Pavlov on his head, insisting that habitualisation, or 'conditioning', is a dead hand on life – 'life is reckoned as nothing' (1965: 12), Shklovsky argues, if lived without active consciousness. 'Art', on the other hand, 'removes objects from the automatism of perception' (1965: 13), exciting the spectator or reader into conscious activity.

The études of Throwing the Stone and Shooting the Bow, with their stretched stories of rebellion, serve precisely this function. They are best viewed as symbols of the general purpose of Meyerhold's theatre, as *ostranenie* in microcosm.

To square this with his declared theoretical basis, Meyerhold had to situate himself outside Taylor's specific environment. Meyerhold's student Arkady Pozdnev explains: 'Taylor built his theory on the economy of the worker's energy, mainly by the rational reduction of the work gesture towards the *least and shortest trajectory*. In the theatre that is not only *not needed* it is *harmful*' (in Law and Gordon 1996: 150). The 'product' in the theatre is the audience's reaction rather than an object fashioned in a factory. Thus, the means by which that product is 'manufactured' must be different. An audience's reaction is best stimulated by 'broad gestures' (ibid.) – those that can be deciphered and understood at a distance.

Such an extension of the gestural language of the actor is intrinsic to the shape of the études. Extended theatricality characterises the runs already described above and underpins the presentation of each constituent action of the étude. The Transition of the Stone to the Knee (action no. 7 in the Throwing the Stone étude) is a good example. In effect, the imaginary stone moves only about eighteen inches – from the left ankle to the left knee. But Meyerhold demands that the stone first travels to the right ankle, then up to the right knee and finally to the left knee. In so doing, the actor's weight is shifted from left to right and back again; strength is needed to support the body in a precarious crouch, and balance is tested as the actor tries to avoid simply kneeling on the floor.

Clearly from Taylor's perspective such an action would be wasteful; the stone would have been thrown hours ago! But for Meyerhold the ultimate aim is different: he wanted to extend the expressivity of the actor, to develop the core skills of balance, precision and dexterity in an illustrative physical task. The extended moves in the étude thus anticipate the ultimate task on stage – to 'excite' an audience and encourage them consciously to engage with the stoniness of the stone.

Neutrality

Whilst he may have resisted Taylorised movement in one sense, Meyerhold did agree with the American on matters of excess – what Gennady Bogdanov calls 'physical trivia'. The goal of *theatrical Taylorism* will be 'the struggle against *superfluous* and *unnecessary* "gestures for the sake of gestures" on the stage' (Law and Gordon 1996: 150), Pozdnev tells us, emphasising the utilitarian aspect of Meyerholdian theatre.

Bogdanov (1999) echoes this sentiment almost word for word: 'We have to free ourselves from superfluous movements and actions. There has to be exactness to your actions – so an audience can read [them].' The way to eradicate superfluity is to become conscious of one's habituated actions; only then can one start to eliminate those unnecessary personal tics that make up natural behaviour. Echoing Shklovsky, Bogdanov rails against unconscious automatic gestures and he extends this to include the often tiny, unconscious actions of his groups when he is elucidating on a theory – crossing one's arms, scratching, playing with one's hair. To develop this regime of constant physical attentiveness Bogdanov punctuates his work with a cry of *stoika!* – a military style 'order' designed to snap his participants into a renewed state of neutrality.

For the *stoika* (*or stance*) the knees must be soft (that is, unlocked), the legs shoulder-width apart and the body erect. Arms are left relaxed by the sides of the body but under control, not swinging. The dactyl, which introduces and concludes the études, begins in this *stoika* position, and the stance is further activated by the actor leaning forward slightly, bringing the weight off the heels. All additional actions, or movements beyond those demanded by the exercise, are to be eradicated. By insisting on this working position throughout his workshops, Bogdanov deliberately creates a culture of self-consciousness, focusing attention on his participants' own physical behaviour and encouraging them to rationalise it.

This neutral state, or *stoika*, is similar to that in Copeau and Lecoq's neutral mask work. Compare, for example, Copeau's work at the Vieux Colombier in Paris, contemporaneous with Meyerhold's in Russia: 'To find the neutral atmosphere within himself . . . the actor would first have to give up deeply ingrained superficial habits' (Zarrilli 1995: 121). The *stoika* is also reminiscent of Copeau in its connection with sport. For Copeau, the state of neutrality is 'a condition without motion but filled with energy, like the condition of a runner in the moment before his race' (Zarrilli 1995: 121). For Bogdanov, the *stoika* is a 'position of readiness, [in which the actor's] physical apparatus is always switched on' (Bogdanov 1999). Thus, the state of neutrality for a biomechanical performer is never static or 'dead'. It is the performative equivalent of the Stakhanovite worker at rest: he may not be moving but he is always anticipating the next call to action.

Rhythm

For the actor, this call to action is best expressed as a reflexive response to the surroundings. Such immediate responsiveness in the actor is inculcated through a process of gradual 'conditioning' – developing a sensitivity to what Meyerhold called 'external arousal'. In performance, the stimulus may be provided by another actor, a sound effect, a lighting change. In training, it comes from the workshop leader, specifically from the use of certain calls.

The rhythmic pattern of the études is set by the vocal signature: *i*, *ras*, *dva*. In addition, the call 'hup' is used at specific moments (before point 10 in Throwing the Stone, for instance), which may be the vestige of a circus influence. *I*, *ras* and *dva* (closely connected to the Noh rhythm of *jo*, *ha* and *kyu*), correspond to the three parts of a biomechanical action translated in many differently ways over the years. Braun's translation in *Meyerhold on Theatre* is the most popular:

1. INTENTION
2. REALISATION
3. REACTION

(Meyerhold 1991: 201)

Significantly, the actual correspondence of 'and', 'one', 'two' with the three parts of the acting cycle is lost here. A performer working from this text would underscore the étude with 'one', 'two', 'three' – as Eugenio Barba does in error in his anthropological analysis of Throwing the Stone (Barba and Raüke 1995). But without the *'and'* the *intention* is not sufficiently differentiated from the other two parts of the action. Any sense of the musicality of the étude rhythms is clouded and, in addition, the fundamental tension between the potential energy of the 'upbeat' and the actual kinetic energy being released in the actions is lost.

To complicate things further, variations on Edward Braun's translation are numerous. Law and Gordon offer another possibility: recoil, settling, fixation (1996: 258) but this seems to be missing the action itself. Van Gyseghem is closer to Braun with 'intention', 'action itself', 'reaction' (1943: 28). And further variants such as 'preparation' for 'intention', 'rejection' or 'refusal' for 'reaction' continue to be used by interpreters.[14] To eschew this confusion Bogdanov insists on using the Russian terms without translating them. Thus:

i: *otkaz*
ras: *posil'*
dva *tochka*

Through practice the meaning becomes embodied: *otkaz* is the preparation before the action, often involving a small gesture in the opposite direction. In Throwing the Stone, for example, the action Preparation to Run begins with a small movement in the right shoulder, against the direction of the run. In early training the *otkaz* should be clearly emphasised. It is the basis for the ensuing action and therefore needs to be strong. As the training continues, though, depending on the nature of the work and the theatrical style of the production, the *otkaz* can become a predominantly mental preparation which lends definition to the *posil'*.

Posil', literally meaning 'to send', is the action itself. Emerging from the *otkaz*, the *posil'* is the physical expression of the intention, the releasing of the energy stored in the *otkaz*: the jump after the squat, for example, or the throw after the aim. In the Throwing the Stone example, the *posil'* for Preparation to Run is the action of taking the stance before sprinting. The resultant shape (the *tochka*) is rather like the standing start adopted by sprinters before the introduction of blocks – an athlete poised and ready to respond to the gun.

Tochka, then, is the finishing point at the end of a phrase of action. As with the *otkaz*, it is to be understood in musical terms, not implying a full stop, but a moment of fixity (a rest, perhaps) before the next phrase of action. The *tochka* is already the preparation for the next *otkaz* and thus the next cycle of activity begins. Each action links with the next in a chain of connected movements.

By way of comparison *jo* (in Noh theatre) is the 'introduction' or 'prelude', *ha* is the 'breaking' of energy or 'development' from *jo* and *kyu* is the 'final section' or 'climax' (Zeami 1984: 264–266). This fundamental rhythm in Noh works at both a microcosmic and a macrocosmic scale, very similar to the *otkaz, posil', tochka* relationship in biomechanics. On the latter scale *jo, ha, kyu* corresponds to the overall structure of the day's performances, beginning with a simple introductory play, a middle placed *ha* play with an emphasis on 'complexity of expression' and the concluding *kyu* – 'the last memento of the day' as Zeami describes it (1984: 83–84). On a smaller scale: 'The pattern of *jo, ha, kyu* is visible even in one gesture in a dance, or in the echo of one step' (Zeami 1984: 138).

Bogdanov's (1999) explanation of the tripartite structure of biomechanics takes us into an altogether different paradigm (Western materialism), but a sense of the Japanese influence remains: 'What is this structure for? It's there so it's easier for you to *build* your movements. Like in music, we count the notes. And it's the same for an actor's movements.' In saying as much, Bogdanov is echoing Meyerhold's musical understanding and indicating the Pavlovian basis of the études. For implicit in his statement is a view of the world which harks back to the Cartesian model of analysis to which Pavlov is also indebted. Pavlov's definition of the building blocks approach: 'the initial decomposition of the whole into its parts or units, and then the gradual reconstruction of the whole from these units or elements' (Pavlov 1932: 102), is echoed as well in Meyerhold's own definition of the *posil'*: the agglomeration of 'all the movements performed by the separate parts of the actor's body' (1991: 201), pieced together into one mimetic whole. At the same time, the likening of movement to music and the process of building up from an essential, nucleic structure of three, to a larger pattern of gestural 'dance' is strikingly redolent of Noh training.

For Bogdanov the construction of an actor's role is a physical task and is facilitated by an understanding of the études. Just as Throwing the Stone and Shooting the Bow 'decompose' the actions of aggression suggested by their titles and reconstruct them as sophisticated and humorous physical studies, so the actor must build up the role from a basis of connected and conscious movements; one might call it a score of physical actions, not in the Stanislavskian sense where causal logic prevails but in the Shklovskian sense where enlightening and novel juxtapositions are stressed.

A pyramid of complexity, similar to that in Noh, thus emerges: from the individual rhythmic triad of each action, to the actor's score of connected actions, and finally to the structure of the play as a whole. What is true at the microcosmic scale is also true at the macrocosmic scale – *otkaz, posil'* and *tochka* still prevail. Meyerhold's production of *Woe to Wit* (1928),[15] for example, incorporated 'a huge *otkaz*', according to Bogdanov (1999), as Chatsky, played by Erast Garin, improvised a 'very long performance before he even said his first line'.

One might read Act 1 of Gogol's *The Government Inspector* in similar terms

– an extended *otkaz* again, preparing the audience for the entrance of the mistakenly identified inspector, Khlestakov. Indeed, in Meyerhold's own production of Gogol's play (premièred in 1926), following the multiple actions and reactions of its episodic structure, the last moments of the play had the entire ensemble frozen in an oft-quoted coup de théâtre. This might be seen as the final *tochka* of the production, which in its grotesque and static theatricality nonetheless invited the audience to anticipate further action.

Reflexivity

From another point of view, *otkaz, posil'* and *tochka* are best seen as the Pavlovian building blocks of biomechanical theatre. They are the basis of a single action but can be joined together in long chains of actions to form the base structure of a play. In the same way, Pavlov reasoned, single reflexes combine to form more complex behaviours in what might be called 'macro reflexes'. This was how Pavlov managed to explain away the otherwise 'strange behaviour' of one of his dogs. This particular specimen was merely exhibiting what Pavlov called a 'freedom reflex' – the agglomeration of a number of smaller reflexes into a large, instinctual response. In the same vein, Pavlov named the ubiquitous curiosity instinct, the 'investigatory reflex' (1927: 11–12), eager, as he was, to reduce the complexity of animal behaviour to a measurable mechanism. It is easy to see from this perspective how Meyerhold arrived at his *Programme of Biomechanics*, peppered with Reflexive terminology. He was simply extending Pavlov's mode of thinking and developing the 'theatricality reflex'.

But it is not simply at the level of form that Meyerhold's biomechanics may be seen to be Pavlovian. Bogdanov and Levinsky, in their different ways, work to instil in their participants a reflexive response – the former through a military style delivery of commands, the latter through a consistent and continual emphasis on the naming of the étude actions and an underscoring of all activity with *i, ras, dva*.

The stimulus to begin an action (or to move to the next) is given by the cry 'hup' (an acrobat might use the same command in the circus). Paused ready to run at a wall, Bogdanov shouts 'hup' to set off each group. Swinging the arm to 'wind the stone', Levinsky shouts 'hup' to indicate the move to the next action: taking aim. Over time, the auditory command 'hup', along with those of *i, ras, dva* to accompany each move of the étude, become unconsciously integrated with the appropriate physical action. The language used is without ambiguity or nuance and relates to a direct physical response. The result is a model of direct communication, effective for both a camp commandant or a theatre director.

Of course, Meyerhold's actors need also to direct *themselves* – the A_1 part of the equation – and thus the 'non-conscious' reactions of the actor are never fully so. As has been indicated above, the spontaneous responses to a given stimulus are held in tension with the self-conscious knowledge of the actor in space. In addition, conscious awareness of the action is brought about by the very strangeness of the action itself and this leads us to the question of resistance or *tormos*.

Resistance

In mechanical terms *tormos* is the brake (its literal meaning in Russian), slowing the action of the machine by offering a resisting counter-force. In theatrical terms *tormos* is responsible for the elongation of the action of the études. As the action itself is carried out, so the restraining force of *tormos* holds it back. Thus, *tormos* provides a controlling influence over the action that can be measured and adjusted by the performer during the very act of performance. For solo études the performer controls his or her own rhythm by making decisions about *tormos*. For pair études, such as The Slap, the level of restraint must be communicated between the performers, and in doing so the mutual rhythm of the étude is established. For this reason the perform-ing pair are divided into active and passive with the former dictating the amount by which the action is slowed through *tormos*. The latter adopts the rhythm set by the active member until half way through the étude when active and passive switch. Each *posil'* in the étude can, therefore, be hugely extended by increasing the level of *tormos*.

In this context, Meyerhold's use of freezes in his productions can be understood as actions slowed by *tormos* to such an extent that they appear to have stopped. The impetus for all such actions is still forward. It is just that this productive motion is being held back in a dynamic tension. In addition to the frozen conclusion of his *Government Inspector*, Meyerhold's production of *Bubus the Teacher*, a year earlier in 1925, may be seen to embody this idea. James Symons explains: 'It was as if one of Charlie Chaplin's early herky-jerky films was suddenly turned down to the super slow motion and stop-action of television football coverage' (1971: 133). Later on Meyerhold articulated the idea in his own writings in his celebration of the comic's art, 'Chaplin and Chaplinism' (1936):

> The object of our experiments was the maximum exploitation of the expressive power of movement. This skill can be acquired from a study of Chaplin. His so-called 'momentary pauses for aim', that peculiar static style of acting, the freeze – it all comes down to the expedient concentration of action.
>
> (Meyerhold 1991: 321)

Significantly, for Meyerhold the expressivity of movement is best exploited through the dynamic use of its opposite, stasis. This, as with other seem-ingly irreconcilable complications in Meyerhold's work, is best understood as a dialectical tension rather than a paradox. Action, Meyerhold is arguing, in its most concentrated form *is* the freeze.

Bogdanov expresses his own interpretation of this 'momentary pause for aim' in his term *powsa*: 'A moment of stillness, an elegant counterpoint to the physical activity. However the body, even in stillness, is never in repose. It continues to radiate the dynamic energy of readiness for the next action' (Baldwin 1995: 188). Stillness and action constantly complement each other. There is never one without the promise of the other. It is this potential, either for stillness to burst out into action, or for action to be spontaneously arrested which characterises the biomechanical actor in performance. It is what leads to the constant surprises inherent in Meyerhold's directorial work.

This interplay of active and resistant forces finds its own parallel in Pavlov's theory of reflexes. For Pavlov, reflexes can be categorised into two broad types: positive or excitatory and negative or inhibitory (1927: 8). The positive reflex to a given stimulus, manifested in his experiments with animals, might be furious barking or the baring of teeth. In other animals, however, an inhibitory reflex is engendered and this can serve to nullify other positive reflexive responses. Pavlov's own words to describe this latter phenomenon are particularly resonant in the current context: 'Other . . . [animals] exhibit a defence reaction of a passive nature – they try to get free and run away or *they stand like lumps of stone, absolutely motionless*' (1927: 46; my emphasis).

All of this returns us to the Newtonian context first established in Part I. Meyerhold is different from Stanislavsky in that his understanding of resistance is predominantly physical, whereas, for his teacher, resistance is achieved by mentally scrutinising the text and finding the *problems* that need to be solved. The brake for Meyerhold, a mechanical metaphor already, is the physical equivalent of the textual inertia Stanislavsky asks his actors to find through his System. But whether the emphasis is in the first instance internal or external, both men may still be seen to be theatricalising Newton, specifically his first Law of motion – the law, we recall, of inertia. Along with Pavlov, who also articulates an understanding of behaviour as being caught between two opposing forces, Meyerhold's and Stanislavsky's acting systems both operate from a root of action and resistance, even if they come to this position from opposite ends of the psychophysical continuum.

Summary

Whilst there may, then, be a case for dismissing Meyerhold's claim for basing his 'art . . . on scientific principles' (1991: 198), there do appear to be sufficient grounds in this analysis of biomechanical practice for a reassessment. Clearly, the Taylor-inspired études borrow only so much from the model of efficiency and organisation imported from the United States and intensified in the laboratories of Gastev, and the view of the body as reflexive 'auto-motor', inspired by Pavlov, is only half the story as far as biomechanics is concerned. But it should now be evident that in matters of structure, rhythm, responsiveness, physicality and control, all key aspects of an actor's training, Meyerhold has embedded the principles of his much-criticised theoretical grounding. I hope examining the work of two contemporary practitioners operating today has served to free Meyerhold of the accusations of opportunism – although these criticisms remain valid in part – and to allow us to evaluate in different times what the value of the theatricality reflex might be.

It is an evaluation that can only fully be made once we have examined the key element missing so far from this assessment: the audience.

Objective psychology and the audience

Whilst the central focus for this chapter has been on training, in the *laboratory*, a brief examination of the place of contemporary science in Meyerhold's *theatre*, specifically his view of the audience, should serve to conclude this argument.

For an audience, the tension between action and restraint is palpable and stimulating. The energy used by an actor to keep the action under control is kinaesthetically regenerated in the audience, as anyone who watches spectacles such as the circus will testify. According to Meyerhold, this process of energy exchange is fundamental to understanding what engages an audience: 'By correctly resolving the nature of his state physically, the actor reaches the point of *excitation* which communicates itself to the spectator and induces him to share in the actor's performance: what we used to call gripping the spectator' (1991: 199). The actor's task is to give form to the emotion of the play, to create a physical shape for it and thus to control it with the material of the body. This physical shape is arousing for an audience and provokes a response. It is the stimulus for a reflex from the spectator.

In adopting such a theoretical position, Meyerhold was once again aligning himself with the contemporary movements in Reflexology and by extension with Watsonian Behaviourism: the science of observed behaviour (Watson 1924: 6). But Meyerhold's belief in this position went further than the simply rhetorical. In the same year as Watson's book emerged, Meyerhold commissioned, via the agency of Vasily Fedorov, a series of audience surveys that were the culmination of a prolonged research period into the reactions of the spectator begun at Meyerhold's RSFSR Theatre#1 in 1920–1921.

For Lars Kleberg, the scientific study of the audience in this period is 'the point where theory and practice meet' (Russell and Barrett 1990: 174) and as such it is the ideal area to conclude our analysis of the theory/practice dialectic in Meyerhold's work. According to Kleberg, these surveys were 'strictly behaviourist in spirit' (ibid.: 178) and adopt an approach that J.B. Watson would have endorsed.

Using a code to identify the various possible responses from the audience, an observer was charged with the task of recording these responses on a chart. The *x*-axis of this chart is related to time and the *y*-axis to the concrete stimulus provided by the actor (see Figure 2.1). The responses intensified in scale from 1) Silence and 2) Noise to 18) Rising from the seats, 19) Throwing objects on to the stage and 20) Climbing on to the stage![16] Thus the passage of the play could be cross-referenced to the observable responses in the audience and then, post-performance, broken down to isolate key moments of excitability. Coupled with additional data, including a Taylorist time-and-motion study focusing on the rest periods in the production (intervals, pauses and so forth), the creative team could work towards the ultimate behaviourist goal described by Watson in *Behaviorism*: 'To be able, given the stimulus, to predict the response' (1924: 18–19).

In an age of productivity a theatre with a political project – as was clearly evident in Meyerhold's adaptation of Verhaeren's *The Dawn*, for example – must make its political point efficiently, without confusion. Thus, the information derived from the scientific observations of the audience had a direct political function, measuring the effective moments and diagnosing the ineffective ones. In the case of *The Dawn*, Meyerhold took particular steps to ensure the spectators reacted in the 'correct' manner, planting 'actor-clappers' within their number whose task, as Konstantin Rudnitsky notes, was 'to react actively to stage events and serve as an example for the rest of the audience' (1981: 269). Some reviewers lost little time in validating Meyerhold's attempts to manipulate the audience, couching their reviews in like-minded terminology. 'This inflames', said one. 'This excites. This sets up currents of living interaction expressed in the audience's applause . . . you can feel the beating of a common pulse, a common rhythm' (ibid.).

Of course, what this particular review (and the research in general) presumes is the homogeneity of the audience. The actors are engaged in a classical causal relationship, with the spectators united as singular 'effect'. As early as 1907 in his article 'First Attempts at a Stylised Theatre', Meyerhold

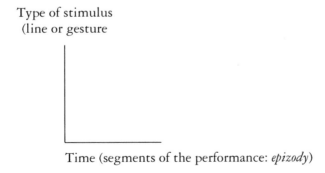

Type of stimulus
(line or gesture

Time (segments of the performance: *epizody*)

Figure 2.1 Meyerhold's chart recording theatrical stimuli and audience responses.

was advocating what he called the 'Theatre of the Straight Line' comprising four theatrical elements: author, director, actor, spectator. This linear theatrical process allowed the actor to stand 'face to face with the spectator (with director and author behind him), and *freely* reveal . . . his soul to him, thus intensifying the theatrical relationship of performer and spectator' (Meyerhold 1991: 51–52). Two decades later, working with very different dramatic material, Meyerhold still saw the theatrical process in Newtonian terms. His audience's reactions were to be consciously manipulated to meet his ideological ends. Meyerhold's pupil Sergei Eisenstein put it in explicit terms: 'Theatre's basic material derives from the audience: the moulding of the audience in a desired direction (or mood) is the task of every utilitarian theatre' (1988: 34). This 'moulding' was to be done by establishing a series of what Eisenstein later called 'attractions' in the performance, designed to 'excite' the audience in predictable ways:

> An attraction . . . is any aggressive moment in theatre, i.e. any element of it that subjects the audience to emotional or psychological influence, verified by experience and mathematically calculated to produce specific emotional shocks in the spectator in their proper order in the whole.
>
> (Ibid.)

Whilst there is not scope in this study to examine Eisenstein's own unique contribution to the cultural environment of post-revolutionary Russia, his statement, drawn from the seminal essay 'The Montage of Attractions' (1923), does capture the spirit of the time and illustrates the fusion of agitational propaganda with the theories of Pavlov and Watson. Reflexology and Behaviourism provide the theory and the means for a politically efficacious product. For Eisenstein, and by implication for Meyerhold, the reactions of the audience can be measured, calculated mathematically and pre-determined in the theatrical equivalent of Lenin's action–reaction dialectic cited earlier.

It may be tempting, then, in this particular context, to see Meyerhold's biomechanical work in the 1920s in strictly mechanistic terms; an actor/engineer works to produce an emotional 'product' in a unified audience. Certainly, we have seen a clear relationship between the practice of biomechanics and Reflexology, Behaviourism and Taylorism and have traced a living link back to the birth of the études to test these theories against the physical record passed down by Levinsky and Bogdanov. But there remain problems with this view of the work, specifically in terms of the audience and the actor studying the études.

Although the behaviourist analyses detailed above indicate a homogeneous view of the audience, Meyerhold also claimed the need to polarise his audience: 'If everyone praises your production, almost certainly it is rubbish. If everyone abuses it, then perhaps there is something in it. But if some praise and others abuse, if you can split the audience in half, then for sure it is a good production' (in Gladkov 1997: 165).

As such, Meyerhold's understanding of the nature of audiences is more complex than it may first appear and closer to the kind of thinking which Lars Kleberg attributes to Mikhail Zagorsky: 'There is no single spectator, neither is there a single performance. The revolutionary current turned on from the stage splits up the auditorium, organises and differentiates its positive and negative elements' (in Russell 1990: 177). Whilst it may have appealed to Meyerhold to have a 'scientific' understanding of how his audiences reacted to his work, underpinned by statistical data recorded *in situ*, he was never committed to reducing his audiences to a collective mass of reflexive responses. At its best his was a theatre that encapsulated the dialectical tensions we have seen in his biomechanical training and central to that dialectic was the audience. Lenin's action–reaction model is, therefore, best situated, *within* the audience itself, and not, as Eisenstein implies between audience and actor.

From an actor's perspective, the classically mechanistic view of biomechanical training raises other questions. Descartes, one of the founding fathers of the mechanistic paradigm, saw the extended body of humankind *as* a machine. Meyerhold, by contrast, saw his actors' physical work to be *like* that of the machine: 'In that they are in need of improvement, in need of gaining complete control over their physical capabilities' (Van Norman Baer 1991: 136). He drew all the positive connotations of the machine under one banner and then added 'freedom'. As Lancelot Lawton stated on a visit to Meyerhold's theatre in 1924:

> The Machine is sober, reliable, heroic, powerful and productive ... The machine-man is also sober, reliable, heroic, powerful and productive. Free him from capitalist chains and, with the aid of the machine that enslaved him in the past, he will build a new society.
>
> (Lawton 1924: 378)

Beyond the explicit Marxist perspective there is a message for the Meyerholdian actor in this statement: that by adopting the positive characteristics of machine-like behaviour, the actor's expressivity is increased tenfold. Strict adherence to rigorous technical exercises in training leads to creative freedom on stage. In saying as much with his own interpretation of the machine age in Soviet society, Meyerhold was differentiating himself from Descartes' model of the past as well as from the view of some of his immediate contemporaries, such as Alexei Gastev and Nikolai Foregger.[17]

While Gastev's industrial system was ultimately considered to be an ironic return to Tsarist oppression, Meyerhold's training never loses sight of the actor's creativity. He may have publicly applauded the work of the engineer, and echoed industrial practice in his attempt to keep his machine-actors in fully working, rhythmically united, order. But as an artist he recognised that his chosen medium was rich with problems, tensions and contradictions. He wanted his actors to engage fully in the dialectics of the actor's craft – consciousness versus reflexivity, A_1 versus A_2, discipline versus freedom – dialectics which are perhaps best expressed by one of the central questions posed by Zeami's writings on Noh: how does the flower blossom within the machine?

3 The System, psychology and the US

Richard Boleslavsky and Lee Strasberg

In 1934 two American theatre professionals travelled to the Soviet Union to find out more about the Russian tradition of acting and to bring back word of the current thinking in actor training. Both were already demonstrably committed to pursuing a Stanislavsky-inspired form of realism on stage but differed in their interpretation of how to achieve it. Both had worked with the Russian émigré teachers of the System, Richard Boleslavsky and Maria Ouspenskaya, and both had striven for ten years to introduce their ideas into the American theatre. The trip was to reinforce the schism between the two and ultimately led to a defining split in the interpretation of Stanislavskian practice in the United States. The two were Lee Strasberg and Stella Adler.

Adler went on to Paris and, through the agency of Jacques Copeau, managed to work for a month with Stanislavsky to develop her acting. Strasberg strangely avoided all contact with Stanislavsky when he was in Moscow, visiting Meyerhold's workshop instead and spending time with Vakhtangov's widow. On their return, the two famously clashed with Adler claiming that Strasberg's understanding of Stanislavsky's theories was tendentious and Strasberg responding that he was 'improv[ing] upon Stanislavsky' (Frome 2001: 28), incorporating the ideas of Meyerhold and Vakhtangov into his work.

Much has been written about this clash and on the subsequent factionalism that later dogged the Group Theatre and the Actors Studio, but the story is re-told here to seed a different set of ideas. In this chapter, the interest is not in personal conflicts, nor particularly in the different claims being made about the Stanislavsky tradition. Here, the focus is on the underlying cultural and scientific tensions exemplified in Strasberg and Adler's parting, more specifically in what their different interpretations might tell us about the science of psychology at the time.

Tracing the roots of this tension back to Richard Boleslavsky and the *early* days of the Moscow Art Theatre (MAT) is a principal aim, for Boleslavsky was singularly important in exporting the Stanislavsky tradition to the US and in developing its most significant outpost there. He remains an elusive figure, however, and his publication *Acting: the First Six Lessons* (1933) has not received significant critical attention, even though it was the first formal pronouncement on Stanislavsky's System in the United States, published three years before his teacher's own book, *An Actor Prepares*.

The journey to America is appropriate for other reasons as many of Stanislavsky's students made the same journey, including Michael Chekhov, the subject of Chapter 4. It is also illuminating because the cultural shift encapsulated in the move across the Atlantic, marks a scientific shift too. As we have seen, the System of Stanislavsky is constantly transformed by its particular context and this is nowhere more evident than in the changing psychological climate of America in the 1920s and 1930s, exemplified by Freud's theories of psychoanalysis on the one hand and by J.B. Watson's Behaviourism on the other. Whilst Freud's ideas may have been enthusiastically received early on by the Bolsheviks, Stalin's rise to power ensured that they were only discussed amongst secret coteries for many decades. In the vacuum, as has been argued in the previous chapter, the Objective Psychology of Pavlov was given support and was taken up by theatre practitioners such as Meyerhold.

There was no such controlling hand in the US, skewing the theoretical base of the emergent science of psychology. Freud's theories flourished alongside the American equivalent of Gastev, J.B. Watson. What follows, then, is an assessment of the extent to which we can examine this tension – between the introspective school of psychoanalysis and the objective school of Behaviourism – through the development of Russian-based actor training methods in the US. The key figures in this assessment are Boleslavsky, as the bridge between Russia and New York, Lee Strasberg as the well-known devotee of introspective techniques of emotion generation, and Stella Adler and Sanford Meisner as two former members of the Group Theatre, who, in their separate ways, have developed action-based, behavioural models of performer training.

That such oppositional perspectives on the System have emerged from the same source is indicative of the complexity of the subject and of the problems any critic faces when analysing the dissemination of the System in America. In no other country have so many different schools and sub-groups developed around Stanislavsky. His writings are 'like the Bible', as Strasberg put it, 'quoted to any purpose' (1988: 42). Jerzy Grotowski develops a similar theme: 'Throughout his numerous years of research [Stanislavsky's] method evolved, but his disciples did not. Stanislavsky had disciples for each of his periods, and each disciple stuck to his particular period; hence the discussions of a theological order' (1975: 174).

Strasberg is as guilty as any of using the System to preach his own gospel but his statement, together with Grotowski's, does pinpoint the status of his master's work in the US. In the Soviet Union stability was forced onto the System by governmental edict; all the state-run theatres after 1934 had to subscribe to the Stanislavsky system. In America no such stability, enforced or otherwise, existed, leaving an expanding group of ex-Laboratory students wanting to teach *their* versions of the System. After the 1930s the 'problem' intensifies exponentially with second- and third-generation post-Stanislavskians setting up in America and establishing their own idiosyncratic readings of his System. Here, the endeavour is to navigate a route through these sub-systems, drawing on the contemporary scientific environment as well as on the theatrical context of these practitioners in an attempt to establish why America has encouraged such a proliferation of different theories.

Before Boleslavsky

One needs to go further back than Boleslavsky to trace the first seed of Stanislavskian thinking in America. Years before he set foot in the US Stanislavsky's ideas had begun to be disseminated by émigré, ex-MAT actors preaching different forms of the System. As early as 1905 Alla Nazimova and Pavel Orlenev toured America with the St Petersburg Dramatic Company, the first Russian troupe to be seen in America. Nazimova had been a student at the MAT and although Stanislavsky had not begun the formalisation of the System when she was there, her style of acting was credited with the stamp of psychological realism for which the MAT was later acclaimed: 'a type of psychologised acting, that was more nuanced and more based on inner life than was customary in the West' (Senelick 1992: 9). Orlenev, too, spoke of the craft of acting with a particularly twentieth-century slant, highlighting a psychically motivated model of acting. The *Boston Evening Transcript* (15 March 1906) quotes him directly:

> Human actions [are] controlled by 'states of the soul': they are the causes, the pure motives; to see them is to see plainly the denouement of the grand tragedy of a human life; to be able to make them be seen and comprehended is the highest achievement of dramatic art.
>
> (in Senelick 1992: 9)

Orlenev's understanding of acting, developed separately from Stanislavsky, is nevertheless in tune with the emotion-driven early work done at the MAT.[1] He neatly presents one side of the psycho-physical actor, lending the inner workings of the soul a causal role in human behaviour. Much of the debate around Stanislavsky in this century has focused on the distinction between this emotion-led model of performance and the alternative model of psycho-physical acting, in which emotion is seen as a by-product of focused action on stage. Indeed, the schism between Adler and Strasberg centred on this distinction, with Strasberg a staunch advocate of the school of Emotionalism and Adler the follower of what was later called the Method of Physical Actions.

Boleslavsky's training with Stanislavsky

Whilst Nazimova was busy forging a career for herself in America, Richard Boleslavsky was auditioning for the MAT. Nazimova had chosen to leave the

MAT in 1905, and, according to Christine Edwards, first acquainted American audiences with the 'new acting' of the Stanislavskian school the same year (1965: 215). Edwards credits her with 'having introduced in this country [i.e. America] the Russian inspired acting of psychological realism which America was to see in full flower in the Moscow Art Theatre performances of 1923 and 1924' (ibid.).

In fact, the psychological school of acting attributable to Stanislavsky was in its very infancy as Nazimova was emigrating and it is unlikely that she would have absorbed any systematic teaching from Stanislavsky.[2] Boleslavsky, on the other hand, the man who was to play an important role in those first American performances in the 1920s, joined the MAT just as the psycho-technique was taking shape. Stanislavsky may have been looking for a 'new' kind of actor that season, for Boleslavsky was one of only three members accepted in the autumn of 1906 (Roberts 1981: 16) and quickly became embroiled in the new approach to training.

It was a crucial time in the development of the System. With eight years of frenzied production schedules behind him, Stanislavsky was taking stock and beginning the first tentative steps towards formalising his thoughts on the acting process. Boleslavsky played an important role in this formative work on the System, arriving in the period directly after Stanislavsky's celebrated 'crisis' in Finland (Benedetti 1989: 22) and observing the practical experiments that followed this crisis – as Stanislavsky attempted to test his acting psychology on the actors at the MAT. This period of 1906–1909, from the beginning of Boleslavsky's apprenticeship to his main-role début as Belyaev in *A Month in the Country*, is important for it marks both Boleslavsky's and the MAT's introduction to the System. Examining Stanislavsky's rehearsal techniques at this time gives us a precious insight into Boleslavsky's particular perception of the System, an understanding that he went on to develop with Michael Chekhov and Vakhtangov at the First Studio and finally exported to America with the help of Maria Ouspenskaya.

For the first two years of the apprenticeship the student actors at the MAT attended classes run by established actors in the company 'under the supervision and periodic inspection of Stanislavsky and Nemirovich Danchenko' (Roberts 1981: 16). These classes covered diction, voice training, fencing and dancing. It was not until the third year that apprentices performed on the stage, as 'contributors' – extras or walk-ons in crowd scenes (ibid.: 18). In the fourth year students could join the MAT as full members following a satisfactory examination. Thus, the main connection with the directors of the MAT (Stanislavsky and Nemirovich-Danchenko), the principal learning forum for the dissemination of the System at this time, was the observation of rehearsals.[3] The importance of this method of learning, for both directors, can be measured by their insistence that students attended all rehearsals in addition to their other classes. As David Magarshack reports: 'Rehearsals . . . were considered to be the actual school of acting in which the young actor of the company got all his practical knowledge' (1986: 305).

This observational model of approach, where *process* rather than product is placed under the spotlight, is reflected in Boleslavsky's practice at his Laboratory Theatre and in Strasberg's at the Actors Studio, where the open rehearsal – or the scene critique – was the dominant method of teaching. It will also feature in the discussions of Vasiliev in Chapter 5.

It is an approach that begs several questions. What can the observer learn from seeing other actors directed and to what extent can this be called 'practical knowledge'? In what circumstances might the practice be seen as inappropriate? Are there hidden issues – of power and hierarchy, for example – caught up in the process? And how does it relate to the particular scientific context of this chapter?

The two productions Boleslavsky watched being rehearsed (before he was to become a 'contributor' himself) were Knut Hamsun's *The Drama of Life* and Leonid Andreyev's *The Life of Man*. Both were examples of what Stanislavsky called 'irrealistic' plays (Magarshack 1986: 287), the one 'an abstract highly symbolic text', the other a Symbolist Mystery, 'even more abstract than *The Drama of Life*' (Benedetti 1990a: 150, 171). That such non-naturalistic plays could serve as the testing ground of the emergent System is testament to the stylistic scope of Stanislavsky's theories. Indeed, as we shall see, the emotional experiments performed whilst rehearsing *The Drama of Life* informed Stanislavsky's approach when he was to return to an early naturalistic text – *A Month in the Country* – two seasons later. For the time being, though, it was the abstraction of the Hamsun and Andreyev texts that best supported Stanislavsky's new inner technique. Magarshack explains the idea:

> It was disembodied passions in their pure and bare form that Stanislavsky tried to represent in this production [*The Drama of Life*]. It seemed to him to do this the actor only needed the help of his eyes and of his facial expression. He therefore forced his actors to 'live' the particular passion each of them represented in the play by remaining absolutely still and relying entirely on their feelings and temperaments.
>
> (1986: 288)

It was an approach that simply ignored the other half of the actor's psychophysical armoury, one that, with its emphasis on the eyes as the window to the soul, recalls the techniques of expressionist acting as much as it does the psychological school.

Nick Worrall notes that during the rehearsals for the play, 'a cult of inner feeling' (1996: 173) arose in the rehearsal room and surrounded the actors' motionless emotionalism. This was the atmosphere that Boleslavsky first experienced as an apprentice at the MAT – originally as an observer but subsequently as the actor playing Belyaev in the rehearsals of the Turgenev play. Boleslavsky's practical introduction to the System, therefore, included an extreme emphasis on the inner work of the actor and, not surprisingly, this is reflected in his own interpretation of Stanislavsky's theories at the beginning of his teaching career. Later, as his understanding grew, he had to reconcile the internal focus stressed when he began at the MAT with the external, physical side of acting – a development that at least one of his students, Lee Strasberg, never made.

A Month in the Country

From a scientific perspective, Stanislavsky's work on *A Month in the Country* is highly significant. It was the first production directly informed by Stanislavsky's own scientific research and this may have influenced his exceptional move to abandon his policy of open rehearsals and create an intimate and ostensibly safe haven for his actors, behind the closed doors of the small studio at the MAT. He clearly felt his cast (including Olga Knipper-Chekhova and Boleslavsky) should not be subjected to public scrutiny during their period of emotional training. Instead, he created a secluded space for his research to experiment both intensively and intimately with his cast's emotions. Stanislavsky cast Boleslavsky for his youth and openness to new ideas but other members of the company found the environment too experimental (in the literal sense): 'Olga Knipper was not the only one to be scared by Stanislavsky's technical terms; some of the older members of the company protested that they were being treated as guinea pigs and that rehearsals were being turned into an experimental laboratory' (Worrall 1996: 185).

The research informing these experiments was drawn from Théodule Ribot's *Psychologie des Sentiments*, published in St Petersburg in 1906 and read by Stanislavsky in the spring before rehearsals began on Turgenev's play in the August of 1909. Ribot (1839–1916) was a French psychologist who taught experimental psychology at the Sorbonne and who has been credited with helping initiate the 'study in France of a positivistic and physiologically-oriented psychology' (Crohn-Schmitt 1986: 347).

There is little evidence, however, that Stanislavsky was influenced by the external aspects of Ribot's psychology at this time. On the contrary, his work on *A Month in the Country* extended the experiments in stasis begun with *The Drama of Life* and drew on Ribot's much debated notion of 'affective memory', the term which was finally acknowledged in *An Actor Prepares* almost thirty years later in the chapter on Emotion Memory (Stanislavsky 1980a: 166). By that time, Stanislavsky had developed his system to acknowledge the role physiology plays in the emotional work of an actor and was looking beyond Ribot's psychology to Pavlov's conditioned reflexes for a scientific model. The cast of *A Month in the Country* did not benefit from this larger view. They were treated to an uncomfortable fusion of Western proto-psychology and Eastern mysticism as Stanislavsky searched for a language to express his ideas. In *My Life in Art*, Stanislavsky describes the challenge posed by the play:

> The lacework of the psychology of love which Turgenev weaves in such a masterly fashion demands a special sort of playing on the part of the actors, a playing that might allow the spectator to see closely into the peculiar design of the emotions...

And then offers his solution: 'One needed some sort of unseen rayings out of creative will ... The actor needs greater strength in his spiritual rayings out' (1980b: 543–544).

On the one hand, drawing on Ribot, Stanislavsky saw the actor's role as playing the through-line of affective memory, scored by him and recorded in his prompt copy. On the other, to enable this process, Stanislavsky looked to Leopold Sulerzhitsky's Eastern philosophy and training methods, coining the Sanskrit term *prana* for the communication of these emotions – the radiation of energy out to an audience.

Such a seamless fusion of ideas needs to be placed in context. It is illustrative of Stanislavsky's eclecticism that he appropriated two divergent schools of thought without compunction. Ribot, working from a Western positivist tradition, is paradigmatically removed from Eastern philosophy and spiritualism but until the materialistic forces of Stalinism impressed themselves upon the System in the 1930s such a pragmatic marriage of occidental and oriental influences remained unproblematic. *Prana* does appear in *An Actor Prepares* but, by the time his first acting volume was published, Stanislavsky had separated out the two influences. The chapter on Emotion Memory (which refers to Ribot) is couched in Pavlovian stimulus-and-response terminology whilst Ray Emission forms part of the next chapter on 'Communion' and is dismissed as unscientific and personal:

> I have no desire to prove whether Prana really exists or not. My sensations are purely individual to me, the whole thing may be the fruit of my imagination ... If my practical and unscientific method can be of use to you, so much the better. If not, I shall not insist upon it.
>
> (Stanislavsky 1980a: 199)

Interestingly, Michael Chekhov, whose work with Stanislavsky's ideas took a spiritual direction, developed the idea of communion in his own system and embraced the concept of Radiation, making it a central tenet of the Chekhov Technique. Boleslavsky also exported the term (slightly amended to 'irradiation') and described it as one of the solutions for the 'spiritual problems' of the actor (Roberts 1981: 141). Lee Strasberg's interpretation of these sources, by contrast, denies the practicality of Stanislavsky's Hindu-influenced ideas. Stanislavsky, Strasberg claims, was unable to suggest 'exercises to facilitate ray emission' (1988: 61). It was a significant misreading of the Russian by Strasberg and will need to be analysed later.

For the cast of *A Month in the Country*, Stanislavsky's mixture of psychological and spiritual sources was difficult to grasp. His prompt book for the show includes illuminating detail of the hieroglyphic language he was developing to communicate his ideas – a language which both Knipper-Chekhova (as Natalya) and Alisa Koonen (rehearsing Verochka) found unhelpful. Worrall's account of the production reveals a harsh, clinical side to the director, conflicting with the popular paternalistic images commonly associated with Stanislavsky and belying the actor-friendly approach chronicled in the acting handbooks. He may have claimed at the end of his career that using abstract terminology with actors was counter-productive (Stanislavsky 1958: 35) but for this production Stanislavsky utilised an abstruse shorthand to convey the emotional content of the play to the cast. The annotations in his prompt book give us a flavour:

?	= surprise	
(?)	= hidden surprise	
−	= apathy	
X	= creative state	
|	= transition from apathy to creative state	
—	= the need to convince someone of something	
O	= the dramatic scene $(a + b + c + d + e + f$, the constituent parts, $= O)$	

(Worrall 1996: 186–187)

There are two things related to this evidence to note. First, Stanislavsky was looking for a formal language to codify the emotional states of the play. He was striving to authenticate his research at first to himself and to his cast but later and more importantly to the surrounding figures of the MAT (including Nemirovich-Danchenko) who had been excluded from the rehearsal process at his own behest.

Second (and intrinsically connected) is the result of this pseudo-scientific codification, measured by Knipper-Chekhova's response. Stanislavsky had set up an even more intimate environment in his own flat for Chekhov's widow to rehearse and had grilled her in this approach in solitude for nineteen out of fifty of the rehearsals held on the play. She broke down under the strain and ultimately under-achieved in her performance. Later, Stanislavsky recanted and admitted in a letter to her that he had overdone the terminology: 'Should you need help I will divide [your role] into sections and promise not to frighten you with scientific terms. That was probably my mistake' (in Benedetti 1991: 277).

Out of this heavy-handedness came the understanding that the logic of the through-line was of primary importance, not the emotional states themselves, or indeed their notation. Besides, Stanislavsky claimed that the suffering Knipper had undergone was not in vain: 'I suffer with you at a distance and at the same time know that this torment brings forth wonderful fruit' (ibid.).

Such a belief in the actor-martyr plumbing their emotional depths for the good of the play ultimately alienated Michael Chekhov from the work of Stanislavsky; Chekhov prioritised instead the Higher Ego and the Imagination as a defence for the emotions. For Boleslavsky, it was a baptism in fire, an intense introductory experience to the embryonic psycho-technique. Nevertheless, his openness to the theory and his ability as an actor meant he survived to get very good notices. Later, Stanislavsky shifted his approach and staunchly rejected the imposition of an alien language on his performers but the same emotional probing – by what might be called the director-analyst – is evident in Boleslavsky's writings and reaches its apogee in the Method of Lee Strasberg. Without knowing it, for Stanislavsky knew nothing of Freud's work,[4] he was setting a precedent for the psychoanalytical interpretation of his System in America.

Boleslavsky in America

It was a further thirteen years before Boleslavsky emigrated to America. After his success in *A Month in the Country* he went on to co-found the First Studio (which later became the Second MAT) and forged a relationship with two other future émigrés – Michael Chekhov, whom Boleslavsky directed in the Studio's first production and Maria Ouspenskaya, his partner at the Laboratory Theatre. The other significant artist at the Studio was Evgeny Vakhtangov, originator of the style of 'fantastic realism' and an oft-cited influence in Strasberg's writings.[5] Thus, a second generation of Stanislavsky-trained actors began to establish their own reputations, using the First Studio as a laboratory for their work. The studio was in effect the first formalised outlet for the reinterpretation of Stanislavsky's ideas. It was supported by the MAT but remained artistically independent. Ultimately, it began the diversification of the System, resulting in the founding of the Chekhov Theatre Studio in Dartington, in Vakhtangov's seminal production of *Princess Turandot* and in the Americanisation of the psycho-technique initiated by Boleslavsky and Ouspenskaya and extended by Strasberg, Adler, Robert Lewis and Sanford Meisner.

Boleslavsky left the MAT in 1920, and arrived in the US in October 1922, a little more than two months before the MAT was to arrive for its first tour of America. In the intervening years, he fled to his native Poland, rejecting the Bolshevik system. He then drifted undetected around Europe before meeting up with a splinter group of the MAT (known as the Kachalov Group) who themselves had been forced into exile from Russia by the civil war.[6]

But although he had been developing his understanding of the System since his time at the First Studio, Boleslavsky recognised that his version of the Stanislavsky System would need to adapt to the specific cultural conditions of New York at the time:

> 1) This theatre must grow here by itself and must get its roots into American soil. 2) It must begin slowly, training young Americans for the stage in all its departments. 3) It must be recognised and organised as a living social force, recreating itself each generation from the thoughts and material of its own times.
>
> (in Roberts 1981: 108)

So what *were* the 'thoughts and materials' of the time moulding his system and allowing it to be more effectively absorbed by the acting youth of America?

One clue is provided in Boleslavsky's article for *Theatre Arts Magazine*, 'Fundamentals of Acting' (February 1927). Aligning himself with Joseph Jefferson's famous statement on the actor: 'to have the heart warm and the head cool', Boleslavsky points to two contemporary factors which made his school a practical possibility: 'the new psychology and psycho-analysis' (Roberts 1981: 134).

On the one hand, then, Boleslavsky owed an explicit debt to Freud and the emergent school of psychoanalysis, an assertion that nevertheless needs testing. But the other influence – the 'new psychology' – is more opaque. What school did he have in mind? It will be argued here, with detailed reference to Boleslavsky's *Acting: The First Six Lessons*, that he was referring to Behaviourism. Indeed, his little book is a sensitive barometer of a very big debate – the shifting ground of psychological thinking in Russia and America in the first half of the twentieth century.

Boleslavsky's original source, Théodule Ribot, is cited in his own explanation of Emotion Memory, first published in 1933 (Boleslavsky 1949: 36), as well as in Stanislavsky's *An Actor Prepares*, but is combined, in Boleslavsky's thinking, with a psychoanalytical approach – a new theoretical basis which does not figure in his teacher's publications. The phenomenon of 'affective memory' is Ribot's but the means by which such memories are accessed owes a more significant debt to the discipline of psychoanalysis. Thus, what Boleslavsky had learnt about the psychology of the emotions from his training in Russia is brought together in *Acting* with the psychoanalytical method of Freud, an approach that emerges in Boleslavsky's practice after he arrived in America.

Later, in the same book, Boleslavsky appears to shift his emphasis again, away from the Freudian school, and towards the understanding of emotions articulated in William James's (1842–1910) seminal essay 'What is an Emotion?' (1884), and in his landmark publication *The Principles of Psychology* (1890) – a behaviourist model of emotion, based not on mental but on *environmental* factors. Just as these two schools of psychology were fighting it out for supremacy in America, so were the disciples of Boleslavsky, divided by their focus on either emotion-driven action or action-based emotion. For Boleslavsky, himself, there exists a less-than-easy alliance of the introspective and objective theories of emotion, a situation which would almost inevitably lead to division in his followers.[7]

Freud in America

As Boleslavsky was making his debut for the MAT in *A Month in the Country*, Sigmund Freud (1856–1939) was making his first (and only) appearance on the American stage.[8] At Clark University's twentieth anniversary conference, Freud delivered his *Five Lectures on Psychoanalysis* (1909), a 'decisive event in the history of psychoanalysis in America' (Hale 1971: 4), which enthused a network of professionals to disseminate his ideas further and which, according to the then president of the University, G. Stanley Hall, 'launched' psychoanalysis in America (Hale 1971: 24). Freud's lectures, reprinted a year later, covered the use of hypnosis in 'catharsis' (the discharging of emotion), non-hypnotic approaches and the notions of 'repression', 'dream analysis' and 'free association', 'child sexuality' and 'transference'. It was a model of psychoanalysis which in a few short years spread out beyond the psychoanalytical movement to the wider medical community and further still to lay practitioners and to those interested in the arts.[9]

New York became the key location for the dialogue between the medical proponents of Freud and those artists and writers who embraced his ideas. Hale notes that New York had the 'largest number of psychoanalytic practitioners' and that his pupil Carl Jung spoke to the Liberal Club in Greenwich Village three years after Freud's Clark University lectures (Hale 1995: 60). He also lists the key writers who were part of this active interchange of ideas. What he calls 'the range of acquaintances who knew something about psychoanalysis' included Van Wyck Brooks, Waldo Frank, Eugene O'Neill and Sherwood Anderson, literary figures who were, in turn, to play their parts in influencing the post-Laboratory work of Strasberg and Harold Clurman.

Thus, just a few years after the Clark University conference, it is possible to detect a leakage of Freud's ideas from the academic world of psychology into the literary community, and specifically into the New York theatre world. The first use of the term 'psychoanalysis' on the American stage has been dated at 1912 and the first direct citation of Freud's name on Broadway, in 'an otherwise conventional comedy', *Good Gracious, Annabelle*, followed four years later in October 1916 (Sievers 1955: 54). The special atmosphere of Greenwich Village, with its collage of cafés, bookshops and theatres proved receptive to the ideas of psychoanalysis and at the same time provided an artistic outlet for such ideas in the form of the Provincetown Players, one of the prototype Art Theatres in America dedicated to a repertoire of indigenous plays. The Provincetown Players moved to Greenwich Village in 1916, reviving Susan Glaspell and George Cram Cook's psychoanalytical satire *Suppressed Desires*, and thereby mining the Village's intellectual enthusiasm for Freud and his student Jung.

That spoofs on 'home-brewed psychoanalysis' or what was known as the 'new fashion . . . among sophisticates' (Sarlós 1982: 15) were being written just six years after Freud's arrival in the US is an indication of the speed in which the ideas were absorbed in this part of America. Whether read first hand or not, Freud's work offered up a terminology that clearly appealed to the intellectual and theatrical coteries of New York. By the time Clifford Odets was writing for Strasberg's and Clurman's Group Theatre in the 1930s the principles of Freud were so well absorbed into common parlance that he was moved to state: 'The best of Freud is so deeply in creative writing that it is bootless to stop for examination of where one always knew or where Freud opened up knowledge of self or others' (in Sievers 1955: 262).

This was the climate in which Boleslavsky began his work in America. His task was to find a meeting point between the Russian school of acting where he had trained and the specific cultural expectations of 1920s New York. His introduction to the latter, significantly, was in part through the Provincetown Players, for he was charged with taking over the direction of their production of *The Saint* in 1924 and watched by a young Harold Clurman as an extra (Clurman 1983: 7). As the first major vehicle for O'Neill's plays, the Provincetown Players were part of the Freudian coterie of New York and contributed to Boleslavsky's immersion in the culture of Greenwich Village and to his introduction to the popular language of the day – the language of psychoanalysis.[10]

Behaviourism in America

Whilst Freud's theory of psychoanalysis focused on the introspective drives of the unconscious, the alternative counter-theory eschewed all references to consciousness entirely, developing instead a theory of Objective Psychology – or Behaviourism – based on the scientific observation of behaviour. The seeds of Behaviourism, at least in terms of its view of emotion, were sown by William James's article 'What is an Emotion?' published in *Mind* in 1884. Six years later he published his seminal collection of writings, *The Principles of Psychology*, in which he expanded upon this theory in the chapter entitled 'The Emotions'. Strasberg refers directly to the latter publication in his autobiography *A Dream of Passion* (1988), selectively highlighting areas of James's theory to justify his own thinking on the subject. *The Principles* set forth a diverse range of theories and by no means constitute a treatise on Behaviourism – that was the role of J.B. Watson's writings twenty years later – but contained within James's texts on emotion are the fundamental principles of an externally stimulated, reactive model of emotion: 'Readers of this Journal do not need to be reminded that the nervous system of every living thing is a bundle of predispositions to react in particular ways upon the contact of particular features of the environment' (James 1977: 3).

And more famously with specific reference to emotions:

> Common sense says we lose our fortune, we are sorry and weep; we meet a bear, are frightened and run; we are insulted by a rival, are angry and strike. The hypothesis here to be defended says this order of sequence is incorrect, that the one mental state is not immediately induced by the other, that the bodily manifestations must first be interposed between, and that the more rational statement is that we feel sorry because we cry, angry because we strike, afraid because we are sorry, angry or fearful, as the case may be.
>
> (Ibid.: 2)

Thus, in James's theory, which later became known as the James–Lange theory of emotion (after its independent co-founder Carl Lange),[11] the physical state of the sufferer *is* the emotion; indeed there would be nothing to speak of without the bodily response elicited by an external stimulus. The physical sensations of crying may be interpreted as grief by the subject but grief does not stimulate the action of crying.

J.B. Watson developed these ideas along Pavlovian lines, adapting the theory of reflex cycles to embrace all human activity. He adopted an oppositional standpoint from the school of Freud in America, launching his theory some three years after the Clark University lectures, at a series of summer lectures at Columbia University in 1912. Watson's key text, *Behaviorism* (1924), indicates his position:

> The behaviorist's main contention is that man's emotional life is built up bit by bit by the wear and tear of the environment on him ... The future development of [behaviourist] methods will enable us to substitute natural science in our treatment of the emotionally sick in place of the doubtful and passing unscientific method now known as psychoanalysis.
>
> (Watson 1924: 194)

For Watson, Freudian theory was 'unscientific' in its introspective (and ultimately unverifiable) focus on the unconscious. Following Darwin, Watson sought scientific credibility by concentrating on observable 'facts' and by measuring things in terms of a linear relationship of cause and effect, or in his terms as stimulus (S) and response (R):

S..R

(Ibid.: 22)

Like Pavlov, Watson believed that both parts of the behavioural formula could be novel (unconditioned) or habituated (conditioned) and sought to underpin his theory with what seems today to be unacceptably invasive experiments on small children. Albert B, for example – an eleven-month-old who was renowned for his gentle nature – became the Pavlovian dog in Watson's laboratory. Having manifested a natural urge to reach out to a furry animal (in this case a white rat), Albert was then conditioned to develop a 'fear response' by associating the entrance of the rat into the room with the sound of 'a steel bar . . . struck with a carpenter's hammer' just behind the child's head (ibid.: 159). After seven days the baby had 'learnt' to cry (a conditioned response) on seeing the rat (now a conditioned stimulus). In so doing, Watson was attempting to put the emotional behaviour of children – what for him were simple models of adults – on a mechanistic footing.

David Cohen summarises: 'The central tenet of Behaviourism is that thoughts, feelings and intentions, mental processes all, do not determine what we do. Our behaviour is the product of our conditioning. We are biological machines and do not consciously act; rather we *react* to stimuli' (in Gregory 1987: 71). Put this way, Behaviourism constitutes the apogee of the Newtonian paradigm in psychology, a mechanical, predictable model of the mind based on rigidly objective criteria and a demonstrable scientific rigour. Watson's infamous belief that he could train a healthy baby to become anything he wanted through his conditioning of their environment[12] is the psychological equivalent of Halley's Comet's predictable return, a measure of the confidence which comes from Newtonian thinking. These tenets of Behaviourism were dominant in the field of psychology at least until the 1950s when alternative theories of emotion and of cognitive psychology grew up. For thirty years, then, from the time Boleslavsky was planning his Laboratory theatre to when Strasberg was setting up his own Actors Studio, there was a significant counter-psychology to that of psychoanalysis.

But despite its oppositional starting point, Freud's psychoanalysis may also be viewed as part of a mechanistic paradigm. Fritjof Capra makes the point explicitly:

> As in Newtonian physics so also in psychoanalysis, the mechanistic view of reality implies a rigorous determinism. Every psychological event has a definite cause and gives rise to a definite effect, and the whole psychological state of an individual is uniquely determined by 'initial conditions' in early childhood. The 'genetic' approach of psychoanalysis consists of tracing the symptoms and behaviour of a patient back to previous development stages along a linear chain of cause-and-effect relations.
>
> (1983: 189)

This causal structure is reminiscent of Stanislavsky's textual analysis and, more significantly in this context, of his own statement on emotion: 'In recalling the past do not try to go forward towards the present. Go backwards from the present to the point in the past which you wish to reach. It is easier to go backwards' (Stanislavsky 1980a: 255). Both views see the mental record of the past as something to be found by following a linear path backwards into the memory, reversing (but not contradicting) Newton's first Law of Motion. The behaviourists may have thought that they were avoiding the capriciousness of the emotions by focusing on the external, causative forces of the environment but they shared with Freud a belief that such forces (with all the Newtonian connotations of the word) were there to be discovered and ultimately manipulated in order to understand and control an individual's mental processes.

Boleslavsky's interpretation of the System

Ribot

Whilst Meyerhold's work veered sharply away from the System once he had left the Moscow Art Theatre, Boleslavsky's development as an artist remained closely allied to his teacher's despite their permanent separation after the MAT tour of America. Indeed, Stanislavsky charged him with the official dissemination of the System in America whilst the MAT troupe was performing in New York. One reason for this kinship is Boleslavsky's adoption of the same scientific sources as Stanislavsky. Boleslavsky, having been trained in the techniques of affective memory at the MAT, adopted the psychology of Ribot and along with it an introspective method of building a character. Emotion memory was 'the prime requisite of the actor's work, the starting point of developing a role' (Roberts 1981: 142) and this was how he presented it in the lectures which he gave on the system as part of the publicity for the American tour by Stanislavsky in 1923:

> After having decided what is the feeling necessary for a certain part of his role, the actor tries to find in his affective memory a recollection similar to that particular feeling . . . Then by a series of gradual exercises and rehearsals he brings himself into a state, enabling him to arouse in the strongest degree the necessary feelings by a mere thought of it and to retain it for the necessary period of time.
>
> (Ibid.)

The very first aspect of the actor's work, then, is to isolate the emotional characteristics of the role. Next, drawing off his/her own mental resources, the actor retrieves an analogous set of emotions by using various stimuli, ranging from the text itself, to the actor's own life. Finally, these emotional states are applied to the lines of the author colouring the text with a 'true' inner life (ibid.: 143). The belief that such mental resources exist, the imprints of an emotional experience of the past, is Ribot's. His theory of affective memory argued that:

The impressions of smell and taste, our visceral sensations, our pleasant or painful states, our emotions and passions, like the perceptions of sight and hearing, can leave memories behind them ... These residua, fixed in an organisation, may return into the consciousness ... by provocation, or spontaneously.

(1911: 141)

In the vast majority of cases this process only happens at an *intellectual* level: the past event is recalled – the circumstances surrounding the emotion – but the emotion itself leaves what Ribot calls only 'a vague affective trace of what has once been but cannot be recalled' (1911: 152). For the few, however, and Ribot interestingly singles out poets and artists in this group, they can: 'Recall the circumstances *plus* the revived condition of feeling. It is these who have the true "affective memory"' (Ibid: 153).

As an oft-cited (but perhaps less well-read) document on emotional psychology, Ribot's voice can be muted by critics who overlook the significance of *his* writing – as opposed to Stanislavsky's appropriation of his writing. Eric Bentley, though generally helpful in pinpointing the problems of translating Stanislavsky, suggests that *The Psychology of the Emotions* should not be recommended reading for actors (1976: 278). And, as a strong disincentive to the lay reader, he quotes Ribot's own admission: 'the emotional memory is nil in the majority of people' (ibid.: 277).

Yet, if probed further – that is, beyond the appendix in which this simplified conclusion appears (ibid.: 171) – Ribot's 'Memory of Feelings' recounts some fascinating observations, even for those actors who are suspicious of scientific theory.

The first is the case study Ribot includes of an artist blessed with the gift of a 'true' affective memory (Case 5). The writer in question (M. Sully-Prudhomme) describes the process he undergoes when composing verses. After leaving his embryonic poetry in a drawer for a period of gestation, Sully-Prudhomme retrieves the writing from his desk, in his words, 'to *retouch* the verses' (ibid.: 154) inspired by a conscious effort of emotional recollection, in this instance of youthful passion and angry jealousy. This, he feels, is the only way to breathe life back into the work, to lend the present poetry an emotional colouring extracted from the past by 'working on the recollection of an affective state' (ibid.: 154–155). Method actors, it seems, were not the first artists to colour poetic words of literature with a real and felt emotion drawn from their own emotional store.

The second notable case study is Case 6 in which Ribot describes the technique another of his correspondents uses to achieve this affective state:

If I wish to repeat the impressions of this time of waiting [for a friend in hospital], which was always disagreeable to me, all I have to do is to sit down in a chair, as I was then seated, to close my eyes and put myself in the same frame of mind, which I can do quite easily. Not half a minute passes between the evocation and the clear and absolute reconstruction of the scene. First I feel the carpet under my feet, then I *see* its pattern of red and brown roses; then the table with the books lying on it, their colour and style of binding; lastly the peculiar atmosphere of the room . . . After this I feel over again all the weariness of waiting, complicated by an intense dread of the doctor's arrival, a state of apprehension ending in a violent palpitation of the heart, [from] which I find it impossible to escape. When once I have entered on this train of thought, I have to follow it out to the end, passing through the whole series of states which I passed through at the time.

(Ibid.: 156)

This passage is worth quoting at length for it describes a procedure which has fundamental connections with the emotion memory techniques of Boleslavsky and Strasberg. It is the only moment in Ribot's thesis where he elucidates upon the stimulation of affective memory – that is, on the *process* of emotion memory. Notable is the slow descent of the subject into the painful memory, at first stimulated by 'reconstructing' the general circumstances surrounding the event and then by an ever-increasing eye for detail, which seems to bring the past events back into the present for the speaker. Once this period of circumstantial recall is completed, the emotions of the past event slowly rise up, become defined and then, finally, are experienced violently. Once this affective abreaction is triggered it seems there is no stopping it. Control of the events is ceded as the emotional sensations are retrieved.

All of this process takes some thirty seconds, after practice, and is self-induced by the speaker in the comfort of her own chair – a kind of auto-hypnosis. For the first case study it is clear why the exercise of emotional recall is undertaken – to 'retouch' potentially moribund written material with an authentic, emotional quality. For the latter, however, the motive is unclear. We do not even know if she is an artist. Nevertheless, as the details of Boleslavsky's acting theory are now considered, the story of the hospital visitor tells us much about Boleslavsky's debt to Ribot and, by extension, about his developing psychoanalytical language.

I and the Creature

The opening of Boleslavsky's text *Acting: The First Six Lessons* recalls much of Stanislavsky's practice with Knipper-Chekhova in *A Month in the Country*. Knipper is transformed in *Acting* into the figure of the 'Creature' – a naive initiate created by Boleslavsky to set up a dialogue, through which his system is articulated. He ('I' in the text) subjects the Creature to a punishing examination of her motives:

I: What right have you to say that you have worked in the theatre? You have destroyed the very conception of the word Theatre.

(*A pause; the Creature looks at me with the eyes of one innocently condemned to death . . .*)

CREATURE: So I must never play?

I: And if I say *Never*? (*Pause. The eyes of the Creature change their expression, she looks straight into my soul with a sharp scrutinising look, and seeing that I am not joking, clenches her teeth, and tries in vain to hide what is happening in her soul. But it is no use. One enormous real tear rolls out of her eye and the Creature at that moment becomes dear to me . . .*)

CREATURE: But I am going to play. I have nothing else in my life.

I: All right then. I must tell you that this very moment did more for the theatre, or rather for yourself in the theatre, than you did playing all your parts. You suffered just now; you felt deeply. Those are the two things without which you cannot do in any art especially in the art of the theatre.

(Boleslavsky 1949: 18–19)

This account resonates perhaps with Stanislavsky's letter to Knipper, after her breakdown over the emotionally intense rehearsal period on Turgenev's play. Suffering is synonymous in both men's books with an actor's genuine commitment to the theatre. For Boleslavsky it is also a prerequisite in emotional terms. The Creature proves herself to be emotionally receptive to his bullying and therefore earns her right to remain.

The extract also makes clear the format Boleslavsky adopts for the vast majority of the text – a series of one-to-one, private sessions controlled by the director in which the Creature slowly 'improves'. She begins her journey, pent up, wilful, emotional 'with wide-open, frightened eyes' (ibid.: 15) and a lack of physical control – she crushes her handbag nervously on two occasions. At the conclusion, she is accomplished, serious, confident in her skills and deeply grateful to her teacher. Not only has she developed as an actress but through the teachings of Boleslavsky she has emerged as a balanced individual.

This is an interesting choice for Boleslavsky to make. First, he avoids the group rehearsal context that Stanislavsky favours in his acting journals, preferring instead to depict the solo tuition of his Creature. Second, and more significantly, Boleslavsky chooses to characterise himself as a paternalistic teacher-cum-therapist, single-handedly addressing the inhibitions of his pupil/patient through a series of discreet private sessions. Their status mirrors this power relationship with 'I' immediately assuming a dominant role and within thirty pages becoming an invaluable ear for the Creature:

CREATURE: Oh, I was so foolish not to come back to you right away.

I: Not at all. It takes at least a year to get the foundation of your technique. You've got enough to be an actress now . . .

CREATURE: May I come tomorrow?
I: No.

(Ibid.: 46–47)

By the conclusion of the second chapter on emotion memory, the relationship between the two is redolent of the popular understanding of a patient's relationship with their psychiatrist – confessional, needy, private. The 'I' of the director (we might say the 'Creator') has become the sensitive support to his Creature's anxieties.

Affective memory and the ego

Significantly, Boleslavsky chooses this very context to establish the notion of affective memory, first through a story and then through exercising the Creature's own emotional memory. Boleslavsky echoes Ribot on the subject of the artist's ability for emotional recall and raises the stakes further. 'It is in every artist' (ibid.: 36), he states, which later elicits a rather disingenuous request from the Creature:

CREATURE: I wanted to ask you if you thought I had memories like that in
    me.
I: Plenty of them – just waiting to be awakened.

(Ibid.: 38)

It is the director who can uncover the creative potential of the Creature by taking her back to a formative emotional experience buried in her unconscious. He does this by regressing her: 'All right. Tell me how the whole thing happened. Start at the moment you left your house. Don't omit any details' (ibid.: 40). The Creature then recounts her first visit abroad. She is charged with a mixture of sorrow and elation being separated from her brother (who sees her off from the pier) whilst anticipating the excitement of a foreign voyage. Gradually, the mechanical rendition of the Creature's story subsides and her narrative becomes coloured with the emotional qualities that originally accompanied her experience: 'her face and eyes are shining ... Tears come to her eyes. She conceals them' (ibid.: 40). This double quality of happiness and sadness is then transferred, at the behest of the director, immediately to the lines of the play where a similar emotional quality is needed.

Thus, the Creature is introduced to Ribot's ideas of affective memory. Boleslavsky follows Ribot in insisting the Creature focuses first on the circumstances *surrounding* the emotion; in her narrative it is the recollection of the noisy and busy pier that finally sparks the emotional recall. The slow process of recall parallels exactly the experience of Ribot's Madame X (Case 6) as the circumstantial details are imperceptibly subsumed under her welling up emotions. She, like Sully-Prudhomme, then colours the work of art with the felt emotion.

But Boleslavsky also lends the moment a specifically psychoanalytical bent. Comparison with Stanislavsky's elucidation of emotion memory is illuminating. Where Stanislavsky has an unsolicited Kostya wilfully offer up his example of an emotion memory – the celebrated street accident (1980a: 170–173) – Boleslavsky's 'I' wrests the recollection out of his Creature. Where Kostya's example is drawn from a recent and neutral experience, the Creature's is specifically connected with a family member. Where Stanislavsky's work with Kostya is done in the public domain of the workshop studio, Boleslavsky's with the Creature is done in the privacy of his own room. And perhaps most significantly, where Stanislavsky and Ribot stress the capriciousness of the emotions, Boleslavsky sees them as subject to control. His particular terminology is enlightening: 'The point is to bring yourself back as you were then, to command your own ego, go where you want to go and when you are there, to stay where you went' (1949: 39).

For Boleslavsky, the ability to control the process of emotional recall is facilitated through a concomitant control of the 'ego'. Freud's term refers to the only conscious part of the mind as he constructed it – the other (unconscious) constituents being 'id' and 'superego' – and points to the area of the mind responsible for volitional activity and perception. In addition, Freud tells us: 'The Ego refuses to . . . let itself be compelled to suffer. It insists that it cannot be affected by the traumas of the external world' (1985: 429). Thus, in Freud's example, the ego is essential in the appreciation of humour – as a distancing influence. Deep empathic engagement with the subject of a joke destroys its impact. Overly powerful emotions can have a similar effect on an actor's performance.

Whilst there is no external evidence to confirm that Boleslavsky read Freud – unlike Strasberg – it is interesting to note the divergence from the Stanislavskian understanding of affective memory and Boleslavsky's developing reliance on a terminology that is well known to have had particular impact and currency in America. The term had been in the air since 1923 from Freud's *The Ego and the Id*[13] and bandied around the Greenwich Village cafés well before Boleslavsky published his book on acting in 1933. The point is not that Boleslavsky understood the term ego in the specifically Freudian sense – although he does attribute it an appropriate role in the conscious 'commanding' of the recollective mind – but that his choice of terminology is coloured by the popularity of Freudian terminology, either understood or not. Coupled with the significantly different context in which Boleslavsky explores the concept of emotion memory (the pseudo-psychoanalytical atmosphere of *Acting*), it is fair to say that, in his desire to root his interpretation of the system in America, Boleslavsky looked as much to Freud as he did to Ribot for a language to explore the actor's psychology.

Action, rhythm and Behaviourism

The opening two lessons of *Acting*, then, reflect a commitment to the techniques of emotion memory and an internalised creative approach: 'your ... work is done in solitude', he informs the Creature, 'entirely inside of yourself' (Boleslavsky 1949: 42). Accordingly, the context of these sessions is private and intimate. But as the focus of Boleslavsky's work shifts – away, in fact, from introspective work, towards a more external, action-based method of working – so too does the working environment of *Acting*. Chapter 3 on Dramatic Action is set in a park, Chapter 4 begins outside the theatre and the final chapter on Rhythm is located on the top of the Empire State Building – a very literal manifestation of Boleslavsky's desire to place his theories at the highest point of American culture!

This shift in context reflects a more significant shift in Boleslavsky's thinking, evidenced in the structure of his book (from an internal focus to an externally driven model) as well as in other historical evidence. The first lectures articulating his understanding of Stanislavsky's System delivered in 1923 end on the subject of emotion memory. By 1925 Boleslavsky was re-evaluating the place of emotion and looking, as Stanislavsky did later, for a more significant role for action: 'You know – and there is no use to repeat – that the main thing and the most important thing and the only vital thing on the stage is action' (in Roberts 1981: 167).

Drawing on the simple, natural behaviour of the actor engenders emotions far more truthfully than the hysteria evidenced in his students' emotion memory work. 'I see nerves – I hear screams. Where is the feeling built?' (ibid.: 166), Boleslavsky asked. To answer his own question, he makes a cultural observation, arguing that the technique of dramatic action is more suitable for an American clientele, especially the younger actors who are 'Exceedingly sensitive as to this simple method of connecting problem and action. In my experience with American actors, particularly those of Anglo-Saxon origin, I have found this is the only effective way of arousing the emotions' (ibid.: 168).

From a scientific point of view the repudiation of emotion memory suggests a shift in the psychological basis of his work away from Ribot and Freud, towards the 'new psychology' of Behaviourism. There is evidence in the latter chapters of *Acting* to support this view, for Boleslavsky's interest moves from emotion memory to the actor's relationship with the environment. The sixth and last lesson, for example, focuses – as Stanislavsky does in his second volume of *An Actor's Work on Himself* – on Rhythm.

For Boleslavsky, an actor's sensitivity to Rhythm is essential. He illustrates this by taking his Creature away from the bustle of the New York streets up to the summit of the Empire State Building to absorb the view in awe-struck silence. I's intention is to illustrate the emotional change engendered by the shift in location from the rush hour streets to the isolated peace of the top floor – from what he describes as the 'terrific tension' of below to a 'broad, streaming magic carpet ... float[ing] in the air to the rhythm of a steady wind'. His conclusion follows: 'our spirit is raised in an upward flash from torment to bliss' (Boleslavsky 1949: 110–111).

Thus, in Boleslavsky's view, the surrounding environment is a powerful emotional stimulus. J.B. Watson might have articulated it thus:

from:

S (Busy New York Street).......................R (Tension)

to:

S (Empire Rooftop).......................R (Elation)

The actor's task is, first, to develop a consciousness of how the rhythmic stimulus of the environment influences behaviour and, second, consciously to manipulate these rhythms to creative ends, to 'condition' him/herself to respond appropriately. This conditioning can be facilitated by music and may ultimately lead to an emotional response: 'Special attention should be given to the results of different rhythms. The best thing to start with is music, where Rhythm is most pronounced ... Give yourself up to the emotions it brings to you' (ibid.: 120). Along with Meyerhold and Stanislavsky, Boleslavsky saw the importance of music in its rhythmic impact. Working with the external stimulus of a sound score can suggest an elaborate set of circumstances in improvisation as well as stirring the emotions of the actor. The musical stimulus is not, in this instance, simply triggering an emotional recollection through the phenomenon of affective memory; rather the emotions are engendered by the very rhythmic structures which underpin the music and which chime with the actor's bodily sensations. Stanislavsky used a metronome to set different tempi and thereby to stimulate a range of emotional responses from his actors. Pavlov also used a metronome in his conditioning of dogs in his famous experiments on Conditioned Reflexes. J.B. Watson, in his work with Albert B., used an altogether more blunt method of sound stimulation. Whilst Boleslavsky's emphasis on Rhythm is a long way from this, the concluding chapters of his work do indicate a more materialistic approach to the problem of generating sincere emotions on stage.

Characterisation

This is true of the fourth lesson too, Boleslavsky's chapter on Characterisation. What is lacking in the Creature's performance is *form*, what Stanislavsky would call *voploscenie*. To dress the part, to give structure to the naked emotions expressed by the Creature, two things are needed: an understanding of rhythm (as might be expected) and a clear 'action' to play in the scene. 'I' challenges the Creature (who is playing Ophelia) on her chosen active motivation in the Gonzago scene of *Hamlet*. The action for this scene is not, as she has decided, 'to *be* insulted' by Hamlet but, Boleslavsky insists, 'not to break down' (1949: 94). Thus, in his reading she is not a passive supplicant at Hamlet's feet (as the state of 'being' suggests) but actively resisting his attempts to humiliate her in the presence of the court. The actions of Ophelia and Hamlet clash rather than complement each other. In saying as much, Boleslavsky is arguing that the emotional score of the role must in some way be organised and controlled by attention to physical action.

All of this is reminiscent of the changes in emphasis to the Stanislavskian System, from the early period of *A Month in the Country*, to the work on *Tartuffe* and the Method of Physical Actions analysed in Chapter 1. The progression of *Acting*, from the introspection of its opening to the concluding chapters on externally motivated means of controlling behaviour, may in fact be seen as a microcosm of the System's development after 1906. Roberts, for one, argues that Boleslavsky is to be credited with the discoveries of Physical Action a decade before his teacher (1981: 171).

Whilst avoiding the overt claim that Boleslavsky was developing a proto-behaviourist interpretation of the System a full ten years before Stanislavsky made the same paradigm shift in his thinking, there is a significant distinction to be made between the development of the System in Russia and its genesis in America. For where Stanislavsky in the last years of his life consistently, if rather contentiously, downgraded the feeling-based approach he had so emphasised during the early years, Boleslavsky retains a commitment to Affective Memory as well as to the more externally directed methods of Tempo-Rhythm and Dramatic Action. In *Acting*, Boleslavsky accords the Ribot-inspired emotional recall of his Creature a prominent place in his thinking, yet in other published sources (in *Theatre Arts Magazine*, for example), dramatic action is seen as an antidote for emotionally under-distanced work, freeing the actor from 'being handicapped by the emotion itself or becoming a nerotic [sic]' (Roberts 1981: 168).

One way of understanding this conflict in Boleslavsky's work is to emphasise, as Roberts does, the progression of his ideas and to recognise that his book was unfinished; what we have in Boleslavsky's *Acting* is a theory caught between two schools. Another explanation is that as a practising theatre expert, Boleslavsky was less concerned with the coherence of his sources and more interested in results – in an outcome for the particular body of students with which he was working. A level of pragmatism entered into his practice, therefore, which coloured both the language he used to articulate his theories – as in the pseudo-psychoanalytical expression of *Acting* – and the methods he adopted for a specific audience. The shift from Ribot-based exercises to an emphasis on action was, after all, initiated by Boleslavsky's assessment of the student-body at his Laboratory theatre, rather than by any theoretical change of heart.

The two approaches to the problem of emotion evident in his book, then, may point to a widening of his theoretical base, rather than to a developing change of mind on his part. Appealing to *both* of the predominant psychological schools gave him more options with his students whilst continuing the spirit of Stanislavsky's teaching: to balance the introspective work of the actor with the physical side of performance training. Indeed, whilst it is possible to detect an understanding of the scientific milieu of America in Boleslavsky's writings, at no time do these influences become explicitly scientific (as they do in Meyerhold's work, for example) or counter-productive – the accusation faced by Stanislavsky during *A Month in the Country*. In Boleslavsky's thinking, science (and psychology specifically) constituted one of the many cultural factors to which he had to be sensitive in bringing the System to America. The touchstone for its success was not whether it was 'tried by science' as Stanislavsky claimed in *My Life in Art*, but whether it produced results in its new context.

For Boleslavsky, then, the 'new psychology and psycho-analysis' coloured the expression of his acting theory, rather than determining his approach. For at least one of his pupils, however, Freud's theories were not so much a source of interest but a methodology. Turning to the second generation of American Stanislavskians will afford insights into how the roots of Boleslavsky's interpretation grew into the Method.

Lee Strasberg's interpretation of the System

As the teacher of so many famous actors and the guru still for some, Strasberg's impact on theatre in the US cannot be denied. His Method has been described as 'the most influential . . . of all American acting styles' (Hirsch 1984: 10), and credited with creating a 'revelation in the theatre . . . something almost holy' (Clurman 1983: 45). And yet consistently such eulogies are qualified in some way, even by those who do not have a specific axe to grind with the Method man. Strasberg's work is 'notorious' (Hirsch 1984: 10), 'controversial' (Krasner 2000b: 135) and the man himself, 'a dogmatic who brooked no heresies' (Senelick 1997: 288). This ambivalence clearly says something about the attitudes engendered by Strasberg's work and by the teacher himself. In the hands of great actors the Method has obvious and startling results but for those with technical needs, with less than robust personalities or simply with opposing views there are questions to be asked. For the purposes of this chapter these questions will be formulated around the claim that Strasberg was continuing the evolution of the System in America.

Completing the project

An indication of Strasberg's ambition as a writer is given early on in his book on acting, *A Dream of Passion* (1988). 'It is not a textbook', he claims: 'It is the first effort to explain what is acting? What is the Stanislavsky system? What is the Method?' (xi). All three counts are difficult to sustain.

It would be impossible to cite the number of texts devoted to the craft of acting published before Strasberg's death in 1982, difficult even to do the same for those dedicated to Stanislavsky in English. Only the last question might be answered by Strasberg's publication but this area too had been extensively discussed before Strasberg put pen to paper.[14] Taken literally, Strasberg's claim is clearly unsupportable. He may of course have meant that his book was the first *successful* explanation of the System but such an assessment raises significant questions over the efficacy and accuracy of his summary of Stanislavskian practice in *A Dream of Passion*.

Academically speaking, Strasberg's explication of Stanislavsky's thinking is careless. He uses long quotations without acknowledging their source, jumps from a cited source to his own interpretation of the source without highlighting any change of perspective and, most seriously in terms of documentation, appropriates secondary sources as his own. Thus, Magarshack's elucidation of emotion memory in *On the Art of the Stage* (1967: 53) is cited verbatim in Strasberg's book (1988: 60) as if it were his own analysis. At other times Magarshack's words are indented and explicitly quoted but the specific source is left undisclosed. On further occasions he paraphrases Magarshack – on the subject of 'ray emission' or 'prana', for example – and then offers a statement of his own in direct opposition to Magarshack's.

From Magarshack:

> As usual, Stanislavsky invents an utterly unscientific term for the definition of this inner and invisible communication. He calls it 'ray emission' ... It is 'as though the inner feelings and desires', he writes, 'emitted rays which, issuing through the eyes and body poured in a stream over other people' ... As for the method of mastering this process, Stanislavsky ... suggests two exercises to facilitate ray-emission and ray absorption.
>
> (1967: 60–61)

From Strasberg:

> Stanislavsky, influenced by some of his previous interest in Hindu philosophy, kept describing this inner communication as 'ray emission and ray absorption' ... as though the feelings and desires emitted rays which issued through the eyes and the body and poured in a stream over other people ... But Stanislavsky was unable to describe his methods of mastering this process by suggesting exercises to facilitate ray emission and ray absorption.
>
> (1988: 60–61)[15]

Either Strasberg did not read as far as Magarshack's next paragraph or he is making a judgement that the exercises referenced by him are insufficient in their aim. Whatever the case, Strasberg's summary of Stanislavsky – or more

accurately Strasberg's summary of Magarshack's summary of Stanislavsky –
is both misleading and inaccurate.[16]

Of course, as a practitioner, not an academic, there is no need for Strasberg to conform to academic good practice in the presentation of his subject
matter. But the inconsistencies in his documentation point to a general
tendency towards distortion in his summarising. Throughout his précis of
Stanislavsky, Strasberg refers to just two texts by the Russian director: *My
Life in Art* and *An Actor Prepares*. The other source, as we have seen, is David
Magarshack's *On the Art of the Stage*, which offers a detailed exposition of the
psycho-technique drawn from *An Actor's Work on Himself Part 1*.[17] Strasberg
does not acknowledge the existence of the second part of *An Actor's Work on
Himself*, translated as *Building A Character*, or the collection of writings
including the summary of the Method of Physical Actions in *Creating a Role*.
Thus, the overriding emphasis of Strasberg's summary of the System is
drawn from a period in the mid-1920s – the time when the MAT arrived in
America, sparking Strasberg's interest in the theatre.[18] In theatrical terms
this was the formative period of Strasberg's life when he began to study seriously with Boleslavsky at his Laboratory theatre and when he 'learned the
principles of the Stanislavsky system' (Strasberg 1988: 84). Strasberg takes
this period of the System's development as definitive and does not update his
reader beyond the theory of the psycho-technique. His summary of the
System, in *A Dream of Passion* is, therefore, weighted towards the introspective techniques associated with this theory. These he claims are drawn from
the Theatre Laboratory: 'The central emphasis in the system set forth by
Boleslavsky was on concentration and affective memory' (1988: 69). From
what has been seen of Boleslavsky's system, it should be clear that such a
definition is misleading. The two areas cited by Strasberg are only the first
two chapters of Boleslavsky's textbook and although Strasberg studied with
the Russian émigré ten years before *Acting* was published, there is other
evidence to suggest that the acting programme at the Lab was more compre-
hensive than Strasberg suggests – even in its infancy. Roberts's account of
the range of lessons on offer during the period includes classes in diction, a
rigorous physical training, Eurhythmic classes, tone and voice production
and ballet. All this was in addition to two hours a day with Boleslavsky. The
programme was further augmented by a series of lectures from outside
speakers including Luigi Pirandello, Norman Bel Geddes and Stark Young
(Roberts 1981: 122).

There is no indication of the richness of this creative environment in
Strasberg's writings. His selection of the practical work done at the Lab sup-
ports his particular view of Boleslavsky's teachings – a view that concen-
trates on the inner work of the actor. In the light of this imbalance,
Strasberg's claims for the significance of the Method seem without foundation: 'Through our understanding, analysis, applications, and additions, we
have made a sizable contribution to the completion of Stanislavsky's work
. . . The Method is therefore, the summation of the work that has been done

on the actor's problem for the last eighty years' (1988: 85). Strasberg's underlying project comes through clearly here. He views the problem of acting as the neo-Newtonians view science – for both there is the promise of a Grand Unifying Theory which will succeed in integrating the previous research done in the area. For Strasberg, Stanislavsky's work needs to be *completed*. He may acknowledge that the Russian director went through different periods of discovery but these periods are evidence of a developmental process towards an ultimate goal of closure – a definitive method or (more accurately) Method.

Although, as has been argued in Chapter 1, Stanislavsky might in his later years have shared such a Newtonian view of the System, a retrospective view of the tradition born out of his practice belies such an argument. The legacy of Stanislavsky, reflected in the diversity of sub-systems interrogated in this book, is characterised by a sense of fluidity, of receptivity to local, national and international influences and by an interrogative attitude to performance. The polysemic term 'system' encourages such a reading. Amongst other things, it connotes a wide programme of activities – a complex or network of ideas. A 'method', on the other hand, has a more limited range of definitions. It tends to operate at a local level, focusing on specific problems. A system can draw on a range of methods to achieve its overall aim, but the reverse does not hold true. Strasberg's claim that his Method constitutes 'the summation' of the previous research on acting (including Stanislavsky's System) seems unsustainable in such a context.

A left-sided approach

A Dream of Passion, then, tells a partial story. Rather than simply locating his own practice on 'the left' (the side of the System known as *perezhivanie* which details the psycho-technique of *An Actor Prepares*), Strasberg disregards 'the right' side of the system – *voploscenie*, from *Building a Character*. In this way he can claim to be following the tradition without deviation. 'I feel as intensely today about the basic discoveries of Stanislavsky as I did then', he states in *A Dream of Passion*, and then lists those discoveries: 'Relaxation, concentration and affective memory' (1988: 82). No account is taken here of the expressive side of the actor's craft.[19]

According to his contemporaries at Boleslavsky's Laboratory Theatre, Strasberg adopted the same selective approach to his tuition. Although his notebooks cited in the book indicate a study period of just over a year, from 13 January 1924 to 6 February 1925, Roberts records him leaving the Lab after a matter of months (1981: 230).[20] Harold Clurman's memoirs, *The Fervent Years*, seem to confirm this, noting Strasberg's employment at the Theatre Guild and his direction of amateur productions during the period (1983: 10–11). He and Strasberg signed up later for the directors' course under Boleslavsky in 1926 but Strasberg's growing commitments elsewhere look to have interrupted his attendance.

Most significant is the attitude he adopted to the classes he *did* attend, for there is clear evidence in his own writings that he was already predisposed to a particular view of the actor's psychology. In one of his many taped sessions with actors at his Actors Studio, Strasberg himself explains:

> By the time I came to the American Laboratory theatre I had already arrived at the essential principles ... At that time Boleslavsky said in his first talk, 'There are two kinds of acting. One believes that the actor can actually experience on the stage. The other believes that the actor only indicates what the character experiences, but does not himself really experience. We posit a theatre of real experience. The essential thing in such experience is that the actor learns to know and to do, not through mental knowledge, but by sensory knowledge.' Suddenly I knew, 'That's it! That's it!' That was the answer I had been searching for. The point is I had already read Freud and already knew the things that go on in a human being without consciousness. I had already picked up everything Boleslavsky had said, but he showed me what it meant.
>
> (1991: 144–145)

There are several things to note in this quotation, beginning with Boleslavsky's statement. His is a theatre of experience, of *perezhivanie*, of 'living through' the part, a theatre underpinned by the actor's sensory knowledge or sense memory. The implicit reference is to Ribot. For Strasberg, though, already well versed in psychoanalysis, Boleslavsky is best understood through Freud. As Strasberg states very clearly, he arrives at the Lab with his questions already answered. He already had an understanding of Boleslavsky *before* he began working with him, an understanding drawn not from Ribot's theories but from Freud's psychoanalysis. Boleslavsky's teachings simply confirmed his pre-designed model of acting.

The latent influence in Boleslavsky's work thus becomes explicit in Strasberg's Method. Like Boleslavsky, Strasberg was a Polish immigrant. He moved to America when he was only eight, the same year Freud visited Clark University. As such, he was steeped in the culture of America (and of New York specifically) from a child and perhaps inevitably had a stronger sense than Boleslavsky of the currency of Freudian thinking. But we can also detect here Strasberg's tendency to model the process of acting around his own theoretical predilections and a habit of reading others' work through these theories. His infamous rejoinder to the Group Theatre that 'Stanislavsky is wrong',[21] made on his return from Moscow, is a case in point.

An analysis of his training method, drawn from *A Dream of Passion* as well as from the testimony of Method actors, will exemplify this sharpening of Freudian thinking in Strasberg's interpretation of the System.

Relaxation

Whilst for Stanislavsky physical tension is primarily a physiological condition, for Strasberg there has to be a psychological cause at the root of the
problem:

> I became curious about the particular problem [an actress] was having
> ... When she put her head back, she experienced a very sharp pain in
> her neck. To investigate, I supported her neck, encouraged her to let in
> rest in my hand and asked her to tell me when the pain started.
>
> (1988: 97)

At first the actress claims a physical condition – arthritis – for her tension
but at Strasberg's insistence she is led back to a moment in her childhood to
isolate a psychological cause. It transpires that as a young child she had to
share a bed with her sister who 'had threatened to kill her if she didn't lie
still' (ibid.). This 'traumatic' childhood experience, in Strasberg's narrative,
then led to a compensatory reaction of physical restriction, which, after years
of habituation, now manifested itself in a physical disability.

In working with the actress in such a way Strasberg, is fashioning her
physical problem as a neurosis, which, after Freud, has been taken to mean a
mental blockage, developed from a past experience and becoming fixed and
resistant to modification (Gregory 1987: 549). Interestingly, Psychoanalysis
is both a theory *of* and a treatment *for* neuroses, involving the regression back
to the original conditions surrounding the 'blockage' and the concomitant
'release' from the neurosis. Freud and his colleague Breuer used such a cathartic technique to treat their most famous patient Anna O, who, according to
Freud in his introductory lectures on psychoanalysis theory, was 'as if set free'
from her 'melancholy' (including paralysis and hydrophobia) once she had
been regressed to the sequence of formative neuroses surrounding her father's
illness and subsequent death (Freud 1995: 8). Strasberg, adopting a similar
role, demands 'the release of those areas [of the actress's traumatic past] to
free her ... from mannerisms and tension ... on stage' (1988: 97).

A little later he questions another actress about her past, again to ascertain the root of her muscular tension. Appealing to what he calls 'most
modern schools of psychology', Strasberg argues that for 'certain types of
traumatic emotional experiences ... no amount of physical exercise can
correct these tensions' (ibid.: 99). Instead, he probes into the actress's family
history:

> Something made me say: 'did you use to be punished?'
> She said, 'Yes'
> 'A lot?'
> 'Yes'.
>
> (Ibid.: 98–99)

There are two points to note here. First, relaxation is viewed as a release mechanism, primarily of *psychological* rather than muscular tension. Strasberg is contesting Stanislavsky's claim in *An Actor Prepares* that relaxation is naturally part of 'the external side of our training' (1980a: 95). He is, in effect, redefining the place of relaxation in the System.[22] Second, Strasberg's emphasis on personal detail is notable. Boleslavsky draws on psychoanalysis in his presentation of the material of *Acting* but he remains committed to Ribot's psychology in his practice. Strasberg veers even further away from the philosophical root of the System by taking an expressly personal line into his actors' psychology.[23]

The conflict of private and public

At the same time, Strasberg ignores the psychoanalyst's principle of non-contact. The first example above begins with the establishing of a physical connection between teacher and student. The focus on the supporting of the neck draws on a technique of corporeal massage used in many warm-up situations. But the physical intimacy established by this position is changed abruptly to one of emotional trust, as Strasberg's questioning opens up the actress's private world. Clearly in some situations the two can facilitate each other but within the current context this approach is potentially more problematic and raises questions regarding the mode of teaching adopted by practitioners. Stanislavsky, we recall, abandoned the practice of open rehearsals when he was probing his actors' emotional resources. Strasberg, by contrast, taught the vast majority of his lessons in an open forum. In doing so, the diverse sources on which he draws in his teaching come into conflict. As a director and teacher, influenced by Boleslavsky and the Russian school of the 'scene critique', Strasberg adopts the tried and tested pedagogical technique of public analysis – what might in Britain be called 'the masterclass'. But as a self-confessed reader of Freud, regressing his actors, even in the context of a relaxation exercise, such a public forum may be seen as inappropriate.

Actors Studio members differ in their response to this conflict. Kim Hunter, for example, believed that it was a safe space for experimentation whilst others (Eli Wallach, for instance) suggested directly to Strasberg that his sessions were closer to public therapy: 'you should not practise psychiatry without a licence'.[24]

Those on the plus side nevertheless describe this safe space as punishing, necessarily so:

SALLY FIELD: I needed to be smacked around a little.

KATHERINE CORTEZ: He seemed to get mad and really come at me, looking at it [now] it looks like an attack but when I was on the other side of it I didn't experience it as an attack.

And on the specific subject of emotion memory:

ELLEN BURSTYN: He would ask a question and then another, and get deeper and deeper into you until finally you reached the point where you were tender and exposed and from that point you act.[25]

Such statements are reminiscent of Boleslavsky's interrogative approach with the Creature, measuring truth by the emotional response of the interviewee, and of Stanislavsky's earlier relationship with Knipper-Chekhova. But where Boleslavsky was writing an illustrative fiction and Stanislavsky conducted his affairs in private correspondence, Strasberg's probing is public. Thus, the emotional work of the actor becomes a learning instrument for the audience – a formula which is far closer to the experimental laboratory of actor/guinea-pigs than that which Stanislavsky was charged with running in the early 1900s.

Also to be noted here is the relationship between power and gender. Ben Gazzara makes the point that Strasberg was tougher on the women than the men in his sessions and, interestingly, the willing victims in the *Reputations* documentary, *Lee Strasberg: Method Man* (1997), are all women. Similarly, Steve Vineberg lists three women 'at the forefront' of the group of Method actors he calls 'the neurosis kids': Geraldine Page, Kim Stanley and Sandy Dennis (Vineberg 1991: 206). That the same dynamic is present with Stanislavsky and Knipper and with I and the Creature should not perhaps be seen as coincidental but rather as evidence of a particular gender-specific power dynamic throughout the tradition.

In Strasberg's case this conflict between two paradigms – spectatorial and private – is encapsulated in the cover illustration of *A Dream of Passion*, a filmic series of photographs of Anna Strasberg (Lee's wife) in the throes of an emotion-memory exercise on a stage in Germany. Strasberg, the teacher/analyst, is seated off stage, outside the view of the actress but still in view of the audience. At one and the same time he is both encouraging the regression of his actress and offering a commentary on it to his spectators, offering private pain as a public spectacle.

Inevitably this deviation from the spirit of Stanislavskian emotion-memory work has led to objections. Richard Durham,[26] one of the members of the Actors Studio who was taught at the height of its success in the 1950s and 1960s, and who attended classes with Ben Gazzara, Rod Steiger, Martin Landau and Kim Stanley, describes the process first hand:

He ... brought in Freud in his sessions with actors in what he called 'Affective Memory'. That is, instead of lying on a couch, the actor sat in a chair (straight-backed), relaxed as fully as possible, eyes closed, while a teacher (Strasberg) led him in a kind of dream-like sensory journey into an incident in the actor's past experience; the exercise being conducted to bring the actor in vital touch with something traumatic, or joyful, or ecstatic in his past and which led him in his acting to be more aware and active (responsive) to his own qualities. This was not always favourable (this exercise) with all the members of the Actors Studio, nor approved of even in the hey-day of the Studio.[27]

Durham then explains *his* objections:

> Certainly, in my opinion, the focus of his teaching was internal rather than physical and while he had great perceptive powers in his teaching and in his comprehension of actors and their fine creative qualities as well as their problems, I later came to feel that he was 'lop-sided' in his teaching in that he shunned, possibly scorned, a fuller body approach, that there was something either too linear and certainly something restrictive in his method, and he didn't want to explore physical avenues.[28]

This hitherto unpublished commentary by an actor also trained in bio-mechanics raises an interesting charge of 'linearity', particularly in the light of the Newtonian reading of Freudian psychoanalysis argued by Capra above. Strasberg's use of emotion memory is linear in that it trains the actor to forge a straight line back to their formative pasts and then to 'return' armed with a 'piece' of emotional and personal truth to adapt to the demands of the text.

But Durham's real focus is on what he calls the lop-sidedness of the Method, echoing the points made earlier. For many of Strasberg's colleagues this introspective bias, the emphasis on *perezhivanie* as opposed to *voploscenie* and the pseudo-psychoanalytical approach adopted by Strasberg were all aspects of an American interpretation of the System which needed resisting. For Stella Adler and Sanford Meisner – figureheads of two of the most prominent alternative schools of American Stanislavsky-based actor training – there were alternatives to Strasberg's emotion-centred Method and pursuing them did not mean a wholesale abandonment of psychology, but a return to the spirit of the latter part of Boleslavsky's *Acting*.

Acting is behaving: Stella Adler and Sanford Meisner

Robert Lewis

In a gesture which was clearly designed to deal directly with the question of a balanced actor training, Robert Lewis pointedly defines Method acting in his own terms, in his book *Method or Madness*, by holding up both parts of *An Actor's Work on Himself*: 'I will attempt first of all to describe what I think the Method is . . . (*holding up Stanislavsky's two books*) There's the bible, *An Actor Prepares* and *Building a Character*' (1960: 7). Lewis, another former member of The Group, then outlines all the problems associated with intro-spective acting amongst which he includes: poor diction and projection – or 'method mumbling' (60), too much analysis (75), no sense of rhythm or of movement (77) and an over-emphasis on the actor's personality rather than the character's (79). His antidote is to follow what he calls 'that right side of the column on his [Stanislavsky's] chart' (84) – an understanding of the Russian's System which is demonstrably more holistic than Strasberg's.

At the same time, Lewis is clearly identifying himself with the counter-school of post-Boleslavskyans who gathered round Stella Adler after her meeting with Stanislavsky in 1934, for the chart to which Lewis refers is the one brought back by Adler from Paris and dictated to her by Stanislavsky (see Figure 3.1). It represents yet another attempt by the Russian director to schematise his developing system in pictorial form and differs in terminology, if not in form, from the other two diagrams referred to in Chapter 1. Spelled out at the top of the diagram, perhaps to add weight to Adler's argument on her return to the Group Theatre, are the outcomes of the work in the System: 'E: THE PART is the outcome of THE TRANSACTION (A) between C: COMPLETE INTERNAL INNER FEELING and D: COMPLETE EXTERNAL' (Lewis 1960: opposite 34).

Thus, there is an interdependency between the elements of an actor's external work (which notably begins with Relaxation – no. 28) and his/her internal work which places emotional memory (no. 17) amongst a further sixteen elements of training. In retrospect, this diagram illustrates clearly Strasberg's reductive reading of Stanislavsky. Strasberg's *Dream of Passion* was written well after this document was published – twenty-eight years, in fact, after Lewis's book and sixty-four years after the original debacle at the Group Theatre. But within the pages of Strasberg's book there is no counter-argument to justify his particular bias, a reflection of the feeling already intimated in this chapter that Strasberg's model of acting was already fixed in his own mind before he met with Boleslavsky as early as 1924.

Interestingly enough, Robert Lewis also challenges Strasberg on his model of emotion, rejecting his Freudian emphasis for something reminiscent of an action-based approach to emotional acting: 'It is a mistake to wait to act until you feel', he argues, 'I think that you must act and feeling will come' (1960: 90). Indirectly, Lewis offers a scientific source for this belief:

> Modern acting, just like modern life has been very affected by the research in psychology that has gone on in recent years. A good deal of our problem now stems from the fact that we have learned a lot about reflexes and the like which did not enter into the earlier arguments ... We can't turn the clock back; we have all this scientific material to deal with and we have to incorporate it somehow into our understanding and our work.
>
> (ibid.: 96–97)

Whilst there is no evidence that Lewis incorporates J.B. Watson's reflex-based model of human behaviour into his work explicitly, his reassessment of the place of emotional training in an actor's work does offer an effective counter-model to the psychoanalytically weighted Method of Strasberg.

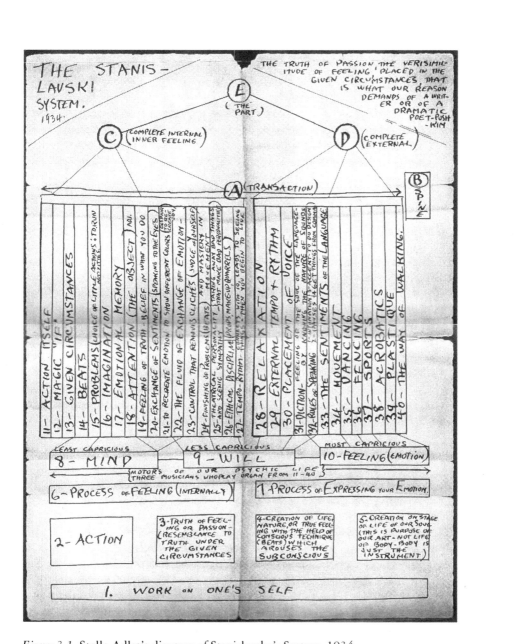

Figure 3.1 Stella Adler's diagram of Stanislavsky's System, 1934.

Stella Adler

For Stella Adler (1903–1992) the same was true, as Mark Hammer, her improvisation teacher at the Stella Adler Conservatory, makes clear:

> She was skeptical of the actor's goal to locate the fullest range of motivating sources merely through experience . . . Adler appreciated passion and the need for it as a motive force [but] . . . she was emphatically convinced that by its nature drama dealt with doing, not feeling, and that feeling was a by-product of doing.
>
> (2000: 300)

Following the approach Stanislavsky took working on *Tartuffe*, Adler places the emphasis on action within the given circumstances, valuing but not becoming beholden to the experience (*perezhivanie*) of the actor and insisting that playing the active score of the role engenders the 'by-product' of feeling, not the other way round. Like the Method of Physical Actions, this approach leads to an initial downgrading of the words of the play in favour of a paraphrased or personal text. The 'actor must lose his dependency on the words' she says, 'and go to the actions of the play . . . Words come out of the actions' (in Krasner 2000b: 141).

Adler was clearly listening carefully when she worked with Stanislavsky in 1934. In her last book, *On Ibsen, Strindberg and Chekhov*, published posthumously in 1999, she indicates her debt to the Russian and highlights her own attitude to the action–feeling debate: 'Actions must be DOABLE. Break down the overall action into its doable elements. Action means doing not feeling' (Adler 1999: 301). And later with an implicit reference to the Method of Physical Actions: 'Pay attention to *sequence* . . . Find the growth in the action through the plot. Emotion comes out of action. Never look for the emotion – you'll drive it away. Let it come out of what you're doing' (ibid.: 303).

Thus, her approach to Chekhov encourages the actor to score his/her physical movements in a given scene – at first in a mechanical sense without motivation, and then by choosing to motivate each action (ibid.: 302). The stress is continually on making a personal connection with the text, not through affective memory but by individualising the given circumstances, breaking them down into simple actions (Stanislavsky would call them tasks) and fulfilling those actions – *doing* the tasks set by the text. At all times the environment is crucial:

> Have a little talent and use the action and truth of the *play's* situation, not the situation in your own bedroom. That's what I fought with Strasberg about . . . The Method is hysterical insanity to squeeze something out of you. That doesn't make you act. This will make you act.
>
> (Ibid.: 280–282)

Adler goes on to describe in rich detail the environment of Act Two of *Three Sisters*, the environment into which Andrei enters, shorn of his dignity and weeping. Significantly it is the 1901 MAT premiere of the play which she recounts, directed by Stanislavsky and characteristically suffused with scenic stimuli.[29] It is dark, the living room of the Prozorov's house (now changed to suit Natasha's taste) is strewn with toys, the fire is going out in the stove and Andrei is realising the extent of his depression – he is married to an unfaithful woman and surrounded by the effects of his unwanted progeny. For Adler, the actor playing Andrei should connect with his environmental context, not with his own emotional past, to stimulate the necessary conditions to capture his character's degradation. 'It's winter. If you only have one thing, it's that the windows are frozen' (ibid.: 283), she argues, and that attention – to the immediate stimulus of the stage space – is what excites the actor to act. It is an approach which consciously distances the actor from any personal emotional material, relying instead on the power of the performer's imagination and on the view that the external surroundings of the stage are a strong stimulus to emotional work.

As such, Adler is closer to the behaviourist element of Boleslavsky's teaching as well as to the bias towards imagination we will see in Michael Chekhov's work in the following chapter. To complete the trio of First Studio directors, David Krasner highlights the influence of Evgeny Vakhtangov in Adler's thinking, specifically his 'idea of "agitation from the essence"' (2000b: 141) or what Vakhtangov defines as a feeling 'aris[ing] spontaneously on the stage, depending upon the situations in which the actor finds himself' (Cole 1955: 119).

Vakhtangov's essay was translated for the actors at the Group Theatre in the 1930s and this is probably the source for Adler's influence, one which Strasberg claims too (1991: 308). It contains the seeds of the dispute which dogged that theatre. For, on the one hand, Vakhtangov speaks ardently for an action-based understanding of emotion: 'the actor must . . . come on stage not in order to feel or experience emotions, but in order to act. Don't wait for emotion – act immediately' (Cole 1955: 118). On the other, the actor is commanded to 'live your own temperament on the stage and not the supposed temperament of the character' (Cole 1955: 120). The former points to a behaviour-based model of acting, founded on the principle that the active completion of tasks, drawn from the given circumstances of the play, prefigures any emotional content. The latter seems to suggest a more introspective and personal route to unlocking the emotional material of the character, the route Strasberg in fact favoured. Vakhtangov squared the circle by creating a particularly stylised and expressive form of 'truthful' theatre. But it is easy to see how the interpretation of Stanislavsky and his disciples, dependent sometimes on just a few nuggets of translated material, may be subject to confusion and selective interpretation.

Sanford Meisner

Where Adler's training implicitly acknowledges a shift away from the Freudianism of Strasberg's teaching towards environmental behaviourism, Meisner's school of acting, taught at the Neighbourhood Playhouse in New York, took *behaviour* as its watchword.[30] Although he makes a point of informing his reader in *On Acting* that he has had 'considerable experience in psychoanalysis' (Meisner 1987: 5) and quotes at length from Freud's writings, Meisner's technique, drawing as it does on the classes Adler taught at The Group, owes more to J.B. Watson's Behaviourism than it does to any Viennese school – not least because in its very essence it encourages a behaviourist eye in the performer.

Two maxims hang up high in Meisner's classroom, framed, like the *perezhivanie* and *voploscenie* banners constructed by Stanislavsky in *Building a Character*, for rumination and cogitation by his students: 'Be specific, says one, and the other, An Ounce of BEHAVIOR is Worth a Pound of WORDS' (Meisner and Longwell 1987: 4). The maxims give an immediate indication of Meisner's emphasis and of his particular interpretation of Stanislavsky, different from Adler's but sharing in spirit a desire to find alternatives to affective memory. Words are once again of less importance than what he calls the 'reality of doing' – the very 'foundation of acting' (ibid.: 16), rooted in simple, *do*able behaviour on stage.

This 'real' behaviour is trained by the central exercise of the Meisner technique: the Repetition Exercise. The actor sits in front of their partner, observes something about them (something about their appearance rather than any value-based assessment), speaks their observation out to the partner and then listens as their statement – their ultra-simple text – is repeated back to them, verbatim. This cycle is then repeated and repeated mechanically until the words become of no interest, whilst the spontaneous and reactive behaviour of the actors takes over.[31] The exercise then moves to repetition from a point of view – '"I'm staring at you." "You're staring at me." "I'm staring at you." "You're staring at me."' (ibid.: 23) – and this, in turn, develops into simple conflict-based improvisations. The point throughout is to generate a sensitivity in each actor for their partner's subtextual, instinctive responses, to take the focus for the work expressly outside of the individual and direct it towards the partner, to read behaviour and respond. David Krasner, a Method actor himself, puts it in revealing terms:

> Impulse is a response to internal or external stimuli ... The actor responds by acting on the stimuli, creating an 'impulsive' behaviour that emerges truthfully and spontaneously from reactions rather than from pre-planned behaviour. This procedure must be performed without intellectual interference, without 'thinking'.
>
> (2000b: 145)

Put thus, the Meisner actor seems to be the very embodiment of the Watsonian Behaviourist project whose central concept, as it appeared in the manifesto of this 'Science of Behaviour', was to: 'Avoid mentalistic concepts such as sensation, perception and emotion, and employ only behavior concepts such as stimulus and response' (Woodworth and Sheehan 1964: 113). Central to Meisner's technique is an action and reaction pattern that is first experienced in rudimentary form in the Repetition Exercise. This fundamentally Newtonian pattern then forms the basis of the actors' engagement with one another, an engagement underpinned by the detailed and perceptive observation of the partner's external behaviour (the stimulus) followed by an almost instantaneous reaction (or response).

Viewed from this perspective the two psychological schools are brought into sharp relief. Where the psychoanalytical bias of the Strasberg Method encourages his actors to focus inward – on their own neurotic past – the behaviourism of Meisner trains the actor constantly to concentrate on the external signs of performance as they shift and evolve through the play. It is perhaps for this reason that Robert Brustein, one of the harshest critics of the Method in America, declared: 'The Stanislavsky System bears about as much relation to the Strasberg Method as caviar does to hot dogs . . . While the Strasberg actor is listening most intently to himself . . . the Stanislavsky actor is listening most intently to others' (in Allen 2000: 127). Brustein is right to focus on the ensemble-led philosophy of the Stanislavsky tradition, something found in Meyerhold's work too. But he might have looked a little closer to home – to the Neighbourhood Playhouse and indeed to the Stella Adler Conservatory, for example – for the counterpoint he was seeking to the introspection of Strasberg: 'really listen', Adler exclaims, echoing Meisner, 'become engaged and respond spontaneously. *To act is to* REACT!' (Adler 1999: 305).

Strasberg's riposte to Brustein

That Strasberg does not offer an alternative to his own introspective approach is not strictly true. The penultimate chapter of *A Dream of Passion*, entitled 'The Method and Non-realistic Styles', does attempt to take into account other approaches to text which derive from different sources, both scientific and theatrical. Strasberg's main approach however is to assimilate rather than to differentiate. Thus Brecht, he concludes, is non-Aristotelian only in his writing with the 'best part of his work with actors deriv[ing] from Stanislavsky and perhaps even [from] the techniques of the Method (Strasberg 1988: 197). Grotowski's work on the other hand in its reliance on 'some hypothetical collective unconscious' creates 'general emotion as distinct from real emotion' and is therefore disappointing (ibid.: 179–181). In effect, Strasberg is only able to evaluate non-realistic styles of theatre in the light of his own practice.

Strasberg uses a similar approach in his treatment of scientific sources.

He is keen to argue that the main alternative theory of emotion to his – the James–Lange theory of emotion – is in fact compatible with the techniques of affective memory. Ostensibly, he shares the same desire as Boleslavsky to integrate the two different theories of emotion in his own acting theory. But Boleslavsky's System has an intrinsic duality in its structure. There is little evidence in Strasberg's work that he sees any alternative to emotion memory as the centrepiece of his Method. Appropriating William James to his cause is therefore more difficult.

Where Strasberg succeeds is in pointing out an interesting correlation between James's opening context on emotion (in *The Principles of Psychology*) and his own theory of emotion memory: 'As with instincts, so with emotions, the mere memory or imagination of the object may suffice to liberate the excitement' (James, quoted in Strasberg 1988: 187). He strengthens his argument by referring to a later section in *Principles* where James seems to be directly referencing Ribot: 'the revivability in memory of emotions … is very small. We can remember that we underwent grief or rapture, but not just how the grief or rapture felt' (ibid.: 187). Interestingly, William James goes on to indicate how 'actual' rather than ideal emotions can be revived by 'summoning up a lively thought of their existing cause' (James 1950: 474), although Strasberg does not quote this.

Given that James and Ribot were contemporaries this similarity in thinking is not altogether surprising. We have already noted that James's book sets out a range of psychological theories and might add here that he was present at Freud's American debut, demonstrating his interest in the developments of psychoanalysis. He clearly had an expansive vision of the emerging science of psychology. But these connections do not amount to any synthesis between the objective and introspective schools nor do they offer a rebuttal to the 'external' schools' opposition to the Method, as Strasberg implies. For the central thesis of James's chapter on Emotion remains as it has been defined earlier, that emotions are the consequence of an external stimulus, or as James puts it: 'the general causes of the emotions are indubitably physiological' (ibid.: 449). Affective memory, by contrast, stimulates emotion from within.

Strasberg's eagerness to claim a theoretical alliance with this view, his attempt to argue that he and James are speaking one and the same language, is evidence of the importance American theatre practitioners lend to the discipline of psychology. Like Lewis, Strasberg acknowledges that some cognisance of the contemporary thinking in psychology must be assumed to reflect the modernity of the training. His aim is different from Lewis's though. Put succinctly, it is to assimilate in order to eliminate. Arguing that Jamesian, and, by extension, Watsonian, psychology is part of the same thinking as his own reduces the range of truly alternative acting systems. The Meyerhold tradition, associated with the James–Lange theory, can thus be assimilated into the same school as the Method – just as Brecht is brought on board later in the chapter. Both styles, in Strasberg's vision, can then contribute to the *completion* of Stanislavsky's work with the summative work being centred on Strasberg's own practice. Viewed thus, his use of psychological theory in his analysis of Method acting becomes a powerful tool in the battle over which interpretation of Stanislavsky is pre-eminent. James and Freud unwittingly become part of the rhetoric exchanged between the feuding schools of Laboratory Theatre alumni.

Whilst much of Strasberg's practice is in conflict with Stanislavsky, as has been seen in this chapter, his desire to 'complete the project' and his overarching vision of a Method-for-all is ironically in tune with the late Stanislavsky's drive for universalism. Both men had a clear vision of the kind of legacy they wanted to leave for the western world of actor training, a legacy traceable back to Newtonian thinking. Although very different in their application, Meisner and Adler form part of the same sub-tradition, rejecting the mechanics of Freud for the mechanics of Watson and thus exemplifying in their respective systems one of the most significant psychological debates of the twentieth century in the United States. As a migrant and an exile Boleslavsky straddles this debate, his own version of Stanislavsky's teachings signifying that any system has to be adaptable and responsive to new environments.

There were, of course, other responses to Stanislavsky's System and other branches of actor training which began in Russia and moved to America. One in particular that should not be overlooked, that of Michael Chekhov, was developed in the 1920s and refined in the context of Dartington Hall in Devon, England. Chekhov represents a very different paradigm to those grouped together here as the Newtonian or Cartesian strain of the Enlightenment tradition. Indeed, his approach to training, the Chekhov Technique, marks a significant turning point in the development of the Stanislavsky tradition of acting, not because it rejected science, but because the kind of scientific principles informing it were demonstrably anti-Newtonian. Thus evolved a counter-tradition (what I will call the Goethean strain), stretching from the 1920s to contemporary Russian practice today.

Part III
The Romantic branch

4 A delicate empiricism
Romantic science and the Michael Chekhov technique

Whilst Meyerhold swiftly and enthusiastically became part of the post-revolutionary theatrical establishment after 1917, Michael Chekhov (1891–1955) lamented the radical changes to his Russia. Indeed, at the very time civil war was raging, Chekhov was playing Malvolio in *Twelfth Night* and was said by Oliver Sayler to have cut a downtrodden figure 'weighed down by Russia's sorrows' (Sayler 1923: 93). Earlier in 1916, he had lost his great mentor and teacher of Stanislavsky's System, Leopold Sulerzhitsky, and the Revolution served only to compound his depression. For Meyerhold, the Revolution brought great hope, for Chekhov it further distanced him from a culture he considered to be materialistic, superficial and mechanical. 'I accepted the theatrical world as a huge organised lie' (Chekhov 1936a: 5), Chekhov says in the opening to his autobiography, *The Path of the Actor* (originally published in 1928), extending his criticism to the surrounding social conditions:

> 'Research', 'experiments', studios, schools, lectures ... and side by side with it money, rank, servility, fear ... all this lives, moves, agitates, shouts (loudly it shouts!), flies impetuously from various points on the surface of the sphere to the centre and there it discharges itself in a flash, a spark, a lie!
>
> (Ibid.: 5)

There was much for Chekhov to be concerned about at this time; the years between the Revolution and his departure from the Soviet Union, a decade later, were some of Chekhov's worst, punctuated as they were with bouts of mental illness and personal crises. His wife divorced him, gaining custody of his daughter. He lost his mother, his cousin and began to lose himself on stage. Finally, Stanislavsky arranged for him to be treated by a team of psychiatrists to cure his depression and the 'fits of uncontrollable laughter which sometimes erupted in the middle of his stage performances' (Gordon 1987: 123).

But it was not the Western medical profession which brought Chekhov back to his senses. Instead, it was a growing interest in Hindu philosophy and in Rudolf Steiner's Anthroposophy or 'Spiritual Science'. Having seen private demonstrations of Steiner's unique voice and movement training, Eurythmy, in Moscow, Chekhov studied Steiner's writing first hand, specifically *Knowledge of the Higher Worlds and its Attainment* (1904). As a result, Chekhov became a practising anthroposophist and began to integrate this new thinking into his actor training. At the same time, as an actor, Chekhov started to develop a sense of perspective and distance and began to turn a critical eye on his own work, a lesson that ultimately had a significant influence on his acting technique. In effect, Steiner's Spiritual Science led Chekhov out of the physical and mental abyss into which he had unwittingly fallen during the First World War years.

Chekhov's public enthusiasm for Steiner's work inevitably led to his clashing with the Soviet authorities. Whereas Meyerhold's appropriation of Taylor and Pavlov was (at least at first) fully in line with the government's reforms, Chekhov was in direct opposition with Soviet ideology from the beginning. If Stanislavsky had had problems with the concept of the 'magic if' (Carnicke 1998: 81), then Chekhov's belief in Spiritual Science and the immortality of the soul, as well as his experiments in Eurythmy, were bound to place him at risk. The questions over Chekhov began close to home: in June 1927 sixteen of his actors left the Second MAT, where he had become Artistic Director, accusing him of idealism and mysticism. At the same time, the press labelled him 'a sick artist' and his productions [were] condemned as 'alien and reactionary' (*The Drama Review* 1983: 13). Whether his actors were critical of Chekhov himself or simply scared that they too would be marked as counter-revolutionary mystics is not apparent. What is clear is that, unlike Meyerhold, Chekhov escaped liquidation, taking up Reinhardt's invitation to work with him in Berlin in 1928 and spending the rest of his life in exile, in Paris, Lithuania, England and, finally, America. For the years which followed it was no longer his productions which were considered alien but the director himself – a point symbolised by his inclusion in the 1936 Aliens Register on his arrival in England.[1]

Chekhov is perhaps best known for his transformational approach to acting. Witness the photo-montage of Chekhov characterisations included in *On the Technique of Acting*. The page of pictures, entitled 'The Many Faces of Michael Chekhov' (1991: 118–119), shows seventeen radically different characters, stretching over thirty-four years of performance. The one unifying factor, beyond the universal glint in the eye of all his creations, is the metamorphosis undergone by Chekhov in creating his characters. A comparison of two of his most famous incarnations, Eric XIV in Strindberg's play of the same name and Khlestakov in Gogol's *The Government Inspector*, may serve to illustrate the point:

> Abnormally dilating eyes, dropping of intonation and the nervous movement of his thin hands betrayed suffering and anguish. At the moment when Eric threw the magnificent royal mantle from his shoul-

ders with one short, quick movement, his boyish thinness, his frailty immediately became apparent. Eric personified weakness itself, impotence itself.

(Rudnitsky 1988: 53)

Chekhov's Khlestakov now dived underneath the table three times in search of money, now skipped across the stage like a young goat, now lusting for the mayor's wife, gnawed the leg of the chair, now mocking Khlopov, moved a burning candle about right under his nose ... His performance stunned with its unbelievable improvised ease and unrestrained imagination.

(Ibid.: 52)

Whereas his portrayal of Eric captures a profound weakness and fragility, Chekhov's Khlestakov is all life and libido. But for each character the *transformation* of the actor is marked. Chekhov is the very personification of weakness or of lust, fluidly transforming as the character moves through the play.

Most significant of all in these two colourful descriptions is Rudnitsky's final statement – that the brilliance of these characterisations is the product of an 'unrestrained imagination', for imagination and its place in the preparatory work of the actor is a key term in the lexicon of Chekhovian acting. Not, as Rudnitsky might have it, a free and unfettered imagination but a concentrated, disciplined, rigorously trained imagination, the sort of imagination Romantic science first harnessed in the late eighteenth century by Johann Wolfang von Goethe (1749–1832):

None of the human faculties should be excluded from scientific activity. The depths of intuition (*Ahnung*), a sure awareness of the present, mathematical profundity, physical exactitude, the heights of reason (*Vernunft*) and sharpness of intellect (*Verstand*) together with a versatile and ardent imagination, and a loving delight in the world of the senses – they are all essential for a lively and productive apprehension of the moment.

(Goethe 1996: 116)

Imagination, Goethe argued, along with a deep intimacy with the realm of the senses, were two hitherto unrecognised aspects of the scientific method. He did not avoid rational and objective observation in his redefinition but strove to marry this conventional scientific approach with an intuitive and creative mode of thinking. This synthesis of reason and imagination Goethe called 'delicate empiricism' (1996: 72), his answer – his riposte, even – to the Newtonian paradigm, which he, like Chekhov, found unacceptably mechanistic and divorced from Nature.

Thus far, we have been predominantly concerned with outlining a Newtonian root to the Stanislavsky tradition. In this chapter the focus will shift radically, tracing a route back not to Newton and mechanics but to Goethe's organic view of the world, a sharp (and conscious) deviation from the mechanistic model of scientific enquiry. Goethe offered an alternative explanation of colour and light to challenge Newton's *Opticks* and through his polemical rejection of Newton's theories in his own *Theory of Colour* (1810) he has come to represent an alternative paradigm to the dominant Newtonian world-view. For this reason alone, his ideas fell on rich ground as far as Chekhov was concerned for the popularity of Newtonian mechanics in the post-revolutionary epoch summed up the state of the Soviet regime for Chekhov – materialistic, linear, law-bound, a world-view divorced from nature and the imagination.

Chekhov's route back to Goethe's art and Romantic science was stimulated by his deep fascination with Rudolf Steiner, the figure who is most often associated with Chekhovian practice. For Mel Gordon, Steiner helped 'fill . . . a dangerous void in Chekhov's creative world' (1987: 124) and for Franc Chamberlain, 'Steiner's theories were to form the basis of Chekhov's personal belief and [had] a significant impact on his theory of the actor' (2004: 14). In the same vein, Lendley Black notes that Chekhov's encounter with Anthroposophy 'had a direct effect on Chekhov's system of acting' (1987: 9). Even Rudnitsky, who omits to mention Chekhov's entire period in England, attributes his important collaboration with Andrei Bely to a mutual 'passion' for Steiner rather than to any theatrical common ground the two men may have shared (Rudnitsky 1988: 194).

Yet, despite this level of agreement over Steiner's influence, there remains precious little information on how Chekhov's interest in Spiritual Science may have impacted on his actors. More significantly, no one so far has sought to trace a route back from Steiner's work to reveal the key principles underlying the Chekhov technique – drawn, as much from Goethean Romantic science as they are from Anthroposophy.

In concentrating on this new and important relationship this chapter will seek to unravel the 'delicate empiricism' adopted by Chekhov in his studio, focusing, primarily, on his time at Dartington. From this perspective it becomes clear how important it was that Chekhov made his move away from the Soviet Union, not only for his own safety but also for the integrity of the philosophical core of his acting system. He did not forget the rich set of formative experiences he had had in Russia, both with Stanislavsky and Vakhtangov, but his particular holistic vision of the acting process needed an alternative environment in which to flourish. That environment was Dartington Hall in Devon, England, where Chekhov practised between 1936 and 1938. It was at Dartington that his system began to be properly documented and it was at Dartington that he found, in the Elmhirsts, a commitment to Art which mirrored his own.

Before examining the specific conditions of Dartington's utopian project, it is necessary to outline the scientific tradition to which Chekhov was indebted. Drawn from Goethe and Steiner respectively, it is a tradition which offers a very different model of the world than so far encountered in this book.

Romanticism, Romantic science and Goethe

Romanticism

With its emphasis on the primacy of the perceiver and on theories of the imagination, Romanticism seems at odds with a 'scientific method'. Indeed, some have gone as far to say that the very term is 'oxymoronic' (Halliwell 1999: 14). The objective model of scientific investigation passed down by Newton and his contemporaries emphasises a clear division between nature – the subject of study – and the observer of nature – the experimenter. Romanticism, generally, offers a different interpretation of humankind's relationship to nature, one based on organic *inter*-relationships, a unity *with* nature rather than a separateness *from* nature. Goethe expresses this sentiment clearly in his fragment *Die Natur* (1782): 'Nature! We are encircled and enclasped by her – powerless to depart from her ... She is the whole' (Goethe 1946: 123–124). To separate the perceiver from the perceived is to sever the organic link between Man and nature, an impossibility if one believes, as Goethe did, that: 'every one thing exists for the sake of all things and all for the sake of one, for the one is of course the all as well' (Goethe 1996: 60).

In saying as much, Goethe's science was aligning itself with the Romantic movement in the Arts, specifically in literature. Compare Wordsworth's *Lines Written Above Tintern Abbey*, published in *Lyrical Ballads* (1798), the volume often labelled as heralding the birth of Romanticism (Day 1996: 2–4):

> For I have learned
> To look on nature, not as in the hour
> Of thoughtless youth, but hearing oftentimes
> The still, sad music of humanity,
> Not harsh nor grating, though of ample power
> To chasten and subdue. And I have felt
> A presence that disturbs me with the joy
> Of elevated thoughts; a sense sublime
> Of something far more deeply interfused,
> Whose dwelling is the setting of the suns,
> And the round ocean, and the living air,
> And the blue sky, and in the mind of man,
> A motion and a spirit, that impels
> All thinking things, all objects of all thought,
> And rolls through all things.
> (Wordsworth and Coleridge 1965: 116)

Here, nature and 'the mind of man' are 'deeply interfused'. Nature is both fluid (a motion) and divine (a spirit), motivating and penetrating 'through all things'. The divisions of subject and object have become clouded, purposefully so, in order to celebrate the vivifying energy of the natural world and to highlight, for Wordsworth, nature's deep connection with humankind.

Romanticism, then, is a holistic philosophy, emphasising the interconnectedness of things and deliberately opposed to the atomistic or 'building blocks' approach in the lineage from Descartes. Where Descartes' dualistic division of *res cogitans* (thinking thing or mind) from *res extensa* (extended thing or body) led to the latter being viewed as a machine, Romanticism strove to reunite the mind and body in an organic relationship:

Lord Quinton expands:

> The Romantic favours the concrete over the abstract, variety over uniformity, the infinite over the finite, nature over culture, convention and artifice, the organic over the mechanical, freedom over constraint, rules and limitations ... Mentally the Romantic prefers feeling to thought, more specifically emotion to calculation, imagination to literal common sense, intuition to intellect.
>
> (in Honderich 1995: 778)

As a set of stimulating oppositions this definition is helpful but these polarities inevitably lead to simplifications as well. Goethe's elevation of the imagination, his view of organic nature and his resistance to the mechanical paradigm established by Newton and his contemporaries all contribute in this context towards his credentials as a Romantic. At the same time, Michael Chekhov's own dramatic credo has much in common with the Romantic principles highlighted here. His own interest in imagination, in eschewing dry intellectuality, in freeing up the actor's creative processes, all point to a Romantic tradition of thinking which will be investigated thoroughly later.

But it must also be recognised that the move towards a freer kind of expression, often associated with Romanticism's debt to the revolutions in France and America, is not synonymous with a wholesale abnegation of form or structure – the 'rules' Lord Quinton mentions. Such a perception is often supported by citing Wordsworth's famous statement in the preface to *Lyrical Ballads* (written in 1800 for the second edition): 'all good poetry is the spontaneous overflow of powerful feelings' (Wordsworth and Coleridge 1965: 246). Yet Wordsworth himself immediately qualifies this statement:

> But though this be true, Poems to which any value can be attached, were never produced on any variety of subjects but by a man who being possessed of more than the usual organic sensibility has also thought long and deeply. For our continued influxes of feeling are modified and directed by our thoughts.
>
> (Ibid.: 246)

In saying as much, Wordsworth is much closer to the kind of definition Chekhov and Goethe may have preferred. Organic sensibility yes, but a sensibility which is focused by reflective thought. Feelings yes, but feelings which are in a dynamic and creative tension with the intellect. Goethe said much the same thing just twenty-four years later: 'We need to develop all the manifestations of human character – sensuality and reason, imagination and common sense – into a coherent whole' (1996: 117). For Chekhov, this kind of tension was evident in the performer's 'dual consciousness', in which the actor can feel deep emotions and yet be distanced enough to 'make jokes with our partners' (1985: 102). For him, the imagination and the development of a Steiner-inspired 'Higher Ego' bridged the gap between sensibility and thought.

But before turning to the details of Chekhov's practice, Goethe's scientific career needs to be sketched in first, specifically within this context of Romanticism, noting here that the concept of a delicate *empiricism* is not as far removed from the Romantic urge as Lord Quinton might imply.

Goethe's Romantic science

Goethe's work spanned many sciences. He was a geologist, a botanist, a physicist and an osteologist. But although his studies embraced the diversity of science, Goethe took a synthetic approach, striving, as Agnes Arber puts it, 'to discern the Whole in the tiniest individual thing' (Goethe 1946: 84). This search to find the general in the particular led Goethe to propose an archetypal form (or *Urorgan*) in each of his disciplines. Thus in his geological essay 'On Granite' (1784) the rock of Goethe's title is described as 'the son of nature' and 'the one solid to the core' upon which all other rocks are founded (in Fink 1991: 15). Significantly, this is a view Goethe had come to perched high on a naked peak with the elements of nature both surrounding and inspiring him, the very quintessence, one could say, of a Romantic location – the type immortalised in the harsh landscapes of the German Romantic painter Caspar David Friedrich, as much as by the green fields of Wordsworth's imagery.[2]

In the same year, 1784, Goethe moved into osteology, the study of bones, coining the term 'morphology' for his comparative anatomy and claiming in 'On the Intermaxillary Bone' that the unity of nature is evident in the common bone-type of the jaw in animals and in humans. In the 'Metamorphosis of Plants' (1790) his search for a unified theory of types continued. The leaf, Goethe argues in this essay, is the archetypal form of the plant. It will assume a number of variations as it develops but these are simply embellishments on a common form. He summarises his findings thus: 'When now the plant vegetates, blooms or fructifies, so it is still *the same organs* which, with different destinies and under protean shapes, fulfil the part prescribed by nature' (Goethe 1946: 114).

Such a statement was designed to challenge the atomistic approach to plant-study, which treated the separate parts of the plant (leaves, stamens, petals) as discrete entities and saw the connection between the parts only in physical terms. Goethe, by contrast, 'saw the plant holistically', as Henri Bortoft puts it: 'He discovered another dimension in the plant, an intensive depth, in which these different organs are intimately related. In fact, he discovered that they are really all one and the same organ' (1996: 77–78). Bortoft's enthusiasm for Goethe's holistic approach is echoed in other recent studies including Jeremy Naydler's (1996) and Fritjof Capra's (1997), and all three men have been eager to reclaim Goethe as a modern scientist. Bortoft, for example, describes Goethe as 'our contemporary' (1996: xi) and Capra highlights the contribution Goethe has made to contemporary organicism and systems thinking, referring to Goethe's archetypal forms in the process: 'each creature . . . is but a patterned gradation . . . of one great harmonious whole' (1996: 21).

Philosophically, Goethe's view of the 'ideal leaf' is indebted to Plato's notion of Ideal Forms (dealt with fully in Chapter 5) and it retains Plato's own distance from reality. Where Plato saw the natural world as a collection of copies, removed from those 'ideal' forms that occupy the reasoned world of the intelligence, Goethe imagined a similar world of formative archetypes. But to suggest this is 'a discovery', as Bortoft does, is rather overstating the point. Goethe's notion of the *urform*, what he later called the *Urphänomen*, is in fact a theoretical construct – ironically something against which Romanticism railed. The now famous exchange of views between Goethe and his friend Schiller illustrates the case very clearly. Asking him what he thought of his theory of metamorphosis, Goethe received the following emphatic response from Schiller: 'that is not an empiric experience, it is an idea' (Goethe 1996: 96). Goethe's reply was typically robust and undeviating: 'How splendid that I have ideas without knowing it, and can see them before my very eyes' (1996: 96). Goethe's response is revealing for it articulates an aspect of his scientific practice which Michael Chekhov intuitively adopted in his acting Technique: ideas and images can consciously be utilised in the real world, indeed *become* part of the real world, once they have been conjured up by the imagination.

Goethe on colour and Urphenomena

This elevation of experience above conventional empiricism was most evident in Goethe's most famous contribution to science, *Theory of Colours* (1810) – what amounts to a wholesale rejection of Newtonian optical theory. Ignoring the mathematical evidence detailed in Newton's *Opticks*, Goethe sought to redefine the theory of colour in psychological terms. The ancient castle of Newtonian theory must be dismantled, Goethe stated in his preface, 'that the sun may at last shine into the old nest of rats and owls' (1967: xxiii). Following his unified theories of osteology and botany, *Theory of Colours* attempts to root the diverse spectrum of colours experienced by the eye in a 'primal phenomenon' once again – the polarity of black and white (Fink 1991: 33). Goethe would not accept that colour came from colourless light and distrusted the prisms Newton used to prove his theory. Instead, he based his theory in terms of his own relationship to his beloved nature. As such, the sky and the sun were his preferred source material for a 'natural' theory of colour: 'People experience a great delight in colour generally ... We have only to remember the refreshing experience, if on the cloudy day the sun illumines a single portion of the scene before us and displays its colours' (Goethe 1967: 304–305). Thus, in his preface to Part 6, 'The Effect of Colour with Reference to Moral Associations', Goethe emphasises experience above experimental data and the emotional delight stimulated by the colours of nature in preference to the dispassionate measuring of wavelengths in the laboratory.

To understand Goethe's approach, then, one has to adopt a different mindset to that implied by Newtonianism, one which eschews the measurable in favour of the phenomenal. Goethe was highly suspicious of mathematical abstractions – and here he deviates from Plato who first applied a rudimentary mathematics to nature in the *Timaeus* (*c.*348 BC). He also rejected causality, the bedrock of Newtonianism, preaching instead that:

> The best way to foster scientific knowledge is to ensure that one is completely familiar with the phenomena before going behind or beneath them in search of causes – that is, one first ought to grasp and conceive the Urphenomena.
>
> (in Sepper 1988: 179)

It is this search for an archetypal form, superior, Goethe believed, to the causal approach of mechanistic science, which is crucial for us here. Across the many disciplines of Goethe's science there remains this unifying quest for a primal phenomenon. From the early hymn to nature, 'On Granite', to the mature and assiduously documented *Theory of Colours*, Goethe's overriding project is to find unity in nature, to uncover archetypal forms which are hidden to the purely rationalistic and intellectual approaches of Newtonian science.

Such a radical overhaul of scientific thinking as Goethe proposed needed a whole new attitude from the scientist. Goethe's alternative approach testifies to his Romantic associations as it allowed the force of the imagination to play a part in the gathering of evidence, a factor which previously would have been considered anathema to any scientific method. As a scientist, echoing the Romantic purpose of Wordsworth, Goethe never separated the subjective input of the observer from the phenomenon under study. This is particularly evident in his earlier writings in geology but also applies in a different way to the approach he took to his later, more serious investigations into light. Goethe's way of seeing was 'to *experience* the *quality* of colours' rather than simply allowing them to be impressed upon us (Bortoft

1996: 42). He wanted the colours of nature to pass through the imagination of the scientist revealing new relationships not readily brought about by a purely objective approach.

To do this, Goethe would run his practical experiments twice, the first time in a conventional empirical manner but on the second occasion he would take his observations, garnered from the 'real' experiment, and re-run them in his mind's eye, transforming them in his imagination. It was a process Goethe called 'recreating in the wake of ever-creating nature' (in Bortoft 1996: 42). Far from compromising the results, this method of imaginative re-creation, Goethe believed, brought the scientist closer to the perpetual creativity of nature. In saying as much, he was arguing that the subjective and indefinable aspects of the imagination are the scientist's best hope of getting close to nature, they are in fact part *of* nature, the prerequisites for what he called an 'intuitive perception', the 'truest and highest' of all the scientist's senses (Goethe 1996: 91).

It is perhaps for this reason that the first translator of Goethe's science into English (Charles Lock Eastlake in 1840) considered the *Theory of Colours* to be a far more significant document than Newton's *Opticks* for those practising in the arts (Goethe 1967: xi), a view echoed by Rudolf Steiner in his own book on colour: 'We can *do* something with Goethe's theory of colour. It means something to us. We artists cannot do anything with Newton's physicists' theory of colour' (1992: 120). As Goethe himself was clearly an artist before a scientist this is not surprising. But note that Chekhov too connects Goethe with the creative force of the imagination – in the second chapter of *To the Actor*, 'Imagination and Incorporation of Images': 'Goethe observed that inspiring images appear before us of their own accord, exclaiming, "Here we are!"' (2002: 22). For Chekhov, as with Goethe, these images emerging from the imagination must not be left untethered. They are to be brought under control, exercised and interrogated by their creator in order that they may yield 'answers visible to [the actor's] inner sight' (Chekhov 2002: 23). Although the intended outcomes of this inner sight are clearly very different for the two men, the importance of a non-intellectual, creative intuition for both Chekhov and Goethe is evident.

Rudolf Steiner's conception of the world

Steiner, like his mentor Goethe before him, was the quintessential polymath. In his relatively short life (1861–1925) the range of his publications is impressive, covering theories of education, architecture, colour and painting, the theatre, agriculture and Eurythmy – before his key texts on religion and philosophy are considered.

In education, a subject for which Steiner had the same universal ambitions as we have seen in the alternative paradigm of Newtonianism, his work led to the founding of an international movement of radical schooling, known as Waldorf education. The first Waldorf/Steiner school opened in

1919 and was followed by over 600 more schools in the years between then and now. Waldorf education, like much of Steiner's thinking, was separated into a trinity with three clearly distinct periods of a child's development – from one to seven, from seven to fourteen and from fourteen to twenty-one. The first period, Steiner argued, is associated with imitation and play (will); the second, with artistic expression (feeling); the third, with the intellect or reason (1928: 16).

As an architect – the designer of the monumental *Goetheanum* – Steiner influenced Frank Lloyd Wright, Le Corbusier and Walter Gropius. *Goetheanum* was Steiner's homage to his Romantic mentor, built to bring together under one roof all of his artistic and scientific interests. Steiner used Goethe's theory of metamorphosis as 'a principle of interior design', as Gilbert Childs puts it (1995: 43), using natural, 'live' materials (including seven types of wood) and a fluid, transformational style of organic design. The second *Goetheanum*, built after fire destroyed the first, still stands today. Surrounded by trees and mountains in Dornach, Switzerland and visible from miles around, it is a romantic statement in itself. Perched high on a hill it recalls the inspirational position Goethe himself took beginning his scientific quest and seems at once to be both witness to and participant in its own natural context.

As an artist, Steiner was both a painter and a playwright. His ideas on colour, drawn from Goethe's own thinking (in this case his *Theory of Colours*), had an impact on the anti-naturalistic painters Wassily Kandinsky and Franz Marc. For Steiner, Naturalism was the art form of Newtonian materialism, which had led to the separation of mankind from his spiritual roots. Reproducing surface 'truths', he reasoned, whether it be in painting or in drama, only served to prolong this stymieing of the creative spirit. In *Speech and Drama* (1924) Steiner articulates his resistance to materialism in terms redolent of Plato:

> Whilst true drama raises all that takes place on the stage, lifts it up to a higher level, and in so doing brings what is human nearer to the Divine, naturalism attains nothing but the imitation of what is human. And no imitation can ever be complete.
>
> (Steiner 1959: 407)

Steiner looked instead to ancient Greek literature and to Homer's epic poetry. Homer, whom Plato calls 'the original master and guide' (1987: 422), is accorded by Steiner the function of 'letting the upper gods speak' and valued for putting his protagonists 'at their disposal' (1992: 134). Epic poetry, for Steiner, kept alive the bond between the spirit world and the material world.

The clearest connection to Michael Chekhov's work is made with Steiner's Eurythmy: a movement-based art form that strives to capture, in physical form, the unseen shapes created in the air by sounds. Eurythmy was a key factor in the training of Chekhov's actors at Dartington and, along with Goethe's *urforms*, played a significant role in the development of the Psychological Gesture (PG) – arguably Chekhov's main contribution to actor training today.

Eurythmy's central aim is to give physical form to the invisible sound patterns of speech and music. Thus, there are two forms: Speech Eurythmy and Tone Eurythmy. Steiner took his inspiration once again from Goethe, believing that the larynx – responsible for the creation of sound in humans – is the *urorgan* of the musical body as a whole: 'What occurs imperceptibly in the formations of sounds and tones in a single system of organs [the larynx] is to become visible as a movement and posture in the whole human being' (Poplawski 1998: 34). Steiner was effectively articulating a holistic under-standing of the actor's voice, paralleled in Rudolph Laban's work and developed fully in training regimes such as Grotowski's.[3]

Steiner's diverse range of thinking was drawn together under one banner, what he called 'Spiritual Science' or Anthroposophy, his alternative to mater-ial science. This huge project, pursued throughout Steiner's life, involved the re-unification of religion, art and science and was fuelled by the belief that the separation of science from the creative and spiritual drives of humankind resulted in a one-sided, materialist mode of thinking. Steiner did not reject the material world entirely but wanted to strike a balance between this world (the sensory world) and the spiritual world (the super-sensory world).

According to his critics it was his deep immersion in Goethe's work at this time which led to the new-found synthesis of spiritual and material worlds in Steiner's thinking. For Arthur Pearce Shepherd, for example, 'There can be little doubt that Steiner's study of Goethe's scientific works over the previous years contributed largely to the awakening of this new experience' (1983: 53).

In a way, Goethe's writing had a similar impact on the young Steiner as his own *Knowledge of the Higher Worlds* had on Chekhov when the latter was undergoing his crisis in Moscow. Both men needed an alternative framework to the materialistic and secular world in which they found themselves, both needed a different way of looking at the world and Goethe offered precisely that: a different mode of consciousness. For Steiner:

> Goethe's basic conviction was that something can be perceived in the plant and animal which is not accessible to mere sense observation. What the bodily eye can observe in the organism appears to Goethe to be ... the result of a living whole of formative laws working through one another, laws which are perceptible only to the 'spiritual eye'.
>
> (1973: 87)

Before considering Chekhov's direct relationship with Steiner it is helpful to review the number of convergent elements in Steiner's religious, artistic and scientific theories. First, the anti-materialist standpoint taken by Steiner is evident across all his writings. His world-view, inspired as it was by Goethe and the Romantics, was fundamentally holistic and organic. This is best expressed in his attempt to draw together the 'three cultures' under one roof in Dornach, an attempt which closely parallels the Dartington project. Second, his rejection of material-based science and positivist philosophy was reflected in the stand he took against naturalism in the arts. Later than most anti-illusory prophets, Steiner called for a theatre based on the folk tale and on the great epics of Homer, favouring the imaginary input needed to engage in such material and celebrating the latter's close relationship with the metaphysical world. Third, Steiner argued that this world is open to all who care to train their minds, the first step being the expunging of any material self-interest. Such an attitude is the prerequisite for gaining the 'spiritual eye' in which both Goethe and Steiner believed so strongly. Finally, for both Steiner and Goethe, a deeply Romantic empathy with the natural world facilitates a vision of its underlying morphological mysteries. For Goethe, these were what he called *urforms*; for Steiner, echoing Plato again, they were the 'spiritual *Archetypes* of all things and beings which are present in the physical . . . world' (1942: 93).

Chekhov and Steiner

It is difficult to ascertain exactly whether Chekhov's first taste of Steiner's work came through practice or through his reading. Certainly in the years immediately after the Revolution he was studying yoga and this led him to the doctrine of Theosophy out of which Steiner's Anthroposophy was born.[4] Where the former refers to 'God-wisdom' and to an external focus for the believer, Steiner's 'Man-wisdom' was based on a belief that spiritual knowledge can be found within. Chekhov's emphasis on the imagination, on drawing on the inner resources of the actor's soul must be seen in the light of this internal spiritual focus.

At the time, there were many private demonstrations of Eurythmy in Moscow and Chekhov became keenly involved in these secret anthroposophical societies (Chekhov 1991: xvi). In his autobiography *Life and Encounters*, Chekhov admits that his reading of Steiner's key anthroposophical text, *Knowledge of the Higher Worlds and its Attainment* (translated into Russian in 1918), did not have an immediate impact and instead it was Andrey Bely who stimulated his interest in Steiner. Certainly by 1921 Chekhov owned a copy of Steiner's text, as he brought it to one of Bely's lectures in that year. By then the impact of Steiner on Chekhov was clear:[5]

> The simple, clear, scientific style makes simple . . . those facts which were the objects of the author's discourse. That which is inaccessible to the sensual perceptions became accessible as a result. I read R. Steiner's

whole series of books and this careful reading gave me the answers to the questions troubling me then.

(in Black 1987: 8)

By the early 1930s, whilst he was in exile in Germany and after his success with Max Reinhardt as Skid in *Artisten*, Chekhov attended a Steiner school and trained in Eurythmy. Through Reinhardt he met Georgette Boner (also an anthroposophist) and moved with her to Paris to create a theatre school. There is little evidence of Boner's and Chekhov's activities during this time but what is clear is that in addition to performing *Twelfth Night* and some short plays by his Uncle Anton, the two worked on fairy tales (Black 1987: 26), following Chekhov's belief that the actor's imagination is exercised most effectively using non-naturalistic folk material. It was a belief which Steiner shared:

> Read a fairy tale ... and you will have the impression, not indeed of something natural, but of something that is gently suggestive, of the eerie, of the ghostly ... We are no longer in immediate reality, we receive the impression of something a little uncanny.

(1959: 78)

It was Georgette Boner who notified Beatrice Straight and Deirdre Hurst du Prey in America that Chekhov was touring his newly founded company, the Moscow Art Players – information which ultimately led to the invitation from Straight's mother (Dorothy Elmhirst) for Chekhov to come to Dartington. Boner then followed Chekhov to Dartington and is listed in the archives there as a teacher of theatre history.[6]

Chekhov had travelled from Moscow to Holland to hear Steiner lecture in 1922 (Chekhov 1992: 15) and had met him in person some years before he moved to Dartington Hall. According to Beatrice Straight, Steiner was instrumental in persuading Chekhov to continue his work in the theatre and although this must have been at least fifteen years before he moved to Dartington, Chekhov felt that Steiner had blessed the venture (Young 1982: 231).[7] It was also Steiner's suggestion (as well as Stanislavsky's) that Chekhov commit his theories to writing, advice which led to the first version of *To the Actor* in 1942, put together with the help of Deirdre Hurst du Prey and Paul Marshall Allen. Allen was another keen advocate of Steiner's theories – a fact which may account for the far more significant voice Steiner has in the unpublished 1942 version of *To the Actor*, housed in the Dartington Archives.[8]

Arguably, it is in Chekhov's early writings that Steiner's influence is clearest. In *Knowledge of the Higher Worlds* Steiner defines the prerequisites for the student of Anthroposophy:

> In all Spiritual Science there is a fundamental principle which cannot be transgressed ... Every knowledge pursued merely for the enrichment of

personal learning and the accumulation of personal treasure, leads you *away from the path*; but all knowledge pursued for growth to ripeness within the process of human ennoblement and cosmic development brings you a step forward.

(1964: 14, my emphasis)

It was a message that clearly spoke to Chekhov's particular circumstances in the early revolutionary years in Moscow, circumstances he describes in his unpublished autobiography, entitled, perhaps not coincidentally, *The Path of the Actor* (*Put' Aktera*, 1928). In it, he plots his own journey away from self-gratification, interpreting Steiner's words from his own theatrical perspective:

Five or six years ago I lived through a feeling of acute shame. I could not bear myself as an actor. I did not reconcile myself to the theatre as it was at that time (it has remained so to this day). I recognised precisely and clearly what it is that stands out as distortion and untruth in the theatre and the actor. I accepted the world as a huge organised lie. The actor seemed to me to be the greatest criminal deceiver.

(Chekhov 1936a: 5)[9]

Steiner is a presence throughout his book (either explicitly or implicitly) and his writings clearly helped Chekhov negotiate himself out of his mental crisis. Later, in the same book he describes his recovery:

My mental stability grew stronger every day ... I had not yet become thoroughly familiar with the new ideas which were coming to me, but I was already understanding the direction in which my inner life was to go ... I knew that my senses were unharmonious, my will untrained and my thoughts wandered chaotically in my consciousness ... Despite the powerful resistance which my character was putting up, I began to transform my mental qualities. Religious moods were already less foreign to me.

(Ibid.: 52)

Beyond the general acknowledgement of an emergent spiritual understanding, Chekhov's words in this passage reveal a deeper debt to Steiner. In the chapter 'The Parturition of Human Personality' from *Knowledge of the Higher Worlds*, Steiner, like Chekhov, divides the personality into three separate entities: thoughts, feelings and will, noting the drastic effects felt by the individual if the balance between these three parts should slip out of harmony. 'A violent nature' is the result of an unbridled will, 'a pitiful vacuity' the outcome of too much feeling and overly thoughtful personalities are 'cold and apathetic creatures' (Steiner 1964: 184–185). Later in his career, Chekhov was able to use this formula in creative terms, defining characters in terms of their reason-feeling-and-will balance (Chekhov 2002:

120) and the actor's body in the same terms: reason (head), feelings (chest and arms) and will (legs and feet), (Chamberlain 2004: 71–73). At this stage in his life, though, the message was personal and he interpreted his lack of direction and private shame as a spiritual imbalance.

What is particularly interesting in this context is Steiner's description of the student of Anthroposophy who *has* managed to achieve a balance of reason, will and feeling. Through the facility of the 'Higher Ego' he is able to *control* his impulses, translating thought into action only if he so desires:

> He can henceforth confront, devoid of feeling, a fact which, before his training, would have filled him with glowing love or bitter hatred; and he can remain impassive at a thought which, formerly, would have spurred him on to action as though of its own accord.
>
> (Steiner 1964: 182)

This level of critical distance is central to Chekhov's technique of acting. What, for Steiner, is a growing spiritual awareness brought about through training, in Chekhov's reading becomes the actor's artistic objectivity – his/her double consciousness. Chekhov effectively offers a practical interpretation of Steiner's Higher Ego in his section on 'The Objectivity of Humour' in *On the Technique of Acting*:

> The more our higher self is trained, the more likely we are to leave personal things behind us. We become objective in our perceptions as the artist should. Many things that previously excited us emotionally, and therefore hid from us their humorous features, now show themselves completely. The Higher Ego frees humor [sic] in us by freeing ourselves.
>
> (1991: 23–24)

Chekhov sees the Higher Ego as a way of dividing the actor's consciousness, specifically in this instance to bring lightness and humour to the work or a degree of self-mockery. But more generally, this developing critical distance between the actor and his/her emotions is a defining feature of Chekhov's system and helps distinguish his approach from that of the early Stanislavsky and from Strasberg throughout his career. Where Strasberg's Method encouraged the reduction of distance between character and actor, promoting a kind of emotional under-distancing, Chekhov, through Steiner, insisted on a clear division. It was perhaps for this reason that Strasberg was unimpressed by Chekhov's work when it was first premièred in America in 1935, stating in characteristically uncompromising terms that Chekhov should go back to the Soviet Union (Black 1987: 28).

Chekhov, of course, did not go back to Russia after his tour. Instead, he was brought to England by Beatrice Straight and Deirdre Hurst du Prey, whom he had met on the American tour. There, in the context of Dartington Hall, Chekhov was able to develop his holistic system of acting, a system suitable for the Romantic roots we have thus far outlined

Chekhov at Dartington

The inspiring context of Dartington

Dartington Hall in the 1920s had much in common with *Goetheanum* in 1914. Steiner's vision for his building was to unite the scientific activity of Anthroposophy with his emergent artistic work in drama and Eurythmy. Dorothy and Leonard Elmhirst, in bringing Dartington's researches in agriculture and forestry together with a highly innovative education and arts provision, were doing something similar. They too believed in the therapeutic influence of art and this conviction informed many of their choices at Dartington. Thus, the staff working in the rural industries supported by the estate were fully integrated into the cultural life of Dartington and encouraged to enjoy both watching and participating in the arts. Members of the estate were provided with the 'facilities or means for enlarging the mind and the sensibilities, through vocational interests and studies and the arts' (Bonham-Carter 1970: 124). There were weekly meetings for the whole of Dartington at which an impressive array of contemporary thinkers was assembled: Bertrand Russell, Rabindranath Tagore and Aldous Huxley are listed speakers in the records of these meetings for the period 1930–1935 (Bonham-Carter 1970: 125). These lectures were frequently held in the estate's theatre – the Barn Theatre, owned by the Dartington Hall Trust and refurbished by the Bauhaus architect Walter Gropius.[10]

In addition to the weekly meetings of the estate, the Barn housed Michael Chekhov's theatre school – the Chekhov Studio – from 1936 to 1938. According to Chekhov it was an inspiring context in which to work, a point stressed to his benefactress, the actress Dorothy Elmhirst, in a clipping from the archive: 'Nowhere in this world will you find such a possibility to work – such space, such air, such buildings, such harmony, such light.'[11] During the period following his emigration from the Soviet Union, Chekhov had developed considerable experience of acting and teaching in Germany, France, Lithuania and Latvia as well as America. Now, in England, he was able to put into practice his individual system of acting, designed to facilitate the kind of transformational acting for which he was so famous in his native Russia. Although he had attempted to establish acting schools elsewhere, specifically in Riga, and had been teaching publicly and privately in Moscow, at no stage had Chekhov had the opportunity to develop a formalised programme of activities or the personnel to record them. Dartington provided both. As head of the Drama department Chekhov was working in parallel with the dancers Kurt Jooss and Rudolph Laban in a newly professionalised arts programme at Dartington. He had the resources and the support to begin to synthesise his ideas for a new approach to acting, drawing on Stanislavsky's System but significantly departing from it in many fundamental ways: first, in its attitude to emotion; second, in its innovative approach to the development of character (through the Psychological Gesture and the idea of an Imaginary Centre); third, in the form of its expression – a hands-on practical dialogue, not with fictional students, or with one favoured 'Creature' (as with Boleslavsky), but directly with the reader themselves.

Chekhov clearly had the credentials to take forward the professional aspirations of the Elmhirsts (and the newly appointed head of the Arts department, Christopher Martin) in terms of the theatre programme.[12] For his part, Dartington offered Chekhov a unique environment to develop his work. In the first instance, the Elmhirsts' commitment to bringing science and art together under the same roof chimed with his own inclusive approach. In a passage in the unpublished 1942 version of *To the Actor*, housed in the Dartington Archive, Chekhov explains: 'One can clearly distinguish a new movement arising, the tendency of which is directed towards the *unification of science, art and spiritual knowledge*' (iv–v). In this version – the prototype of the 1953 New York publication – Chekhov's debt to Steiner is much more explicit – in fact he goes on to praise the 'initiator of this movement, Dr. Rudolf Steiner' (ibid.) for offering the practical support for him to achieve such a fusion in his teaching.

The Chekhov Studio: policy and curriculum

Further evidence of the connection is provided in Chekhov's Theatre School Policy written in 1936, although again not freely available in any published form. For this reason alone, it is worth quoting in detail but also because it stands as a unique testimony to his theatrical philosophy at this crucial time in his development:

> Present-day naturalism in the theater represents, to a certain extent, a turning-point. The theater goes back, for its origin, to religious mysteries. The descent to the present naturalism has occupied centuries. The religious, spiritual interest of the theater at its beginnings have faded into interests that are psychological and concentrated in a rather narrow aspect of the daily life of average persons. The figures of gods and heroes have been misplaced and the protagonists of today tend to be sickly or misplaced or superfluous.
>
> To escape from this unfertile path there are various efforts which may be grouped according to two different directions in which is being sought the theater of the future.
>
> In one class may be grouped experiments in merely technical progress, based on a materialistic conception of life. Its object is not to present the living soul or a person or a society, but rather to give instead a conventionalised or stylised symbol of it.

The other branch of change is in the opposite direction. Its aim is to give back to the theater its spiritual content: at the same time using all the advantages and achievements of technique, in so far as this can be done without allowing mechanics to become the ideal and without sacrificing to technical effects creative human individuality.

(Chekhov 1936b: 1)[13]

Chekhov's categorisations are interesting. His repudiation of naturalism as trivial and psychological may be aimed at Stanislavsky whilst the sickly protagonists to whom he refers recalls the popularity of the neurasthenic character actors on the Russian stage at the turn of the century (Schuler 1996: 104–105). If the former reference is to the Stanislavsky school of acting, then Chekhov had not kept up with the developments to his system since he left the MAT in 1928. For Stanislavsky shared Chekhov's sentiments regarding the triviality of naturalism claiming as early as 1926 that its excessive use of detail was 'poisonous to the theatre' and to the imagination (in Gorchakov 1994: 333).

On the other hand Chekhov bemoans the loss of a very different theatre tradition to Stanislavsky's – one that populates the stage with Gods and heroes, the theatre of the ancient Greeks and of Goethe's Romanticism, the very same theatre, in fact, which Steiner was attempting to rekindle. Steiner used Eurythmy in his own production of Goethe's *Faust* and believed that its use in training his actors was instrumental in solving the problems of Part II, specifically for the scenes based 'beyond the earthly plane'. For one Steiner critic, *Goetheanum* became 'the Bayreuth for the performance of Goethe's work' (Poplawski 1998: 52).

Chekhov's criticisms are then turned against what he called technical materialism in the theatre, an alternative to naturalism but one that, for Chekhov, was soulless in its commitment to stylisation. This appears to be a direct reference to Meyerhold's school of theatre. As early as 1907 Meyerhold had published on the Stylised Theatre (Meyerhold 1991: 58–64) and, as noted in Chapter 2, he developed a performer training based on an understanding of the actor's material possibilities. Chekhov's comments at the end of his career indicate that he remained in opposition to Meyerhold, at least philosophically: '[Meyerhold] was just as certain of his own imagined feeling of truth as Stanislavsky was of his photographic sense of truth. If something was actually true to life, it didn't interest Meyerhold' (Leonard 1984: 39). For this reason Chekhov considered Meyerhold's productions to be 'diabolical', not in the popular sense of the word but in the literal sense – they revelled in the presentation of evil. He may have admired Meyerhold as a theatrical visionary but the dialectical materialist basis from which Meyerhold was working was antithetical to his drive for a spiritual renaissance of the actor.

Chekhov's alternative was to synthesise the lessons learnt by Stanislavsky and Meyerhold with his own focus on spiritual and moral values, to define

what might be called a 'delicate empiricism' for the actor. Thus, the technical rigour of the Stanislavsky and Meyerhold schools remained central to
Chekhov's approach. He concurred with the former in celebrating the 'delicate and exact ANALYSIS of artistic material' and with the latter in demanding the actor should train his/her body by having instruction in 'fencing . . .
and in elementary acrobatics, such as tumbling'. At the same time, Chekhov
declared that 'all means of expression must be RE-SCRUTINIZED and RE-
SPIRITUALIZED'. To do this, the external work of the actor must reach a
special level of expressiveness, not over-exaggerated but 'permeated by the
power of a living spirit' (Chekhov 1936b: 2–6).

There is an indication here that the utopian atmosphere of Dartington
was seeping into the language Chekhov used to define his curriculum.
Without the pressures of a commercial set-up, Chekhov could afford to wax
lyrical on the purpose of drama as he saw it and clearly viewed this policy
document as an important vehicle to outline his particular direction. The
curriculum for the school in Ridgefield, Connecticut, by contrast, was far
more 'pragmatic' (Black 1987: 35), reflecting the financial and cultural shift
brought about by Chekhov's move to America. But as such, the Dartington
curriculum did reflect a kind of ideal in Chekhov's thinking and is, therefore, an extremely valuable measure of what, in perfect circumstances, the
spirit of Chekhov's work would embody.

The headings of the proposed curriculum of the three-year acting course
are cited below:

1   A system of exercises to develop:
    A. ATTENTION
    B. IMAGINATION
    C. SPEECH
    D. BODY
2   DRAMATIC ÉTUDES AND IMPROVISATION
3   EXTERNAL PREPARATION AND PRODUCTIONS
4   LAWS OF COMPOSITION, HARMONY AND RHYTHM
5   SHORT LECTURES ON THE HISTORY OF ART, THE
    THEATER AND PLAYWRITING
6   TALKS ON THE SIGNIFICANCE OF ART IN GENERAL AND
    THE THEATER IN PARTICULAR
7   EXPERIMENTAL WORK
8   APPEARANCES BEFORE A SELECTED AUDIENCE
9   PUBLIC APPEARANCE.

(Chekhov 1936b: 5–9)

There is much here that betrays Chekhov's past. The juxtaposition of the
two aspects of inner work – Attention and Imagination – with the development of technical skill in the body and voice – the outer work – recalls the
division Stanislavsky makes in *An Actor's Work on Himself Parts 1 and 2*. The

development of harmony and rhythm and of the discipline of improvised études also takes us back to Chekhov's teacher, who encouraged his actors to think and move musically using exercises in tempo-rhythm. There are close similarities with Meyerhold's own curricula too, not so much in the use of the term étude, for Chekhov meant something akin to a developed 'improvisation on a theme' rather than a repeated physical study, but more so in the scope of the work. Both men had in mind a rounded theatrical education interweaving cultural history and dramatic theory with exacting practical work.

The place of Eurythmy

For Chekhov, work on the body (1.D.) moved from purely technical exercises to work specifically on Eurythmy. Year 1 began with fencing. In the second year an instructor was required for light athletics whilst in the third year the predominant work was based in Steiner's integrated sound and movement training. In the event, Chekhov was forced to leave Dartington in 1938 by the growing likelihood of war with Germany and the proposed third year of the course was never run. It is evident, though, from his curriculum that a significant stress was placed on the complementary discipline of Eurythmy both in terms of the planned progression of the course and in the actual records of the first-year classes which did run. A typical day for the students looked like this:

June 17th 1937
9.30–10.00:	Eurythmy
10.15–12.15:	Rehearsal on text e.g. *Peer Gynt*
12.15–12.45:	Mr Chekhov
3.15–4.00:	Speech
4.00–5.00:	Rehearsal on text e.g. *Peer Gynt*
5.00–5.15:	Tea
5.15–6.30:	Rehearsal on text e.g. *Peer Gynt*
6.30–7.00:	Mr Chekhov[14]

It should be said that the timetables were not the same each week and Chekhov's own input was not always as little as two half-hour sessions. On other occasions he would work the whole afternoon with the students. The one constant in the students' schedule, however, was the class in Eurythmy.

In practical terms, this meant Chekhov's actors were engaging each morning with Steiner's psycho-physical gestural alphabet, literally embodying consonants and vowels in their Eurythmic movements. 'I' (ee), for example, is performed with the arms in a diagonal plane with the right arm up and the left down, 'O' has the arms in a circle stretching forward and 'A' (ahh) is performed with the arms raised overhead in a 'V'. The vestiges of the latter gesture can be seen in Nikolai Remisoff's Drawing 2 in *To the Actor* in the chapter dedicated to the Psychological Gesture (2002: 72–73). Chekhov describes this particular gesture as being 'opened to influences from above' and 'filled with mystical qualities'. At the same time, he argues, he 'stands firmly on the ground and receives equally strong influences from the earthly world' (1953: 68).

In saying as much, Chekhov offers a reading of the gesture which is reminiscent of Steiner's own predilection for Homer. The protagonist's function, we recall, is to mediate between the earth and the gods, following the Homeric Epic. In Chekhov's hands, Odysseus becomes an archetypal gesture, a Classical *urform* from which the actor can evolve a new character and a new body.

Remisoff's drawings in *To the Actor* fulfil a significant function in this process for they translate what, at first, sounds like an arbitrary semaphore of Eurythmic correspondences into a powerful gestural stimulus for the actor. It is for this reason that Chekhov embraced Eurythmy. He saw the gestures associated with the alphabet as having an emotional and imagistic aspect to them. 'A', for example, conjures up a feeling of awe, whereas 'I' was associated with a sensation of power and an image of 'energy streaming to the sky' (Gordon 1987: 141). Sound (and its attendant gestural expression), is a stimulus for the imagination and for the feelings – in that order.

Imagination and the fairy tale

Beyond the stress on Eurythmy, Chekhov's choice of text for rehearsal is notable. Ibsen's epic fairy tale *Peer Gynt*, depicting, as Michael Meyer puts it, 'the struggle between the divine purpose and our undermining passions and egocentricities' (1992: 290), was the ideal text to develop the imagination of his actors. Like Goethe's *Faust*, Ibsen's play is often considered unperformable and indeed was not written with performance in mind. In asking his students to engage with the particular challenges of *Peer Gynt*, Chekhov was highlighting his own predilection with the supernatural and with the fairy tale. He was also asking his actors to make an imaginative leap into the world of goblins and trolls, to enter into his fantastic theatrical landscape.

It is here, with the question of imagination, that we reach the very crux of Chekhov's acting philosophy. As early as 1922, in his notes on Stanislavsky's System, produced whilst he was working at the second MAT, Chekhov stressed the significance of the imagination: 'the bolder the artistic imagination, the greater the power of the work' (Cole 1955: 113) he declared, ostensibly summarising Stanislavsky but more obviously communicating his own credo. Later, in *To the Actor*, Chekhov followed his opening chapter on the body with the chapter dedicated to imagination, citing Steiner as a prologue: 'Not that which *is* inspires the creation, but that which *may* be; not the *actual* but the *possible*' (2002: 21).

In *On the Technique of Acting*, the second revision of *To the Actor*, after the

1942 version, imagination comes first although the Steiner quotation is dropped in favour of the German Romantic historian Rudolph Meyer:[15] 'Man feels himself younger and younger, the more he enters into the world of his imagination. He knows now that it was only the intellect which made him stiff and aged in his soul expression' (Chekhov 1991: 1). With its emphasis on the anti-intellectual rejuvenating force of the imagination, Meyer's statement recalls Lord Quinton's definition of Romanticism and connects Chekhov directly with the Romantic tradition and the free creative spirit. Steiner's declaration extends this connection and crystallises the distinction between Chekhov and Stanislavsky on the subject of imagination. Stanislavsky's view of imagination, drawing, as has been argued, on a Newtonian view of the world, operates to piece out the 'imperfections' of a text. The actor creates an 'inner chain of events which [they] themselves have imagined' (Stanislavsky 1980a: 64) and which psychologically cements the text together. The emphasis remains on the textual given circumstances or what might be called the *actual* world of the text. Chekhov, by contrast, demands a more radical role for the imagination, exploring the *possibilities* of fantasy beyond the text. He invited his actors to train their imagination so that it could be both expressive and intuitive as well as being subject to the actor's control. Chekhov's imagination exercises cited by Mel Gordon exemplify this expansive approach:

- After reading a Shakespeare play, let your imagination rewrite or rearrange its plot, language and characterizations.
- Try to create something that does not exist: an animal, a flower, a landscape, a figure.

(1987: 168)

In both cases the imagination functions either to destabilise or reinterpret an original form. Rather than bringing into focus an object that is partly drawn – the aim of the Stanislavskian imagination – Chekhov's exercises actively encourage a free fancy. Chekhov sees the imagination as an autonomous creative tool, not simply a support to the playwright. Put another way: the actor should 'become the student of his imagination' (Merlin, 2000)[16] – an emphasis which is evident in his practice at Dartington (well before any of his published writings emerged), in the 1936 theatre curriculum.

Delicate empiricism: attention and imagination

The very first skills to develop in the actor are what Chekhov called in his outline curriculum the two 'basic forces in the creative process' (1936b: 5). These are attention and imagination (1.A. and 1.B.), and they form the central dynamic of the technique, underpinning the voice and body work. The very core of his acting technique in this period is, then, based on the creative tension between the expressive force of imagination and the controlling influence of attention. There is nothing revolutionary in this of course. The craft of acting is often expressed in similar polarities: spontaneity versus discipline, inspiration versus technique, talent versus training. But in the current context, the interplay of a free imagination with a rigorous method of focusing that imagination recalls the delicate empiricism of Goethe and the Spiritual Science of Steiner. Goethe saw no paradox in the notion of 'imaginary experiments' – a classical scientific approach embellished by the intuitive force of the imagination – and Steiner's anthroposophical practice was geared to applying a scientific method to his spiritual philosophy.

It remains for this chapter to evaluate the practical value of this delicate empiricism. To be true to Chekhov's own credo, it is clearly important to assess the significance of this Romantic acting model for the performer in the theatre laboratory. After all, this is the context for which it was devised. This final section, then, before the conclusion, draws on my own practical experience with the Chekhov Technique, focusing on one Chekhov practitioner in particular – David Zinder. It may be viewed as a conscious acknowledgement of Chekhov's affirmation in *To the Actor*: 'Many of the questions . . . can best be answered through the practical exercises prescribed herein. Unfortunately, there is no other way to co-operate: the technique of acting can never be properly understood without practicing it' (2002: liii).

Romantic science and the actor: David Zinder's interpretation of Chekhov

David Zinder is head of the acting programme at Tel Aviv University. Here, Zinder worked first under Peter Frye, the Chekhov-trained actor who was one of the group of performers making up the cast of Chekhov's *Lessons for the Professional Actor* (1985) in the early 1940s. Frye had introduced Zinder to the concept of the Psychological Gesture in 1963 but it took thirty years for the link to be made explicit in his thinking. Before 1993 Zinder had been working with Michael Chekhov techniques 'intuitively' until Mala Powers,[17] Chekhov's executrix, pointed out his close affinity with the Chekhov Technique at a conference in Philadelphia (Zinder 2002: xii). Zinder then began consciously utilising the documented workshop approaches of Chekhov and is now a significant figure in the international family of Chekhov teachers. This intuitive absorption of practical technique obviously continues in Zinder's practice (as it does for all of us, perhaps), as there are clear associations with Gennady Bogdanov's biomechanics and Keith Johnstone's improvisation in his work. He acknowledges both sources (and many others) to differing degrees.

As such, Zinder's workshops are a fusion of Michael Chekhov and his own actor-training techniques, culled from a range of sources.[18] In my work with him, he described the latter as 'pre-Chekhov' work arguing that his own preparatory training – which includes work with sticks and balls and movement-in-space exercises – is essential to understand Chekhov today.[19] Whilst the need for an induction into Chekhov is by no means accepted by all the recognised teachers of the technique, Zinder's defence (which implicitly acknowledges Johnstone's work in improvisation) is to argue that his preparatory work, emphasising spontaneity and responsiveness, offers a contemporary precursor to the 'pure' Chekhov Technique. From the purist's perspective, Zinder is implying that Chekhov's holistic system is somehow lacking something today. From an eclectic's viewpoint, he is simply engaging creatively with Chekhov's system, an approach that must be in the spirit of the Russian's work and in tune with the fluid, evolving tradition of actor training.

Of particular interest in this context is the work on *imagination*, the bedrock of the Chekhov Technique as the following exercise of Zinder's exemplifies:

- Begin to make bodily movements of all your limbs, feeling the energy for the movement emanating from your centre.
- Punctuate your movements with a neutral position – a zero point.
- Ensure each new movement is different (between zero points) by changing pace, level and direction.
- Create whole movement sequences by finding a beginning, middle and an end – the 'feeling of the whole'.
- Perform the whole sequence and repeat.
- Continue the repetition in sets of two.
- Then perform the sequence and repeat *in your imagination without moving*.
- Continue in sets of two.

The exercise is typical of Chekhov's in that it connects a number of different practical principles in one exercise – the Imaginary Centre, Attention and Imagination, specifically – and anticipates the key aspect of his work, the Psychological Gesture.

Imaginary centre

The work begins with the actor's body. It is only later that Zinder moves to words and finally to text – the trajectory he describes as 'from physical, to physical/vocal, to physical/vocal/verbal (2002: 5). In beginning thus, Zinder is echoing Chekhov's own progression in *To the Actor*, from Chapter 1, 'The Actor's Body and Psychology', to Chapter 10, 'How to Approach the Part'.

The exercise demands a physical reaction to an imaginary stimulus drawn from the actor's own imagination. The actor's work is given focus by imagining that this physical response stems from the centre of the body. For Chekhov this centre is located in the chest, for Zinder in the midriff. The difference, though small, is significant. Chekhov draws on Steiner in locating the actor's core in the heart or chest – that is, between the nerves (corresponding to the spirit) and the limb system (corresponding to the body), according to Steiner's taxonomy:

	Physical Expression	Psychological Expression	Spiritual Expression
Spirit	Nerves/senses	Thinking	Waking
Soul	*Heart/Lungs*	*Feeling*	*Dreaming*
Body	Metabolic/Limb System	Willing	Sleeping

(Childs 1995: 51, my emphasis)

The chest or heart, from an Anthroposophist's viewpoint, is where the soul is located: the centre of our dreams. Thus, the chest centre effectively mediates between the body and the spirit, between willing and thinking, in practical terms between the bodily expression of the actor and the thought impulses of the imagination.[20]

Zinder argues that the Imaginary Centre of the actor should be lower (in the midriff) as the chest is too close to the personality of the actor but this seems misjudged when one sees Chekhov in the context of Steiner. For moving the actor's centre away from the chest moves him away from the feelings and away from the aim of Chekhov's opening physical work: to unleash the emotional potential of the actor. As he argues in *To the Actor*:

> See that all the movements you make are actually instigated by that power which flows from the imaginary center within your chest . . . This exercise will gradually give you a glimmer of the sensations of *freedom and increased life*. Let these sensations sink into your body as the first psychological qualities to be absorbed.
>
> (1953: 7)

The shift may be influenced by Zinder's work with Gennady Bogdanov and it is interesting here to compare Chekhov's Imaginary Centre with Bogdanov's biomechanical centre, the *gruperovka* or 'commanding point', located in the sternum. Whilst Chekhov's thinking locates the centre of the actor in his/her soul, Bogdanov's centre is a material reference point, used as a navigational tool to locate oneself in space. As such, Bogdanov's centre is fixed and remains so when the actor is in motion – to fulfil its locatory function. Chekhov's Imaginary Centre, by contrast, although based in the chest may be moved about by the force of the actor's imagination to create different characters: 'The center can be placed anywhere: in the shoulder; in one of the eyes (e.g. Tartuffe or Quasimodo); in the stomach (Falstaff, Sir Toby Belch) . . . All variations imaginable are possible' (Chekhov 1991: 101). Thus, where Meyerhold's biomechanics locates the actor in the physical present, Chekhov draws on the fluid imagination to site his actors in a present of their own creation. The material basis of Meyerhold's art is contrasted with the anti-material 'soul drama' of Chekhov.

Chekhov places great trust in the actor's imagination when it comes to training or developing the Imaginary Centre. There are no 'spiritual exercises', as it were, but mental images offered in order to kick-start the imagination. This, in turn, influences the body's movement which re-stimulates the imagination in a circular, organic relationship. 'Imagine the centre is warm, gold, or glowing', Zinder suggests to begin the process, facilitating the leap of faith needed to feel the power of the centre flowing out to the rest of the limbs. Once a sense of the Imaginary Centre is evoked in the actor, the physical behaviour must then change, directed by (and from) the centre.

Most significant in the current context are the results of this imaginative leap, for locating a centre is the first step towards finding a formative core, or '*urcharacter*', out of which all the actor's chosen characterisations can emerge:

> The imaginary center in your chest will also give the sensation that your whole body is approaching ... an '*ideal*' *type* of human body ... You will have the feeling that your 'ideal body' enables you ... to give it all kinds of characteristic features demanded by your part.
>
> (Chekhov 1953: 8, my emphasis)

It is this archetypal centre which provides a locus for all the variants of character born from the actor's imagination. As the actor moves the Imaginary Centre away from the chest to the other parts of the body, so new characters emerge from this 'ideal'. The Imaginary Centre is, therefore, the foundation for the rest of the work. It must be 'felt' by the actor, not in directly physical terms (one can see how centring in this way might lead to an artificial stiffening of the performer's upper body) but in 'spiritual' terms – and by this I mean in Goethe's sense of an external form translated and transformed in the imagination. It is no coincidence that Zinder evokes the Centre with terms such as 'glowing' and 'warm' for these are the qualities popularly associated with an inner spirit, just as their opposites, 'dull' and 'cold', traditionally sign the absence (or departure) of that spirit. Without signing up to any particular religious doctrine, these qualities can be stimulated in a workshop context through the power of the imagination.

Attention and imagination

To return to the Zinder exercise cited above: in punctuating the creative responses of the actor with what he calls 'zero points', Zinder is fusing his training in Meyerhold with Chekhov's approach. Here, though, it *is* in the spirit of Chekhov's work. Zinder's zero point is identical to Bogdanov's *stoika* or neutral stance. It is a moment of pause, held by the actor in an erect position with soft knees, concluding one moment of activity and preparing for the next. It is, 'the highly charged median point between one action and another when fateful decisions are being weighed in the imagination', as Zinder puts it in *Body Voice Imagination* (2002: 11).

In a physical sense, the zero point constitutes the closure of a specific passage of movements – actions which may have become too comfortable for an improvising actor. In an imaginary sense, the zero point places a rest in the flow of ideas, forcing the actor to give up the previous pattern of gestures and to create anew. Effectively, the zero point brings a sense of order to the creative imagination, demanding that the series of movements created by the imagination are treated as a microcosmic piece of theatre with a defined beginning, middle and end, or in Chekhov's words as 'a little piece of art'.[21] The actor's explicit attention to detail and structure is therefore brought to bear on the material in the very moment it is created, attention and imagination supporting each other simultaneously.

The exercise then builds up the material created by repeating patterns in sets of two, finalising and polishing the sequence. Finally it is performed in its entirety *without moving*. Here, there is a strong reminder of the scientific method of Goethe detailed earlier, for having experimented physically to create a movement passage, the Chekhov exercise then asks the actor to perform it again, in a virtual re-run, 'moving' through each step of the piece in the imagination. In doing so, the performer both trains the imagination to review physical material and re-creates that material, as Goethe put it, 'within the living dynamic of the organ' (1996: 119). Necessarily, the choices of movement are coloured by the artistic imagination when they are performed 'in the mind' and this leads to unexpected creative aberrations which can then be fed back into the work. The result is a very different interpretation of psycho-physical action than we have encountered so far in this book, where the inner processes of the actor stimulate and then refine external action.

Such an organic interplay between the physical and the psychological is best understood through the concept of the Psychological Gesture or PG.

The Psychological Gesture

According to Deirdre Hurst du Prey, Chekhov's PG has associations both with Stanislavsky who 'stumbled on the fringes of something akin to it' (du Prey 1979: 3) and Vakhtangov who, in working with Chekhov in *Eric XIV* (1921), experimented with something similar as a directorial tool at the First Studio. By 1938, the concept was fully developed and was part of the teaching classes at Dartington.

As with all of Chekhov's acting exercises, the PG is intimately connected to many of the other aspects of his system, in this instance to Qualities of Action, to Atmosphere and, of course, to Imagination. In essence, the PG is a physicalisation of the overriding superobjective of the character – the 'I want' in mime – although it may be used for separate scenes, or specific moments in the play. Like the biomechanical études, the PG is a training device and is not designed to be seen on stage. Instead, it acts as a kind of mental morphology of the character, retained in the mind's eye of the per-

former. Du Prey appeals to nature to explain: '[The PG is] not only a movement of the body – [but] movement <u>and</u> feeling <u>and</u> will and other elements
. . . gesture in everything, in a plant, a tree, a chair' (du Prey 1979: 4).

The PG avoids drawing on the personal experiences of the actor as,
Chekhov reasons, it is an archetypal not an individual gesture: 'Your father
in a play is a character whom you have to portray with all your skill, and
make it individual. But if you don't have the archetype of the father, your
father will become a very small, dry, insignificant figure' (1985: 113). The
archetype is the fundamental, ideal form of an object or a character. Behind
all the possible variations of, for example, lions, Chekhov argues 'there is an
idea of a lion which is the source of all lions' (1985: 112). The line back to
Steiner, Goethe and ultimately to Plato is very clear here. For Steiner, the
archetype is like the idea of a painter 'existing in the mind before it is
painted' (1942: 93). For Plato, the urforms of all things in nature populate a
similarly virtual world (the intelligible realm), opened up not by the physical senses but by the 'eye of reason' (1987: 314).

But for Chekhov, the PG is anything but abstract. The actor's task is to
find this archetypal form in a physical gesture – the archetype of a king, for
instance, if he were playing Lear. Only after this gesture has been found,
through practical experimentation and improvisation, can the character be
individualised. The individual characterisation is, then, *born out of* the
general archetype, specifically by lending the gesture different Qualities of
Action or by relating it to imaginary Atmospheres.

David Zinder introduces the work on the PG by focusing on eight archetypal gestures, what Chekhov teacher Joanna Merlin calls 'the mothers and
fathers of all gestures' (2000). The work then develops in the following
manner:

- Find an exaggerated physical gesture for each of the Archetypal Ges-
  tures: open, close, pull, push, press, penetrate, scatter, tear.
- Repeat the gesture until it is exact and well defined.
- Add qualities to the gesture: to penetrate *tenderly*, to pull *aggressively*.
- Repeat the gesture until the quality suggests itself: change the tempo –
  note what happens.[22]

The complexity of the gesture in Zinder's exercise is built up through the
work as separate layers of meaning are added. Note that it also possible to
find a quality simply by repeating the exercise – that is the 'how' of the
gesture emerges from the 'what' of the action without, at first, any intellectual choices being made. The Chekhovian actor must be sensitive to these
chance intuitive creations as they are the product of an organic process.
Later, though, as the gesture begins organically to metamorphose, the critical attention of the actor does begin to make choices, bringing the gesture
under control in a delicate balance of imagination and concentration.

Note, too, that at no point is there a concentration on feelings. Changing the *quality* of the action clearly changes the emotional content of the gesture but this shift in tone is effected without any direct reference to the actor's emotional store.[23] Feelings emerge from the exercise when the gesture is performed effectively – that is with strength, clarity and expressiveness. When Chekhov describes this exercise he develops it in the same manner as the physical imagination work analysed above:

> Perform the Gestures with their Qualities again . . . Do each of them as necessary to call forth the reaction of your Will and Feelings. Then go on doing them, but only in your imagination, remaining outwardly immobile. See that your Will and Feelings react upon the imaginary gesture as they reacted upon the real one.
>
> (1991: 42)

Once again, the Goethean technique of imaginary experiments applied to the actor's craft can be seen. The internal processes of creativity (in this case Will and Feelings) must impose themselves on the external action already created. In doing so, the actor reaches, in Chekhov's words, a 'superconscious' level of creativity (du Prey 1979: 18). Goethe would have called it a 'spiritual eye', Steiner a 'supersensory' sensitivity to the world. In each case the search is for a synthesis of two worlds: the material and the imagined.

Having prepared the ground in archetypal gestures, the work on the PG can then move to the text. Here, Chekhov shows his debt to Stanislavsky in the relationship of his own PG to Stanislavsky's superobjective. 'Ask yourself what the *main* desire of the character might be', Chekhov demands in *To the Actor*:

> And when you get an answer, start to build your PG step by step starting with your *hand* and *arm* only . . . Having once started this way, you will no longer find it difficult (in fact it will happen by itself) to extend and adjust your particular gesture to your shoulders, your neck, the position of your head and torso . . . Working this way, you will soon discover whether your first guess as to the main desire of the character was correct. The PG itself will lead you to this discovery without too much interference on the part of the reasoning mind.
>
> (2002: 67)

What is clearly different from Stanislavsky's early approach here is the eschewing of intellectual analysis – table work – in respect of the character. For Chekhov, the accuracy of the PG is found through physical experiment; there is no need for the actor to be deeply informed about the character or the play as the aim of the exercise is to find a bold, ideal gesture, the *idea* of the character, one might say, out of which the individualised character can be born. The physical body works in tandem with the imagination, organically refining the gesture as the exercise proceeds.

In my case, the work with Zinder produced a PG for Gogol's Khlestakov (from *The Government Inspector*) – a character I had already developed up to performance using biomechanics. I had identified Khlestakov as having the fundamental (negative) qualities of an adolescent – an unbridled will, an unfocused libido and a callous disregard for others. Working from the archetypal gesture of pulling, I developed an all-embracing grabbing gesture, seizing sustenance from all directions and pulling the spoils towards my stomach and groin – the two Imaginary Centres of Khlestakov.

Developing a PG for Khlestakov offered an interesting counterpoint to working biomechanically on the character. Both systems allow elements of the grotesque to emerge: for Meyerhold, through an exaggerated gestural language drawn from the études; for Chekhov, through the extended archetypal moves detailed above. Both systems effectively work from a bodily prototype, a physical form foreshadowing the character on stage whilst remaining exclusively part of the *rehearsal* process. But in *individualising* the gesture, in tying it into the superobjective of the character (albeit in general terms), the PG can act in a way which is impossible in biomechanics – as a diagnostic tool for both actor and director. In a rehearsal context my grabbing gesture could be reframed, extended or changed as both the actor's and the director's interpretation of the character emerges naturally through the process. Unlike the fixed étude of biomechanics, the PG can, then, act as common reference point for director and actor, a statement of intent in physical terms, related to the text. As such, it is a powerful tool in the rehearsal room, making explicit and material, the inner life of a character and facilitating a creative debate.

But although this process is exploratory and fluid, Chekhov does see an end to it. Once the developmental work is done, the actor emerges with what Chekhov calls 'the entire character in *condensed* form'. S/he is now master of the character's '*unchangeable* core', possessor of its 'very spine' (Chekhov 2002: 68). In the current context such statements suggest a strong affinity with Goethe's own search for an archetypal form in nature. Where Chekhov is seeking a character's 'urgesture', through an organic imaginative process, Goethe, with a similar emphasis on the intuitive imagination, is looking for the 'urforms' behind nature, in the leaves of a plant, in the bone structure of animals. Indeed, in *On The Technique of Acting*, Chekhov asks his students to observe in plants and flowers 'the Gestures and Qualities that are contained in them' (1991: 40) and in *To the Actor* Chekhov acknowledges that he is familiar with Goethean science and with Goethe's stress on archetypal phenomena, connecting Steiner in the same sentence (1953: 95).

It is unsurprising that Chekhov should mention Steiner and Goethe in the same breath. He may well have been introduced to Goethe's science through Steiner's writings if not through his father's own wide reading. Certainly it is true that, as well as having close affinities with Goethe, the PG owes a debt to Steiner's theory of speech formation. Steiner's contention that 'if speech is to be made plastic on the one hand, musical on the other . . . then this is first of all a matter of bringing gesture in to speech' (Chekhov

1991: 67) is interpreted by Chekhov in the following practical exercise related to work on *Hamlet*: 'At first execute the Gesture without words, then the Gesture with words together, and, finally only the words without the Gesture' (ibid.: 68).[24]

Summary

On the surface of things, Chekhov's PG may appear to have associations with the school of behaviourism outlined in the previous chapter, specifically in its externally biased approach to character development, and its generation of emotion through physical action. David Zinder's fusion of Meyerholdian training with the Chekhov technique may add weight to this reading and other critics have developed arguments along similar lines. Robert Leach, for example, has developed a materialist reading of Chekhov's work, stating in *Contemporary Theatre Review* that the PG 'might not exist if Meyerhold . . . had not been so pervasive in Russia at the time of Chekhov's greatest creativity' (Leach 1997: 83). But although both men are right to stress the influence of physical gesture over psychology any reading of Chekhov's PG which suggests a materialist root to his work I believe is misplaced. There is strong evidence, both in Chekhov's writings and in the practice of his teachers, to suggest a review is needed of the formative influences on Chekhov's contribution to actor training, evidence which is gleaned from following the roots of Steiner's influence back further, to Romantic science and to Goethe's *Urphänomena*.

The final piece of this evidence is to be found in the Dartington Archive and relates to Chekhov's hitherto unknown interest in colour theory.

On colour and light

Chekhov's faith in the universality of the PG was extensive. We have already stated that he considered the PG to be an invaluable support when defining a character's superobjectives and objectives. But he also suggests PGs can be found for more intangible things: for atmospheres for instance, and even for colours. Chekhov makes the latter claim in an unpublished lecture entitled 'Colour and Light' (1937), drawing directly from Goethe and Steiner. The lecture, housed in the Dartington Archive, illuminates, more brightly than ever, the depth of Chekhov's commitment to Romantic science and interestingly prioritises Goethe above Steiner in its use of primary sources. In it, Chekhov picks up on the contention, first suggested in Goethe's *Theory of Colours*, that colours have moral associations, as well as directional impulses:

> YELLOW is powerful but if we add a little bit of RED it increases all its qualities . . . In this <u>RED-YELLOW</u> is the tendency to high glow. It has some of the qualities of the sunset – warmth and bliss – beatitude. Another interesting quality of this colour is that we want to go forward

with it. All of these things, of course, are psychological gestures and we must try to transform them into such.

(Chekhov 1937: 3)

Chekhov sees colour as a physical stimulus to the actor, as well as having innate spiritual qualities – there is a touch of 'God's wrath' to orange he says at another moment (ibid.)! He also, more interestingly, describes this physical stimulus as manifesting itself in a PG, ascribing colour an archetypal significance in his scheme of acting. In doing so, he was intuitively embracing the principles of Goethean science and echoing Goethe's contention that colour itself is the product of an archetypal principle (polarity). He goes on to detail the PGs of twelve more colours, following closely the taxonomy established by Goethe in *Theory of Colours*:

> If we look at nature on a very gloomy day through a YELLOW glass it is able to change the day to a happy one.
>
> (Chekhov 1937: 3)

> The eye is gladdened . . . particularly if we look at a landscape through a yellow glass on a grey winter's day.
>
> (Goethe 1967: 307)

Or

> Blue gives us the feeling of concentration . . . It recedes from us.
>
> (Chekhov 1937: 4)

> Blue seems to retire from us. But as we readily follow an agreeable object that flies from us, so we love to contemplate blue.
>
> (Goethe 1840: 311)

These parallels show clearly that Chekhov was not just paying lip service to Goethe's science or simply aping Steiner's own interest in Goethe. He had clearly read the *Theory of Colours* at least three years before the 1942 version of *To the Actor* was written and closer to fifteen years before any of his theories were published. More importantly, he understood the underlying principles of his science – Goethe's morphology and his sense of delicate empiricism – and found in them something that spoke to his own creative concerns. His concluding shot in the lecture on colour gives a flavour of why he felt such an affinity with the German Romantic, as well as signing where he diverged from Goethe's thinking:

> Imagine the colours without any connection to real things. Imagine them flowing into unlimited space – pure type of imagination . . . Try to be the colour.
>
> (Chekhov 1937: 6)

Inspirational acting

Viewed as a whole, Chekhov's system of acting echoes Goethe's Romantic notion that 'If you seek comfort in the whole, you must learn to discover the whole in the smallest part' (Goethe 1996: 59). 'We can take any point in the method and turn it into a gesture', Chekhov asserts in *Lessons to the Profes- sional Actor* (1985: 108), suggesting that the PG is a kind of 'urform' for the whole of his acting system. Such a possibility would clearly accord with the holistic context argued in this chapter and is substantiated by the view of Chekhov's work evidenced in his 'Chart for Inspired Acting' (see Figure 4.1), composed by Chekhov late in his career in 1949 and annotated by Mala Powers in *On the Technique of Acting* (1991: xxxvi).

Chekhov's system evidently exhibits a unique interconnectedness. It is a kind of web of practical skills for the actor. These varied skill areas are all interdependent, such that, if the actor is paying attention to Atmosphere and Radiation, for example, many of the other 'lights of inspiration' will be illuminated without special attention (Chekhov 1991: xxxvii). As such, it is a non-hierarchical system which models acting rather like modern science models the brain: as an organic web of connections. Each of these connec- tions is not causally related but organised holistically with each element of the system contributing as a whole to a harmonious outcome for the actor – 'inspired acting'.

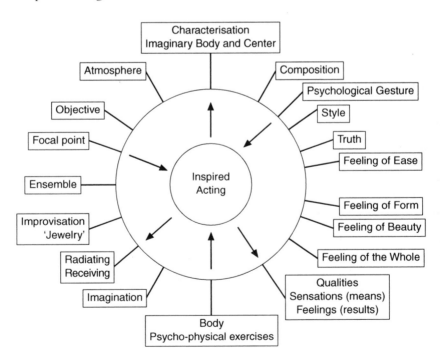

Figure 4.1 Michael Chekhov's 'Chart for Inspired Acting', 1949.

It is a term that deserves some attention, given its (literal) centrality in the system of Michael Chekhov. On one level, Chekhov clearly means a state of consciousness that is responsive to all the demands of the stage – Stanislavsky called it the Creative State or the Superconscious. On another, Chekhov seems to be referring to the literal connotation of the word inspiration: that is, to breathe in. The arrows in the diagram clearly reinforce this idea and the words he uses in *To the Actor* to sum up his thinking further strengthen the view:

> Art is a sphere which suffers most . . . from such an imbalance [towards materialism]. Nobody can exhale without inhaling. Nobody . . . can refus[e] to be strengthened and uplifted by the 'impractical' intangibles which are basic to the creative spirit, which are a kind of psychological 'inhaling'.
>
> (2002: 177)

Breathing in, for Chekhov, is synonymous with being infused with a life force, one which redresses the balance of material and immaterial in an individual and allows the intangible forces of nature to combat the stultifying effects of 'dull materialism'. The beauty of Chekhov's system is that these intangibles, which can seem impenetrable in the mouths of Goethe or Steiner, are made perfectly accessible through his psycho-physical system of acting.

Significantly, the circular form of the chart contrasts sharply with the diagrammatic representation of Stanislavsky's system discussed in Chapter 1. Much of Stanislavsky's thinking is linear – from the through line of action (*skvosnoe deistvie*) to the magnetic supertask (*zverkhzadacha*). Chekhov's, by contrast, is circular. Despite its nineteenth-century roots, Chekhov's 'organic' system seems all the more contemporary for this holistic organisation.

A utopian context for a harmonious system

How, then, might the significance of Chekhov's first theatre school at Dartington be evaluated and why did it have to be developed outside Russia? In a letter to Anatoly Lunacharsky in 1928 Chekhov offers a frank response to the second question:

> I have finally been driven out [of Russia] by the simple fact about our day-to-day theatre life which is truly unendurable: its senselessness . . . Those who control the theatre have become completely hostile to all the interests essential to the art of the theatre . . . A whole range of purely artistic moods and colourful spiritual nuances have been lumped together under the heading of 'mysticism' and banned . . . There is nothing to challenge an actor or stretch him (and no point in his trying

to develop), while the public has nothing worthwhile to watch, nothing to delight it, and nothing to stimulate its grey matter.

(in Smeliansky 1993: 162–163)

The letter is worth quoting in detail as it illustrates how clearly divergent Chekhov's views were from those of the artistic and political ruling bodies of Russia. Once mysticism had become a term of abuse (and a challenge of legality), the country which trained Chekhov could no longer support his radical thinking, for much of his training was mystical, in the wider sense of it encouraging the actor to draw on hidden reserves and in developing a language that helped him/her gain access to that 'supersensory' plane. Where the spirit of the time in post-revolutionary Russia encouraged an increasingly explicit, didactic and accountable form of theatre (at least on the part of the artists), Chekhov was tapping unseen forces, staging fairy tales and calling for the craft of acting to renew its spiritual base.

At the same time the Romantic tradition of science, towards which Chekhov naturally leaned, was anathema to the materialistic mindset of Russia; if he was to develop his own unique acting philosophy he had to find a context more sensitive to such a tradition. It has been argued here that the ideal circumstances of Dartington Hall in the late 1930s offered precisely this, not because the Elmhirsts were anthroposophists – Leonard was deeply suspicious of spiritual science and thought that the wider community might use any such influences as a weapon to undermine the overall project[25] – but because of the freedom it offered Chekhov in the formative years of his system, freedom to develop an acting school that did not have to subscribe to any overall dogma or party line. Dartington was *the* environment for experimentation, in education, agriculture and in the arts, and in this sense Chekhov and the Elmhirsts were deeply united in their overall pursuit of harmony – the fruitful organisation of parts to the whole. For the Elmhirsts, this pursuit informed their progressive education programme and the political organisation of their estate. For Chekhov, harmony was the antidote to the separatist theatre from which he had escaped, a point made vehemently in the aforementioned Theatre School Policy of Dartington: 'The aim of the new theater will be to achieve complete harmony of all the elements of expression ... Its production will be intelligible to every spectator, regardless of language or of intellectual content' (1936b: 3).

Chekhov's Policy gives us a powerful insight into his theatrical mind and direction before the practicalities of the teaching imposed themselves upon him in America. There is clearly an idealism evident in the final sentence which testifies more to his enthusiasm for the project than it does to any pragmatic instinct. The Theatre Policy, in essence, is a position statement outlining the principles underlying the technique. What is evident from the policy is the extent to which Chekhov is prepared to take his holistic vision. Chekhov's actors are charged with understanding all the constituent aspects of production, they 'should, to some degree, be also a director, a scene painter, a costume designer, even an author' and conversely 'the author must know the psychology of the actor, the director, the scene painter and the musician' (ibid.). Thus, the key players in the theatrical process should be linked in their understanding of each other in a profound manner, a relationship which extends to the audience: 'The new theater will develope [sic] ... the power to carry the moral RESPONSIBILITY FOR WHAT ARISES IN THE SOUL OF THE SPECTATOR' (ibid.: 4). For Chekhov, even the spectatorship is drawn into the holistic alliance, their very souls the subject of his moral edification.

In promoting such a mutually interdependent model of theatre, Chekhov was plumbing his own soul for a method of acting that answered the issues he had raised with Lunacharsky in his letter of farewell. He was drawing on his understanding of Goethe and his reading of Steiner to create an approach to acting which was not Romantic in itself – in the deeply emotional sense associated with Talma for example[26] – but which drew on the holistic principles of Romantic science (and on its mystical offshoots) to create a truly ensemble-led theatre. He developed this method in the ideal environment of Dartington, hidden away from the urban life of Moscow and London.

Chekhov then took his findings over the Atlantic to Connecticut and ultimately to Hollywood, to a theatre culture which ironically epitomised in many ways the materialistic egotism and emotional introspection which he despised. There he offered a much needed counterpoint to the developments in Stanislavsky-based teaching in America and an alternative to the native Method school of acting led by Lee Strasberg which, as recounted in Chapter 3, drew on Freud for its inspiration.

Without knowing it, Chekhov's work constituted a turning point in the Russian tradition of acting. His espousal of Goethean ideas and his association with Romantic theories of interconnectedness, took him away from Stanislavsky's philosophical foundations and from the work of his compatriots, Meyerhold and Boleslavsky. From Chekhov onwards, two dominant strains become identifiable within the Stanislavsky tradition. The Cartesian or Newtonian paradigm was sustained in Boleslavsky's work and developed into the Method in the US; the Goethean or Romantic strain, begun by Chekhov as he developed his technique in Dartington, is traceable today in the work of Anatoly Vasiliev, evolving via Maria Knebel. The review of this practitioner in Chapter 5 brings the evolution of the tradition up to date and examines what the only trained scientist in this book does in his 'laboratory'.

5   The laboratory as sanctuary

The theatre of Anatoly Vasiliev

> Everything I do is a development of Stanislavsky. I am reconstructing
> Stanislavsky's system.
>
> Anatoly Vasiliev, 1996

Vasiliev's declaration, made as he began a week-long masterclass at the
Royal Scottish Academy of Music and Drama in Glasgow, strikes a central
chord with the theme of this book. Like so many key theatre practitioners in
this and the last century, Vasiliev acknowledges his debt to Stanislavsky,
taking his place within a tradition that is as diverse as it is potent. He
defected from the sciences to join the theatre in the late 1960s and has been
feted with creating a 'virtually unique feeling in today's theatre' (Smeliansky
1999: 202). To do so, he, like the rest of the practitioners considered in this
book, has had to reinterpret the tradition in which he locates his practice,
responding to the contemporary context of modern Russia at the same time
as recognising its complex and rich history.

Vasiliev's particular choice of words (note: 'reconstruction', not 'reinterpretation') is striking for it clearly signs his own development away from the
psychological school, towards what he calls the 'ludo' system.[1] At the same
time, in using the resonant word 'reconstruction' – the Russian term is, of
course, *perestroika* – Vasiliev is positioning himself in a specifically post-
Soviet political context.

But although Vasiliev has prospered in the period immediately following
Gorbachev's reforms (1985–1991), and particularly under Yeltsin
(1991–2000) and Putin (2000–), any political project is vehemently
denied by him. Indeed, his own description of *perestroika* is anything but
positive:

> It was a tragic period ... It was a time when everybody was looking
> forward to reorganization, to a radical change. I have never shared this
> opinion ... In other words, the events in connection with this 'Second
> Russian Revolution' completely destroyed the theatre.
>
> (Vasiliev 1992: 50)

Unlike his compatriot, Lev Dodin of the Maly Drama Theatre, Vasiliev's *perestroika* has little or nothing directly to do with contemporary politics in Russia. Instead, it is a reformulation of what a Russian audience might expect of 'performance' itself, as well as a reconstruction of the actor's approach to text. This chapter will interrogate both aspects of Vasiliev's practice and point to some of the key influences which have driven this reconstruction of Stanislavsky. Perhaps most significantly, it will bring us up to date, for Vasiliev is working *now* and he therefore functions as a contemporary measure of the place of Stanislavskian thinking in post-Soviet Russia. Like Chekhov's, his is a particular development away from the Newtonian legacy of Russian actor training discussed in Part II. There are, of course, others too. But as a growing presence as a teacher and practitioner in the West, due in part to the International Workshop Festival's support of him,[2] Vasiliev's work is due some considered criticism. As yet, there is next to nothing published in English on his work, beyond some reviews of his productions in translation, an interview and a short section in Smeliansky's book on *The Russian Theatre after Stalin* (1999).

What follows, then, is an attempt to augment the available critical material on Vasiliev, drawing heavily on my own experience of working with him as well as on unpublished sources, interviews and transcripts of three appearances he has made in this country. Unlike previous chapters where the practical analysis has necessarily been centred on the interpreters of Stanislavsky, Meyerhold, or Michael Chekhov (Desnitsky, Bogdanov, Levinsky, Zinder), here the focus is on Vasiliev's system as he himself teaches it – an analysis of Vasiliev on Vasiliev. Thus, fittingly for a final chapter, a direct connection with the Russian acting tradition is sustained, following one idiosyncratic branch of Stanislavskian thinking up to the present day.

As a relative unknown, Vasiliev must be placed in context with specific reference to the tradition he is claiming to reconstruct and to the consistent emphasis within this tradition on 'laboratory work'.

Laboratory theatre: from Stanislavsky to Vasiliev

In many ways Anatoly Vasiliev (1942-) brings together some of the key players of this book. He was trained at GITIS (now RATA), the institute Meyerhold founded in the 1920s, and served his apprenticeship under Maria Knebel – the pupil of Michael Chekhov and Stanislavsky. For a study tracing the scientific influences of the period, Vasiliev is important for he is the only practitioner in this book who is actually trained in a scientific discipline (chemistry) and the approach he takes to his work – if not the content – owes much to this training. He has, in addition, dedicated himself to the development of a laboratory theatre in Moscow (the School of Dramatic Art) which allows us to trace this phenomenon up to the present day, setting Vasiliev's practice against those already discussed to examine the efficacy of such work.

Stanislavsky

Stanislavsky's ceaseless desire to experiment resulted in his forming yet another satellite research group to investigate the acting process just three years before his death. The Opera-Dramatic Studio, as it was known, was the last in a series of creative projects initiated by Stanislavsky, all of which operated tangentially from his work at the MAT.

The First Studio was formed in 1912 by Vakhtangov, Chekhov, Boleslavsky and Ouspenskaya, as a forum to experiment with elements of the emerging System and to share what Stanislavsky called 'the results of . . . research into stage techniques' (Benedetti 1990a: 207). Three more studios followed: the Second Studio in 1916, the Third in 1920 and the Fourth in 1921.[3] Stanislavsky's last project, for which eleven young actors and directors were hand picked to work with him, began in 1935 and continued his preference for working with young blood.

What distinguished the work of the Opera Dramatic Studio from its predecessors was the emphasis on 'pure' research. As Benedetti notes:

> It was to be the laboratory [Stanislavsky] called for in his essay, *October and the Revolution* . . . He made it quite clear to the young actors and directors he gathered around him that there could be no question of gearing their work to performance; it would be done for its own sake, as research.
>
> (1990a: 338)

The fruits of the work done at the Opera-Dramatic Studio constituted the last period of Stanislavsky's work – the Method of Physical Actions[4] – reviewed in Part I of this book with reference to Newton and the materialist paradigm of Soviet Russia. Of interest here, though, is not so much the content of Stanislavsky's System but the forum in which it was taught – the laboratory – for this is a term which all of the pupils examined in this book use at some time in their career and which has been taken up *in extremis* by Anatoly Vasiliev.

Meyerhold

In Meyerhold's work, the appropriation of scientific terminology was both explicit and calculated. Indeed, of all Stanislavsky's associates, his was the most emphatic use of an interdisciplinary language, fusing theatrical 'laws' with scientific laws – Huntley Carter called biomechanics 'the science of motion in acting' (1929: 49). Meyerhold was founder of GITIS, the State Institute for Theatrical Art, which grew out of his attempts to realise an 'exemplary model' of revolutionary theatre. Meyerhold's vision was of a mutually supportive, interactive organisation incorporating a stage, a workshop and a training school in which 'the discoveries in the workshop would affect the training in the school as well as what was exposed on the stage' (Leach 1994: 104) in a three-fold symbiosis. Erast Garin's description of the school, known as the State Higher Director's workshop (GVYRM), is reminiscent of the atmosphere at the Opera-Dramatic Studio: 'Everyone learned – students and teachers alike. It was a laboratory for working through the foundations of a new aesthetic' (in Leach 1994: 105).

By the time Meyerhold's own aspirations were merged with those of Nikolai Foregger, the rhetoric of the Revolution had intensified, although the theme remained constant. GITIS was to be: 'A place unique in the planet, where the science of theatre is studied and drama is built. Exactly: "science" and not "art" – "built" and not "created"' (Leach 1989: 22). Clearly for Meyerhold, the laboratory walls extended much further than the building in which he was working – the Zon theatre – for the experimental attitude he was adopting at a local level was reflected on a much grander scale – the huge social experiment of the October Revolution itself. Central to this commitment to science was the emphasis on outcomes which may in part explain the popularity of the machine as a 'symbol of the new age of mechanical and scientific industrialism', as Carter puts it (1929: 69). The machine stood for productivity, for the benefits technology can bring a new society. The work of the laboratory was not, then, seen in isolation; the laboratories of the Russian Revolution fed the technological advancement of the society – the electrification of the country, for example. From a theatrical perspective, Meyerhold's work at GITIS established the same principle. The experimental findings in his workshop informed the presentations on the stage – the 'product' of a theatre industry.

Boleslavsky

Boleslavsky, in graduating from the First Studio, had developed his own understanding of the System in the safety of the theatre laboratory he shared with Vakhtangov, Sulerzhitsky and Michael Chekhov. Here, he tested out the emotion-led work that he later exported to America, whilst continuing to produce work on the small stage. By the time he reached the States he was clearly committed to a forum for innovation and experimentation which he considered to be lacking from the commercial stage: 'There are no laboratories of the theatre [in the US], there are no tense experimentations and achievements . . . There is no creation' (in Roberts 1981: 113).

Such was his enthusiasm for the term that he called his first creative venture in America the 'Laboratory Theatre', viewing the establishment of the Lab as an antidote to the pure, financial pragmatics of the commercial stage.[5] The laboratory, for Boleslavsky, was synonymous with a spirit of invention and creativity, an understanding which acknowledged both the freedom of a laboratory and the incessant work which goes on inside its walls to discover new forms.

Michael Chekhov and Maria Knebel

Michael Chekhov, as co-director of the First Studio, was part of the same organisational arrangement as his compatriot Boleslavsky. His work developed along very different lines from the Pole's but his commitment to a holistic training for the actor led him to a similar set of conclusions in terms of the value of laboratory work. His enterprise at Dartington was notable for its creative solitude. His students benefited from a seclusion at the Elmhirsts' which allowed them to develop their talents without the pressures a large producing theatre might bring. Dartington was, in effect, Chekhov's laboratory. It was the ideal forum for the testing of his system and for the exchange of creative ideas with other significant artists. If the Bohr Institute had been the model laboratory for Jerzy Grotowski, 'where physicists from different countries experiment and take their steps into the 'no man's land' of their profession' (Grotowski 1975: 95), then Dartington was Chekhov's Bohr Institute, allowing him the freedom to do some of his most radical performance research and have it valued by his patrons for its creative potential.

Viewed thus, Dartington was the natural progression from Chekhov's first workshop in his apartment on Newspaper Lane in Moscow in 1918 where Chekhov worked with Maria Knebel and several other 'young, wholesome people who were in love with his creative individuality' (Padegimas 1994: 2). Through this first 'studio', Knebel argues, Chekhov began what would become 'a little creative laboratory' dedicated to the art of the actor (Padegimas 1994: 3). Knebel has done much to disseminate the Chekhov technique since, through her writings and teaching. In addition to her connections with Chekhov, she was 'one of Stanislavsky's most remarkable colleagues late in life' (Benedetti 1990a: 348), working with the MAT for twenty-six years from 1924 to 1950 before becoming artistic director of the state Children's Theatre in 1955.

Knebel provides the missing link between the tradition of Stanislavskian thinking we have followed so far in this book and the work of Anatoly Vasiliev, a lineage he himself makes clear in an interview for *Theaterschrift*: 'I am a student of the student of Stanislavsky ... Her name is Maria Knebel' (Vasiliev 1992: 46). In addition to writing on Stanislavsky and Chekhov, Knebel also taught both systems at the State Institute of Theatrical Arts (GITIS) from 1948 until her death in 1985.

Anatoly Vasiliev

At GITIS, twenty years into her teaching career, Knebel took on Anatoly Vasiliev as a directing student, and alongside Andrei Popov introduced him to the theories of Stanislavsky and Chekhov. Vasiliev was twenty-six when he began his work with Knebel and Popov in 1968. Already a graduate of organic chemistry and launched on a career in the navy, he left for GITIS at the recommendation of a friend: 'If you work for one more year in the Navy, you'll never become a land-lover again', Vasiliev recalls him saying, 'because the sea has such power' (Vasiliev 1996: I, 2).[6]

Vasiliev's move from oceanographer to director resulted in his learning first hand the technique of the Method of Physical Actions, for along with Toporkov, whose *Stanislavsky in Rehearsal* (1979) documented the late work on *Tartuffe*, Maria Knebel was a key figure in this last period of the System. Through the four decades of her tenure at GITIS, Knebel trained actors and directors in the connected techniques of improvisation, active analysis and étude work. She carried forward the method of textual analysis which Stanislavsky was using at the Opera-Dramatic studio with a new generation of practitioners. As such, rather like Deirdre Hurst du Prey's work with Chekhov, Knebel is best understood as 'transmitter' of the System, not as an active reinterpreter of the training. Her role was to preserve the line of thinking not to develop new branches of practice. Vasiliev, by contrast, first appropriates and then subverts the tradition of Stanislavskian practice taught by Knebel. 'I have chosen a different path', he states, indicating his deeply introspective approach:

> I have never really wanted to work in a repertory theatre. What I always wanted to do is laboratory work. I really only have in mind the path of the theatrical theory which I am trying to follow. Generally, it's a path of research [and] investigation.
>
> (Vasiliev 1999)

Below, then, is the first sustained attempt in English to evaluate Vasiliev's pedagogy in the light of this lofty heritage, the first critical assessment of a training which is both dedicated to and divergent from the theatrical tradition of Stanislavsky.

Vasiliev as philosopher-pedagogue

In order to capture the essence of Vasiliev's pedagogy it is necessary, from the outset, to redefine what might be meant by the term 'workshop'. In his 1996 masterclass Vasiliev took the principle of 'table work' established by Stanislavsky in his early productions of Chekhov and made it the core of his approach; it was an exercise in mental stamina, at the other end of the continuum from Gennady Bogdanov's rigorous physical training. *Practice* might also need to be redefined in Vasiliev's system, at least in terms of a student's experience of a masterclass, for the opportunity to *explore* the key concepts of his approach – his 'ludic' approach to Dostoyevsky's *The Meek One*[7] – was highly restricted. The course in Glasgow ran for a week with just thirty minutes of that time devoted to active reading from the text, during which time we (the readers) remained in our seats.

A flavour of his pedagogical style may be derived from his introductory words to the workshop group:

I wanted . . . to try a different approach [from the 1991 masterclass] with you based on the 'action of the word'. This is a quite different theatrical methodology so I chose a monologue and I thought it would be complicated but nonetheless this text is harmonious with my current position on the theatre. So what is essential for this? Well, first of all, *the thing is that you should listen to me.*

(Vasiliev 1996: II, 1)

For the 'participant' the result of such an intense cerebral focus is to encourage a view of the intellectual exchange of ideas *as* practice, with Vasiliev adopting the Socratic role of philosopher-pedagogue, putting both his own and the group's cognitive muscles under strain.[8] His sessions were exacting, deeply theoretical and intensely interrogative in their approach to text.

Whilst physicality played no part in the work, Vasiliev's practice is not psychologically orientated in the sense the term has been used in this book. Vasiliev's 'ludic' theatre eschews conventional psychology in the early Stanislavskian sense of inner emotional content and in the materialist sense favoured by the late Stanislavsky and by Meyerhold. Instead, Vasiliev's work establishes what he calls a 'spiritual' line through the text, breaking up its emotional content and stressing abstract ideas rather than concrete actions.

This distancing of the emotions from the process of character building invites parallels with Brecht, as does the language Vasiliev uses to distinguish between the psychological school of Stanislavsky and his own ludo system: 'When you use the psychological system you are inside the character you are playing, when you use the ludo approach then you are outside of the character' (Vasiliev 1996: II, 3). Given, Vasiliev's opposition to a politically conscious theatre, it is hardly surprising that he resists any further comparisons with Brecht: 'There is no need to talk about Brecht in this context because I am not concerned with the socio-political context when I refer to these systems. We are outside of that context' (Vasiliev 1996: II, 4).

The distance between actor and character in Vasiliev's work is not, then, to allow for a critical attitude to be established between the two in the pursuit of social truth. Rather the opposite, in fact. Vasiliev's spiritual line through the text imposes a structure of *faith* on the actor, asking him/her to view the actions of the text purely in terms of their religious significance. Thus, as students at his masterclass we were invited into the Orthodox religious symbolism of Dostoyevsky, re-created by Vasiliev through his own Christian faith.[9] The choice of Dostoyevsky allowed Vasiliev to articulate this project explicitly, tapping the religious imagery of his writing and avoiding a psychological interpretation of his literature:

If I study Dostoyevsky using the psychological system the result is people who feel they have been hard done to by life. But if I work on him with the ludo system I don't notice that these people have been badly done by. The dialogues convey the conflicts of ideas but in the psychological system arguments between characters lead to conflicts between people.

(Vasiliev 1996: II, 11)

Clearly, a theatre which diverts an audience's attention away from the plight of the socially disadvantaged is a theatre contra-Brecht. We may also view it as a system far removed from the materialist, politically conscious tradition of Soviet actor training embodied by Meyerhold. Given the affinities between Brecht and Meyerhold's work, Vasiliev's opposition to the latter is perhaps not too surprising. But at the same time as putting distance between himself and Meyerhold, Vasiliev is also challenging, in a very direct manner, the hegemony of the psychological school. Indeed his rejection of action-based conflict strikes at the very heart of drama – at the Aristotelian model itself, not as Brecht did in order to unpick the cathartic pacifying of an audience but, as we shall see, to substitute Aristotle's teacher, Plato, as the founding philosopher of the theatre.

What, in effect, we are witnessing with Vasiliev's religious emphasis is his specific reaction to the 'tragedy' of *perestroika*. His is a clear theatrical response to the resurgence of religious activity in Russian culture, begun by Gorbachev in the late 1980s and developed by Yeltsin in the 1990s, although in truth it was never entirely extinguished during Bolshevik times. Vasiliev considers his retreat into laboratory work a necessary reaction to the instability of contemporary Russia as well as a function of the kind of work to which his company is dedicated:

> As soon as you start thinking about something seriously you isolate yourself ... During the past few years ... I stopped examining life outside the theatre. I have been concentrating on studying only the life in the theatre, life in the art world ... As a consequence I locked the doors of my theatre. And the more you close the theatre doors, the more it reminds you of a monastery.
>
> (Vasiliev 1992: 62–63)

Solitude leads to introspection and to self-examination, in short, to a monastic meta-theatre. Yet this self-imposed seclusion, the barring of the doors of his theatre against the natural economic and cultural forces which surround him, has not left him entirely isolated. In the *glasnost* era, Vasiliev's deeply religious reformulation of the System, drawing as it does on Russian Orthodoxy and on Platonic metaphysics, was well supported. His School of Dramatic Art was founded in 1987, two years after Gorbachev took the helm as General Secretary of the Communist Party, following the abrupt demise of Andropov (in 1984) and Chernenko (in 1985). A year later, Gorbachev met with Orthodox religious leaders and began the process of formally reinstating the Church.

Gorbachev was ousted dramatically by Boris Yeltsin in 1991, two years after the fall of the Berlin Wall, but Yeltsin continued his predecessor's work in recognising the Church. Whilst the economic climate worsened considerably during his Presidency, the Yeltsin government subsidised Vasiliev through two costly refurbishments of the Uranus cinema, creating one of the 'finest modern theatrical spaces in Moscow' (Freedman 1997: 134). It is a trend that has continued under Vladimir Putin, the finished theatre finally being unveiled in March of 2001, a year into Putin's rule. All this state support has not, remarkably, been contingent on Vasiliev sharing the results of his experimentation. As we shall see later in this chapter, any performance by the School of Dramatic Art is a highly exclusive (and exceptional) occasion. Whilst Vasiliev may, then, appear to be a non-political player, his track record of survival in the most unstable of circumstances is notable.

For now, Vasiliev's perspective on Dostoyevsky can set the agenda for this chapter: first to define exactly what he means by the psychological system and the ludo system; second to consider the significance of this shift away from Stanislavsky and his reinterpretation of the Newtonian model of conflict; third to assess the outcomes of Vasiliev's approach both in terms of his teaching and his performance work.

The psychological system versus the ludo system

For Vasiliev, theatrical performance operates on three planes of action: i) the psychological, ii) the physical and iii) the verbal. Thus, the binary model of psycho-physicality we have considered up to now is extended in Vasiliev's thinking to include the verbal plane — what he calls 'word movement'. These three planes of action are intrinsically connected and self-supporting: 'theatre ... exists as a synthesis of these different planes' (Vasiliev 1991: 2), he argues, with one or other of the planes taking precedence at any one time. It is the choice of text which determines what will be the predominant plane of action for a particular project, allowing for a range of styles to emerge from the same system, or, more accurately, from different sub-systems.

There is an important point to be made here, for what is notable in the theatrical thinking of Vasiliev is not so much that it leads to very different outcomes — Stanislavsky's System was applicable to a wide range of styles from opera, through melodrama to the naturalistic school — but that the system itself may differ from project to project. From a theoretical point of view, at least, two opposing attitudes to the treatment of a text coexist in Vasiliev's mind, allowing for a constant set of comparisons to be made by him when illustrating his theories. We have seen this with the Dostoyevsky quotation above: a psychological reading yields one set of results, a 'verbal' or ludic reading another set.[10] Rather than developing one system which may evolve to change with the times, Vasiliev accrues a series of systems as he goes along — accumulation rather than evolution:

A system is a key which enables you to open something. When I talk about the ludo system it also involves reliving and psychology [like the psychological system] but to open up a ludo play you need a different key. There is a different structure. Let's take a maple leaf and a cactus. They are different leaves because they have different structures. And if we make a ludo structure, then let's say you find a cactus leaf and if it were a psychological structure you find a maple leaf. But you can use both approaches for one and the same play, of course, if the play permits it.

(1996: II, 8)

One such play for Vasiliev is Chekhov's *The Seagull* (1896). Through his own practical experiments Vasiliev is confident to claim a special status for Chekhov's play: 'I am convinced I do understand what [Chekhov's] intentions were when he wrote this play. I have studied this over a very long time. And I have rehearsed *The Seagull* using the two systems' (ibid. 1996: II, 10).

Like Dostoyevsky's texts (and, Vasiliev argues, Shakespeare's *Hamlet*), Chekhov's work allows for both systems of interpretation. His comments on the results achieved in applying the two approaches offer us a measure of the distinction Vasiliev draws between the psychological system and the ludo system:

Let's take *The Seagull*. If you choose the psychological system as a member of the audience I will experience the story of these people. If I direct *The Seagull* and I use the ludo system I will observe the story but I will experience a story about these ideas – I will be an observer; I will experience the story of the life of these ideas. I'll explain it once more. You can stage *The Seagull* in two ways. You can present it as a play about art – you could do it like a Pirandello play. But you could also stage it as a play about people who make art.

(Ibid.)

Thus, according to Vasiliev, the psychological system focuses our attention on the characters' lives – a model of empathetic engagement with the stories of individuals. The *ludic* approach diverts attention away from the character, placing the spectator in the role of observer to appreciate the ideas of the play in abstraction – art and its function, rather than the suicidal exploits of the artist, Treplev. The former, we would associate with a plot- (or *muthos-*) driven, Aristotelian theatre – one based in the material world where characters' actions define their individuality. The latter, is a concept-bound, philosophical theatre in which reason (*dianoia*) predominates and attention is focused on the realm of ideas – we might call it a Platonic theatre.

Whilst Vasiliev himself is rather opaque on the subject of what plays lend themselves to both a psychological and a ludic approach, one unifying element is their meta-theatricality: Hamlet's staging of *The Murder of Gonzago*, as well as the passages analysing the craft of the actor (Vasiliev 1996: III, 2), Treplev's debut as a symbolist experimenting with 'new forms' and Pirandello's exploration of the illusion of reality through the Actors and the Director in *Six Characters* (1921) all indicate the extent to which Vasiliev's preferred texts are theatrically self-reflexive.[11] Indeed, each play consciously positions its audience as an observer at specific times. In *The Seagull* whilst we (the audience) watch, the guests on Sorin's estate are themselves watching Treplev's play. In *Hamlet*, similarly, we, the audience *at* the play, are invited along with Hamlet himself to scrutinise another audience *in* the play (the court of Elsinor, gathered for the Players' performance), for evidence of Claudius's guilt. And in *Six Characters in Search of an Author* the entire play dramatises the Father's pursuit to have his and his family's lives staged, that is put up for observation by an audience.

Such layering of theatricality facilitates the distancing of spectator from character which Vasiliev is seeking, for it frames the latter as 'a fiction', as Hamlet puts it (II, 2, 546), one further remove from real passion than the naturalistic character. This may explain his predilection for meta-theatrical texts for they are already one step removed from the material plane of action, one step closer to the removed realm of what Vasiliev calls 'philosophical dialogue', by which he undoubtedly means Platonic dialogue.

Ludus and ludo

Before this contention is further explored, it may help here to examine the term 'ludo' itself. For Vasiliev, the term simply connotes play or game, from the Latin 'I play'. At a simple level, then, he is calling for a more spontaneous, fluid relationship between the text and the actor, for a sense of fun and playfulness to be injected into the work. At the same time, he states, 'a game does have rules' (Vasiliev 1996: II, 3) and thus, like many other practitioners in this book, he is calling for a balance of spontaneity and discipline in the actor's approach.

Roger Caillois, in *Man, Play, and Games* (1962), makes this distinction to provide a helpful taxonomy of game-play. For Caillois, the unfettered spirit of improvisation is defined as *paidia*, from the Greek root '*paid*', or 'child'. This spirit is held in tension with the converse quality of *ludus*, or 'the primitive desire to find diversion and amusement in arbitrary, perpetually recurrent obstacles' or rules (Caillois 1962: 33). Thus, the forces of infantile chaos combine with an adult predilection for structure to make 'play'. Caillois then illustrates how this continuum can be applied to four different categories of games: games of competition (*agon*), of chance (*alea*), of simulation (mimicry or *mimesis*) and of risk, or what he calls 'vertigo' games (*ilinx*). The theatre in Caillois' taxonomy is located in the category of simulation alongside other games of fantasy and transformation (see Figure 5.1). Descending the column, the element of *paidia* decreases whilst the element of *ludus*

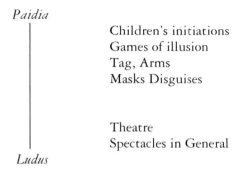

Mimicry (Simulation)

Paidia

Children's initiations
Games of illusion
Tag, Arms
Masks Disguises

Theatre
Spectacles in General

Ludus

Figure 5.1 Roger Caillois' taxonomy of game-play.

increases. The unencumbered and fluid game-play of children gives way to the rule-bound play of the theatre and of spectacles.

Caillois' purpose is to examine the sociology of games and as such he takes his statements on theatre no further but his overarching theory is helpful here for two reasons: first, from a vertical perspective, because it allows for a more inclusive understanding of the term *ludo* (from the entirely free to the constrained); and, second, from a horizontal perspective, because it allows for games to cross categories, to be part simulation (*mimesis*) and part chance (*alea*), for example. Caillois thus offers a helpful terminology with which to examine Vasiliev's 'ludic' theatre.

A further aid to the task of analysing Vasiliev is afforded by Johan Huizinga's *Homo Ludens* (first published in English in 1949), whom Caillois acknowledges as a key influence whilst being sharply critical of what, for him, is a restricted definition of the game. There may be some justification for such a view but later in his book, when Huizinga comes to analyse the etymology of the word 'play', he is more inclusive and, ironically, very close to Caillois' own categories: 'Latin has really only one word to cover the whole field of play: *ludus* ... *Ludus* covers children's games, recreation, contests, liturgical and theatrical representations and games of chance' (1970: 55). Here, Huizinga clearly acknowledges that games of chance are part of the term *ludus* and lists mimetic and competitive games too.

For Vasiliev, this range of meanings of *ludus* is significant in a number of ways. Importantly, he favours the ancient root of the word to the Russian verb to play (*igrat*) – a preference which may underlie his enigmatic statement that the 'ludo theatre is the oldest form'.[12]

First, the association of *ludus* with games of chance speaks directly to Vasiliev's own self-assessment: 'My approach of course [is] very risky because it's rather like the work of a gambler – he likes taking chances' (1999). Interestingly, he casts himself in the role of the gambler here, not his actors. As a producer, he is engaging in the aleatoric aspect of play, in this instance in piecing together the work at the last minute. His appeal highlights his own boyish daring with the production – Caillois would call it 'paidiac' playfulness – but it remains to be seen whether his actors engage in the same kind of play or whether Vasiliev's construction of events imposes a ludic constraint on proceedings.

Second, that both theatrical and liturgical representations are part of the definition of *ludus* is also pertinent, as much of Vasiliev's later work appears to be making the shift from the former to the latter as we shall see when we look at his staging of the biblical story *The Lamentations of Jeremiah*. The religious aspect of play is an area that Caillois does not investigate explicitly although Huizinga's understanding implicitly includes the same divide between *paidia* and *ludus*: 'In play we may move below the level of the serious, as the child does; but we can also move above it – in the realm of the beautiful and the sacred' (1970: 38). Here, I believe is the real reason for Vasiliev's pursuit of a *ludic* theatre and the key to unpicking his statement about its antiquity, for it is precisely this latter realm, the realm Plato associates with forms and with 'good', to which Vasiliev sees his actors aspiring. 'Play', specifically *ludic* play, is the bridge between the material and the spiritual. As Plato suggests in the *Laws* (Book 7):

A man should spend his whole life at 'play' – sacrificing, singing, dancing – so that he can win the favour of the gods and protect himself from his enemies ... He'll achieve both these aims if he sings and dances in the way we've outlined.

(Plato 1970: 292)

Significantly, it is music that Plato outlines as the key organiser of play because, he argues, it is 'infinitely improved by the imposition of *form*' (ibid.: 290, my emphasis). It is a disciplined expression or, in Caillois' terminology, a ludic expressivity.

Vasiliev's use of the term ludo, therefore, is far more complex than the simple playful definition noted at the outset. It carries connotations of the sacred as well as of the disciplined or formally organised. It signs a process in which psychology and the material earth-bound actions of men can be raised up to a level of spiritual abstraction and it begs questions as to the balance of unconstrained and directed playfulness. These are connotations which must be kept in mind when Vasiliev's attitude to text is examined.

Reinterpreting the Newtonian model: the ludo system and *The Meek One*

It was noted earlier in this discussion that in theoretical terms Vasiliev entertains the possibility of using two contrary systems of actor training depending on the nature of the text to be studied. In practice, however, he exhibits a clear bias towards the ludo system of theatre. His choice of texts for the masterclasses run in Britain clearly indicate that, whilst he may consistently acknowledge the psychological system of acting, he does so only to elucidate the differences with his own system. Each one has used Dostoyevsky texts: *The Gambler* (1991), *The Meek One* (1996) and *Uncle's Dream* (1999) with the two most recent workshops devoted to Vasiliev's ludo system.

Initial and main events

Vasiliev's analysis of text hinges on finding two key events: the Initial Event (IE) – in Russian *iskhodnoe sobytie* – and the Main Event (ME) – *osnovnoe sobytie*. The actor's role exists between the two. The psychological line of the play develops *from* the IE: the stimulus for the play's action. Thus, in Strindberg's *The Father*, for example, Nöjd's first entrance as he raises the question of paternal doubt in Adolph's mind would be the IE, or in *The Seagull* Treplev's staging of his play. This event – in Russian the word has biblical connotations: point of 'exodus' (*iskhod*) – sets up the conflict between characters and this conflict leads to the action of the play. Working from a flip chart throughout the masterclass, Vasiliev illustrated this idea diagrammatically (see Figure 5.2). The ME, then, is the culmination of all the actions set off by the IE: 'It is the moment of catharsis/catastrophe ... [which] often changes the protagonist's philosophy of life' (Vasiliev 1991: 3). In *The Seagull* this is Treplev's suicide, the tragic outcome of all the play's moments of action or what Vasiliev calls 'sub-events' (see Figure 5.3). There is

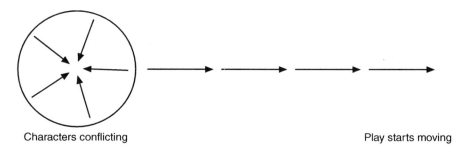

Characters conflicting   Play starts moving

Figure 5.2 Initial event leading to main event: a psychological model of drama.

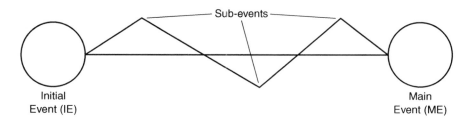

Initial   Main
Event (IE)   Event (ME)

Figure 5.3 Sub-events and the causal model of drama.

nothing new in such a causal modelling of the text. Indeed, this diagram might well have been lifted almost unchanged from Stanislavsky's *An Actor Prepares*, specifically from the chapter on the Superobjective. But this, of course, is what is interesting. To illustrate the tradition of theatrical play analysis in Russia, Vasiliev is compelled to adopt the persona of Stanislavsky. Compare the passage referred to above with Tortsov/ Stanislavsky's performance at the drawing board. 'Perhaps it would be more graphic if I made a drawing for you', he says (see Figure 5.4). In Part I it was proposed that the causal linearity of this drawing echoes the structures of Newtonian thinking and Vasiliev stresses this further: 'the conflict [of the IE] is the cause and the plot is the effect', he argues. Or alternatively, and equally Newtonian in concept, 'the conflict sets the development of the play *in motion*'.

Vasiliev thus returns us to the roots of Stanislavsky's science of acting. He takes his terminology, what he calls 'the concrete practical rules' of textual study, from the Moscow laboratory for actor training, GITIS, as it was inter- preted for him by his teacher Maria Knebel, Stanislavsky's colleague. Sharon Carnicke, working from Knebel's exposition of Stanislavsky's active analysis, makes the lineage clear in her definition of 'events':

> The 'inciting' (*iskhodnoe*) event sets the play in motion. A 'main' (*osnov- noe*) event is one without which a scene could not conclude.
>
> (Carnicke 1998: 173)

The *iskhodnoe sobytie* and the *osnovnoe sobytie* are thus part of the specific termi- nology passed down from theatre lab to theatre lab since Stanislavsky's time in the Opera-Dramatic studio, a terminology which may continue to evoke the Newtonian model just as it did when Stanislavsky coined the language in the late 1930s. It is an important measure of the weight of Stanislavsky's ideas in Russia today that Moscow's main theatrical training programme at GITIS preaches this conflict-driven method of play analysis and that for a self-confessed heretic and radical, even Vasiliev's ludo system has its founda- tions in the mechanistic model.

Determinism in the psychological model

In the psychological model, according to Vasiliev, the actor becomes immersed in the causal development of the piece. S/he is part of the active motion of the play, travelling from sub-event to sub-event (we might say

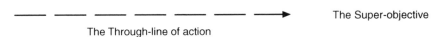

The Through-line of action   The Super-objective

Figure 5.4 Stanislavsky's through-line of action, 1936 (source: Stanislavsky 1980a: 276.

from task to task) to reach the end point or ME.[13] Vasiliev's reading, however, has negative connotations: the actor using the psychological system is 'at the mercy' of the action of the play, 'unable to direct events'. Following the Newtonian metaphor, the actor is set in motion by the IE to run his/her linear course to the end. This critical interpretation of the psychological model of analysis seems to emerge from Vasiliev's resistance to its determinism. There is no freedom for the actor when working inside a character, he argues, no room for alternatives, for play. The role binds the actor to one inevitable set of circumstances initiated by the opening event of the plot and culminating in the resolution of conflict at its denouement.

But whilst this deterministic trap may be the lot of some of the characters in psychological drama – witness the famous last words of Jean in Strindberg's *Miss Julie*, for example: 'It's horrible. But there's no other way out' (Strindberg 1958: 119) – is it true for the actors playing within a psychological system? Certainly, in his fatalistic reading of psychological acting, Vasiliev is not allowing for the 'double consciousness' the actor needs to adopt during performance, at one and the same time being both inside and outside the character. Nor, perhaps is he valuing enough the freedom of the actor to carry out the actions that lead up to the ME *differently* each night, as Michael Chekhov famously did in his interpretation of Hamlet.

At least in terms of his masterclass work, there is an irony in Vasiliev's opposition to the restrictions of the psychological system. My own experience in Glasgow was not characterised by a sense of freedom either physically or mentally – the lecture/demonstration mode of the masterclass was constraining and Vasiliev's dominant, spiritual reading of Dostoyevsky left little space for other interpretations. In this respect his spiritualism is of a different kind from Michael Chekhov's who was careful not to impose his own faith in Steiner's Spiritual Science on his students. Vasiliev's energy and charisma, by contrast, come from his zealotry, and the outcome, according to John Freedman reviewing his student's performance of the Biblical text *Joseph and his Brothers*, by Thomas Mann, is not always to produce free-thinkers but passive disciples:

> The new students he is trying to form outside the traditional theatrical educational system are better at imitating their teacher's 'terrible, swift' aura than creating convincing performances. Most of the men sport the same long black hair, the same flowing beards and the same scowling looks that have made Vasilyev's image famous. Even the women have adopted the 'Vasilyev look'. What appears to be lacking are strong creative personalities who might enter into a fruitful dialogue with a man of vision and talent.
>
> (Freedman 1997: 38)

The performance work of Vasiliev is the subject of analysis below, but here the tension in Vasiliev's ludic approach needs noting. Vasiliev is looking to destabilise the determinism of the text, to encourage a feeling of play in his actors' interpretation of the material. But here 'play' is perhaps better understood in terms of tolerance or distance – how much play do you have in the length of a rope before it becomes taut? – rather than in the sense of a boundless improvisation with the text. That tolerance was governed very carefully by Vasiliev in Glasgow and although he was always interested to receive alternative readings of the text from the masterclass group, it remained clear that the ultimate reading was his. Freedman's assessment that Vasiliev's students are unable to challenge the visionary director chimes with the sense I gained as a participant at the masterclass: that the flow of ideas was predominantly one way, that *ludus* dominated over *paidia*.

I put this allegation to Monika Koch,[14] one of the few actresses in Britain to have worked with Vasiliev for a prolonged period of time in an interview conducted in May 2001. In her response Koch defended Vasiliev against the charge of despotism, arguing that 'you put up with his arrogance because there is this incredible sense of energy' in his teaching. But later she tempered her defence, acknowledging that of those people who disagreed with Vasiliev: 'a lot of them had nervous breakdowns and disappeared'. The parallels with the early laboratory, set up by Stanislavsky with Knipper-Chekhova and Boleslavsky, are striking. Where Stanislavsky reduced Chekhov's wife to tears in a series of intensive and probing rehearsals, Vasiliev, Koch recalled:

> Made you feel like some scientific object in a big laboratory which is going to explode any minute![15]

The laboratory, clearly, does not always allow for a democratic, two-way exchange of ideas. On the positive side, however, the scientist in Vasiliev is clearly evident in the clarity of his expression. His complex theories are elegantly communicated by his consistent use of atomic models and his dialectic approach, interspersed with rich metaphors – like the leaf above – provides a constant intellectual challenge.

The ludo model and The Meek One

With characteristic symmetry, Vasiliev's ludic technique 'reconstructs' the psychological system, reversing perfectly the process analysed above. Thus, where a psychological analysis of the play details the pushing influence of the initial given circumstances, a ludic approach pulls the role towards the culmination point. Instead of feigning ignorance of the ME as in the psychological model, the actor 'adopts an attitude' to the culminating ME. Every event of the play is in effect coloured by the ME through a kind of conscious prospective awareness (see Figure 5.5).

The difference is evidenced by reference to the key text for the 1996 workshop: Dostoyevsky's *The Meek One* (*Krotkaya*). Dostoyevsky's short story

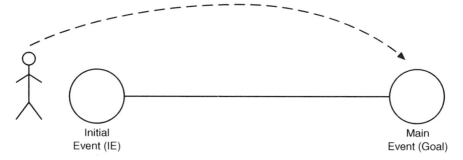

Figure 5.5 Vasiliev's ludo approach.

documents the suicide of a young woman, described in detail by the Woman's husband, a pawnbroker, as he recounts, more or less over her dead body, the events leading up to and including his wife's death. The Woman is an orphan, forced through her own destitution to pawn the remainder of her possessions, including a religious icon, to survive. The Pawnbroker takes advantage of her circumstances and proposes marriage. Although he is forty-one and she is sixteen, he is rankled by her delay in responding, believing himself to be a better catch than others might credit. The Pawnbroker's pride is constantly juxtaposed with the humility of the Woman, a structure which is key to Vasiliev's reading of the text. The Pawnbroker subjects his new wife to a regime of discipline designed to bolster his own status and sense of self at the expense of her dignity: 'In accepting her into my house I required total respect. I wanted her to kneel before me in prayer for my sufferings – and I merited that' (Dostoyevsky 1995: 72). The intensity of the domestic situation precipitates an illness in the Woman who is bedridden for six weeks, supported (although not 'cared for') by her husband. There follows a period of 'rebellious' behaviour on behalf of the Woman, including a silent duel in which she holds a revolver to the Pawnbroker's temple as he feigns sleep. Following this act of defiance, the Pawnbroker satisfies himself that his wife belongs entirely to him, as she chooses not to pull the trigger. Finally, the Woman reaches a state of equilibrium, of happiness even, before she takes her own life by throwing herself from the window of their apartment, clutching her icon.

As with the example of *The Seagull* above, the text can be read either from a psychological or a ludic perspective. A psychological reading would suggest that the IE of the text is the first meeting of the Pawnbroker and the Woman, the event which triggers all the ensuing action. The ME, then, as with *The Seagull*, is the Woman's suicide, the culmination of all the actions witnessed in the story, the final *effect*, so to speak, which arrests the forward motion of the plot. This leads to a dark, emotionally strained atmosphere – the mood captured by Penguin's cover blurb for their version of the story: 'A man lays bare his tortured soul . . . [a] compelling study of despair based on a real-life incident' (1996). The events are shown diagrammatically in Figure 5.6.

Conversely, a ludic reading realigns this structure of events, advancing that the IE is the suicide of the Woman and the ME is the response of the Pawnbroker to this event, his ultimate humbling or, put another way, his spiritual epiphany. The atmosphere is thus transformed from the dark, tortured feeling favoured by Penguin to one of lightness and hope – that is, of course, if you subscribe to Vasiliev's theism. The choice of text is demonstrative of this reversal of Initial and Main Events as the retrospective form of Dostoyevsky's eye-witness account opens (very briefly) with the death of the Woman. The progression here, for the Pawnbroker, is towards spiritual salvation and the forgiveness of God (see Figure 5.7). A performer adopting the ludic approach must, therefore, view all the actions of the narrative in the light of the ME – the Pawnbroker's enlightenment. Rather than stressing the death of his wife as the causal result of an unfortunate marriage, this death (miraculous as it is and with no visible injury) becomes the stimulus for the Pawnbroker's personal re-appraisal.

'*The Meek One* is a confession', states Vasiliev. 'On the surface it is as a story of the relationship between a man and a woman but this is incorrect, it is a story about a man's relationship with God.' The distinction is, once again, communicated by Vasiliev diagrammatically (see Figure 5.8). For Vasiliev, simply to play the horizontal line of the play is seriously to misconceive Dostoyevsky's work. Following his own faith, Vasiliev insists on the realignment of the horizontal, linear model outlined for Stanislavsky, turning it through ninety degrees to represent his philosophical shift away from the material relationships of people to the domain of metaphysics.[16] He has some justification for this, at least in respect of Dostoyevsky whose literature is studded with Christian imagery and whose Christ-like idiot, Prince Myshkin, shares many similarities with *The Meek One*: 'The main features of the prince's character', Dostoyevsky records in his notes for *The Idiot*, '[are] a feeling of oppression, fright, humility, meekness' (1955: 19).

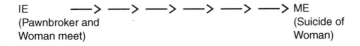

IE   —> —> —> —> —> —> ME
(Pawnbroker and   (Suicide of
Woman meet)   Woman)

Figure 5.6 Initial and main event in Dostoyevsky's *The Meek One*: a psychological reading.

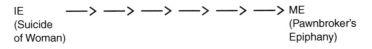

IE   —> —> —> —> —> —> ME
(Suicide   (Pawnbroker's
of Woman)   Epiphany)

Figure 5.7 Initial and main event in Dostoyevsky's *The Meek One*: a ludo reading.

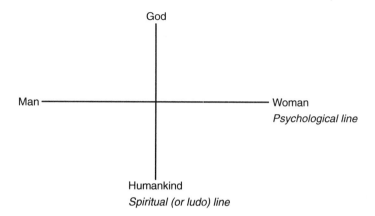

Figure 5.8 Dostoyevsky's *The Meek One:* ludic line versus psychological line.

Symbolism and vocal work in the ludo theatre

In this context, Vasiliev's adoption of a cruciform shape, to illustrate his theory may not be coincidental. Certainly, the diagram represents a dialectic encountered before in this book in the work of Chekhov and Steiner – the tension between the material and the immaterial, the sensible and the super-sensory – and Vasiliev may be drawing from this aspect of his training. It also points to the distinction already drawn between the *muthos*-based Aristotelian drama on the horizontal plane and the Platonic vertical line, directed towards ever-increasing abstraction.

But Vasiliev may be looking closer to home as well, to the theatre of Symbolism. The symbolists – powerfully influential in Russia in the early 1900s – were also opposed to Naturalism and to a theatre of simple plot-based action. They too looked to shun conventional psychology in favour of establishing a connection with a higher plane – a vertical line of development as opposed to a horizontal one. Their ultimate aim for the theatre, as Fyodor Sologub defined it, was 'to bring it closer to communal drama, to the mystery play, to liturgy' (in Green 1986: 150).

To do this, the art of the actor must be changed, particularly (and here the parallels with Vasiliev are striking) in terms of vocal work:

> We find acting that is too much in earnest ridiculous; splendid declamation ... excessively painstaking reproduction of the particulars of everyday life ... For this reason there must be no acting. Only a level word-by-word delivery. The calm enactment of situations, scene by scene.
>
> (Ibid.: 156–157)

The problem of dialogue is central for Vasiliev and surfaces continually in his theoretical discussions. Central to the question of speaking on stage is the role emotion plays in the process. Actors always move from words to emotions, Vasiliev argues: 'So I founded a new class [at the School of Dramatic Art] on 'how to do dialogue' in 1988. Since then I have completely stopped working on how best to convey an exchange of emotions' (1999). Vasiliev's school within a school, where he experiments with his ludo system, is specifically for actors already trained in the psychological system of Stanislavsky. This foundation is both necessary and at the same time unwanted for his actors need 'retraining', as he puts it, 'to imbue them with a different theatrical consciousness' (ibid.). The psychological approach is, of course, dedicated to finding strategies for underpinning the text with truthful emotional content, whether this is derived from Ribot-based affective memory exercises (as with Boleslavsky and the early Stanislavsky), or from the material activity of 'doing' (as Adler, Meisner and the late Stanislavsky practised). Either way, emotions are a significant part of the picture. For Vasiliev, emotions cloud the issues of the text, they colour reason and misdirect the audience's attention. Thus, although training is needed to inculcate an appreciation of the relationship between emotion and the dramatic text, Vasiliev's system is designed to break the hegemony of emotion-driven acting by breaking the natural rhythms of the spoken text.

The following example, taken from the Glasgow masterclass and the work on *The Meek One*, exemplifies the point. One by one the following sentence was read: 'Well what do you mean a handful [of blood]' (Dostoyevsky 1995: 100). The line itself is one of the key symbols in Dostoyevsky's story, for this is the startled reaction of the Pawnbroker elicited by the near-miraculous death of the Woman in *The Meek One*. She falls from a great height and yet bleeds very little. She is the sacrifice and her blood is the blood of Christ. The icon, still lying in her arms after the fall, is a symbol – as Vasiliev interprets it – of her ensuing resurrection. It is this moment which turns round the proud Pawnbroker and begins his spiritual restitution.

An actor wanting to emphasise this miraculous death would naturally lay stress on the substantive noun 'handful': not rivers of blood but a tiny sample, a spoonful, one might say, recalling that the Russian Orthodox communion is given in a spoon not a goblet or glass, as in Roman Catholicism. But for Vasiliev such a stress is to play on the psychological plane. He is interested in the ludic plane or, in this example, in what he calls a 'conceptual' reading. Thus, to break up the natural flow of the sentence and to accentuate the extraordinariness of the line, the ludic actor must stress the interrogative pronoun 'what', not the substantive noun 'handful': 'Well *what* do you mean a handful [of blood]?' As actors trained at the very least to communicate the meaning of a line, if not directly in the Stanislavsky System, all of the participants at his masterclass read the extract with the stress on the noun, only to be corrected by Vasiliev.

His argument is that in speaking Dostoyevsky in this broken mode of delivery, the ludic actor stresses the 'epic' side of the text (another implicit debt to Brecht) and therefore focuses the spectator's attention away from the material sensation of a roadside tragedy towards a deeper, or higher, meaning. Effectively, Vasiliev is trying to do with words what Meyerhold, looking to Shklovsky, was doing with movement, to break up the habituated rhythms of speech and 'make strange' the text.

In a review of *Uncle's Dream* and *Amphitryon* (1995) John Freedman, the *Moscow Times* theatre critic since 1992, offers a view of this technique in performance:

> Most striking – or perhaps most irritating, depending upon one's point of view – is the highly stylised speech that all of the actors have learned as if by rote. It is a choppy manner of chant in which at least minor stress falls on every word, no matter what its semantic value, and every word is separated from those around it by a mini-pause or hesitation. By and large those words which receive major stress are pronouns . . . While superficially creating the feel of a philosophical dialogue, over a period of time, this inflated, oratorical style actually begins bleaching the text of meaning.
>
> (1997: 132–133)

Coupled with Freedman's observation that the actors in this production spent the entire time 'seemingly nailed to their chairs' (1997: 133), the sense one gains is that both Vasiliev's teaching and his direction may succeed in limiting the physical and intellectual space of his actors, leaving them (and the audience) unwittingly in darkness rather than opening them up to the light. The same criticism might well be levelled at the Symbolists, whose aim, as Meyerhold saw it in his dimly lit experimentations with Maeterlinck, was to create a Static Theatre in which 'the word must be coldly "coined", free from all tremolo and the familiar break in the voice' (Meyerhold 1991: 54). The aim of both Meyerhold and Vasiliev in combining physical stasis with verbal disjuncture is, in Mallarmé's symbolist rhetoric, to 'evoke feelings and ideas greater than those the words usually stand for' (Styan 1981: 3).

For Vasiliev, this elevated speech may be seen as an attempt on his behalf to evoke the atmosphere of a Russian Orthodox mass, in which, as with some high Catholic churches, the priest chants rather than speaks the service. The obvious danger with this is ironic: that in pursuing the goal of a novel and defamiliarised vocal delivery, a different kind of habituated, rhythm is established.[17] In the context of a church, where textual understanding may be taken as read, this simply serves to enhance the ritual experience. But in a theatre like Vasiliev's, where ideas not actions are being exchanged, repetitive rhythms can alienate (in the pejorative sense of the word) an audience, or in Freedman's words 'bleach' not brighten the production's meaning.

Vasiliev and Plato

For a practitioner who is so demonstrably committed to theorising as Anatoly Vasiliev, it is fitting that he should shift the philosophical foundation of Stanislavsky's system from the action-based, emotionally driven model of Aristotle to the pure thought of Plato. In both theory and practice, the Socratic dialogues are a central set of texts for Vasiliev. He began developing his ludo system by working on them in his laboratory. He has staged certain dialogues for an audience and insists his students become familiar with Plato's writings as part of their training. At the same time, the training he puts his students through is drawing on an essentially Platonic premise: engage deeply in a distanced and rational investigation of something and you will leave the material (for Plato the 'illusory') concerns of the world behind. Vasiliev's laboratory is as much a sanctuary from the mundanities of everyday life as it is a centre of exploration.

Plato and The Republic

From a theatrical perspective Plato is best known for his rough treatment of the dramatic poet in *The Republic* and for his richly allegorical Simile of the Cave, viewed in conjunction with the metaphor of the Divided Line. Poetry, and particularly poetry written for performance, should, Plato argues, be banished from his ideal state – the Republic – as it appeals to the baser side of humanity: that is, the irrational, emotional side. Aristotle argues that the emotions (specifically pity and fear) are balanced by the cathartic processes of (tragic) drama. Plato maintains that exposure to such theatrical spectacles heightens the emotional response and thus widens the gap between the spectator and his/her reason: 'We are therefore quite right to refuse to admit [the poet] to a properly run state, because he wakens and encourages and strengthens the lower elements in the mind to the detriment of reason' (1987: 435).

Plato's dogmatism has led to similarly intransigent statements from his critics. Iris Murdoch, for example, in *The Fire and the Sun*, labels Plato a 'puritan' for 'like all Puritans [he] hates the theatre' (1977: 13). More recently, though, Tony Gash has drawn attention to the implicit theatrical aesthetic Plato embodies. Interestingly, Gash points to the kinship between Brecht and Plato, arguing that in Plato's anti-emotionalism, and specifically in his criticism of tragedy, 'are the germs of what Brecht meant by an "epic" theatre' (2000: 19). We have already noted some similarities in Vasiliev's own commitment to a dispassionate and estranged mode of performance and his self-confessed disinterest in the emotional training of the actor must be viewed in the same light. Both Vasiliev and Brecht are in search of an anti-Aristotelian theatre: for the latter, this search takes him into political didacticism; for the former, to a no-less efficacious religiosity.

Plato's Simile of the Cave is the central theatrical image in the *Republic*.

Socrates, Plato's mouthpiece in *The Republic*, asks his sounding board, Glaucon, to imagine a cave, populated with people with their backs to the opening. They are fettered so that they cannot turn away from the inside wall of the cave. The only light in the cave comes from a fire which is behind the imprisoned populace. Between the fire and the people there is a road and in front of this road a 'curtain wall' has been built. Here, Plato makes the connection with performance explicit for the wall is 'like the screen at puppet shows between the operators and their audience, above which they show their puppets' (1987: 317). The prisoners are thus treated to a shadow play created by the puppets in the light of the fire – they do not see the puppet play directly – and this is Plato's metaphor for the lowest of the levels of human consciousness: illusion (*eikasia*). To exemplify the ascent to a higher level, the visible realm, Plato has one of his prisoners released from his fetters to turn around within the cave. Gazing on the artificial models of the puppets corresponds with Plato's concept of belief (*pistis*) which is further extended when the prisoner is brought out of the cave entirely. At first dazzled with the sunlight, he later becomes accustomed to the change and can look at real things in the region outside of the cave – synonymous with the development of reason (*dianoia*). Later still, he can gaze directly at the planets and finally the sun, thus leaving the shadow world of illusions behind and entering into the realm of intelligence (*nous*) and the abstract realm of Form.

Platonic theatre

For Gash, Plato's startling image is intrinsically theatrical due to its compound complexity. The situation described in the Cave Simile is, he argues, 'Obviously that of spectators in a theatre who are both seeing something happening in front of them and, at the same time, interpreting intentional signs' (2000: 11). Gash's point is that Plato demands the same kind of double consciousness when reading his Simile as an audience naturally adopts whilst in the darkened atmosphere of the theatre. The images of puppets, planets and fires operate as props do in the theatre on (at least) two levels: at a denotative level they contribute to the overall picture of the poor prisoners, while at a connotative level they correspond with a meta-narrative of philosophical development.

Vasiliev, in his detailed ludic reading of Dostoyevsky, is saying something similar. *The Meek One* can be read as a simple tale of a dysfunctional marriage but, in doing so, the reader would only be engaging with the story at the most superficial level – the level of *eikasia*. The vertical line of analysis favoured by Vasiliev, by contrast, uncovers the religious meta-narrative inscribed in Dostoyevsky's story. The further one ascends above the trivial lives of the characters to the metaphoric meaning of their experiences – the icon as a symbol of resurrection not simply an object of affection – the closer one comes to the Platonic realm of intelligence.

Conversely, a psychological reading with its basis in the material and emotional world of the characters is synonymous with the darkened cave of illusion. By focusing on the feelings of the Pawnbroker and his wife, the reader is basing his/her understanding on capricious sense-perceptions. By extension, the Stanislavsky system exemplifies the lowest of the realms pictured in the cave simile. For Plato, our senses cannot understand the world in any reliable way. We see only *images* of things which may be distorted by circumstances in many different ways. Our senses, then, are already at one remove from 'truth'. True knowledge, Plato argues, lies in the ideal form of something – an abstract universal construct which unlike our sense-perception is stable and constant: the table of all tables which we 'see' not with our eyes but with our capacity for abstract thought. Chekhov's Psychological Gesture, drawing, as has been seen in Chapter 4, on Goethe's notion of the *ur-form* is descended from the same line of thinking.

Theatre, then, particularly a theatre which appeals to the senses and the emotions (a theatre like Stanislavsky's, for example), must be twice removed from these ideal forms, given that what it represents on stage – tables, chairs, murders, breakdowns – are already representations of the ideal form of these things. Put another way: 'the tragic poet, if his art is representation, is by nature at third remove from the throne of truth (Plato 1987: 425).[18]

Of course, Vasiliev's theatre is no different – any theatre which serves the smallest mimetic purpose, must be an illusory one in Plato's world-view. But in recognising that the theatre *is* essentially a fiction, rather than pretending that it is not (as much of the Stanislavsky tradition has done), the meta-theatrical practitioner exposes the layers of meaning – reveals that there *are* different levels – and thus brings the spectator closer to the practice of philosophy as Plato conceived it.

Plato and the ludo system

For Vasiliev, the ascent the prisoner makes towards the intelligible realm and, by extension, towards God is analogous with the vertical line of the ludo system. Although he resists saying as much, the imagery is clear in this passage on *King Lear*:

> In the case of the psychological system then you are gradually going to descend towards the main event to the bottom – Lear descends to the hell of his feelings. In the ludo system you gradually climb upwards towards the main event. In the psychological system you are going to be moving down into the darkness. You are moving out towards the light if you use the ludo system.
>
> (1996: II, 9)

Again this is illustrated using the flipchart (see Figure 5.9).

In Dostoyevsky's *The Meek One*, the same imagery persists. As the Pawn-

Figure 5.9 Climbing or descending – the ludo approach versus the psychological approach.

broker laments his ill-timed arrival at the scene of his wife's suicide – 'just
five minutes too late' (Dostoyevsky 1995: 100) – he describes the transi-
tional period in his relationship with her, and by extension with his relationship with God:

> If I had just a little more time, if she had just waited a tiny bit longer I
> would have dispelled the darkness! . . . She was afraid too, very much so.
> I won't argue . . . But I paid no attention to her fears, *a new sun was
> shining*!
>
> (Ibid.: 96, my emphasis)

Of course, this is a symbol in Russian Orthodoxy of spiritual enlightenment,
but it also lends itself to a Platonic reading, particularly as this passage
follows the section subtitled 'I Understand Only Too Well' and may therefore be interpreted as the Pawnbroker's release from his own cave of ignorance and his concomitant ascent towards the light of understanding – the
symbol for which, it will be recalled, is Plato's sun.

In practice, achieving this ascent to the light outside Plato's cave is an
arduous task. Indeed, in the short time of a masterclass with new students,
the participants may align themselves with the fettered cave dwellers of
Plato's simile, rather than with the enlightened philosophers, staring not at
shadows but at the flipchart of Vasiliev! His own training takes four years, of
which at least eighteen months is spent 'breaking the actors in' before they
can fully absorb the system of ludic theatre – an indicator of the elongated
time-structures Russian theatre has enjoyed (and exploited) since
Stanislavsky.

But, if Freedman's assessment of the Vasiliev performer is taken at face
value, some of the troupe of actors who have trained with Vasiliev for years
in his Moscow school also exhibit an uncanny resemblance to the unenlight-
ened inhabitants of the cave, not quite fettered but 'seemingly nailed to
their seats' and doing little more than facing out to the audience, chanting
their lines. To what extent, then, do Vasiliev's actors reach the state of
philosophical autonomy a Platonic training implies? How far are they the
agents of their own destiny or simply the prisoners who remain in the darkened cave – those to whom the enlightened philosopher (AKA Vasiliev)

eventually returns to show 'some care and responsibility' (Plato 1987: 324)?
An answer to this question will be sought in the 'results' of Vasiliev's ludic
approach, exemplified in performance.

Summary

Following the indications in *The Republic*, a Platonic theatre must eschew
emotionalism. It must find a 'higher' level of exchange between spectator
and actor from the concrete, material level suggested by the Cave – a level of
abstraction analogous to the language of mathematics which is sufficiently
removed from the natural world to compel the mind 'to use reason and not
sense-perception in surveying the subject matter' (Plato 1987: 315). Accordingly, part of its project must be to reveal its own processes and thus to
engage at a level at least one step removed from straight illusionism. Given
this demand for abstraction, a Platonic theatre might also be a minimalist
theatre, shorn of mimetic devices and pregnant with intellectual, not visual
stimuli. It will not focus on characters (*ethos*) or on the actions they perform
in the *muthos* of the piece but instead direct attention to the metaphorical
significance of a character's deeds. To what extent, then, are these principles
evident in the performances of Vasiliev's School of Dramatic Art?

The results of a laboratory theatre

First, let it be made clear that not all of Vasiliev's work could be described
as Platonic. In fact, his performance work has evolved along similar lines to
his teaching, exemplifying the same development away from the psychological theatre and towards a ludic abstraction.

Vasiliev's first real success was Gorky's *Vassa Zheleznova*, staged at the
Stanislavsky Drama Theatre (not the MAT)[19] in 1978 and described as his
attempt to 'save' psychological realism. Produced at the theatre which grew
out of the Opera-Dramatic Studio and where Maria Knebel had a significant
influence, the *Vassa* project was very much a product of Vasiliev's
Stanislavsky-based training – detailed, gritty and linear. By contrast, Victor
Slavkin's *The Grown-up Daughter of a Young Man*, produced a year later at the
same theatre, is described by Vasiliev with typical mathematical neatness as
a 'half-way house' between psychological realism and ludic theatre.[20]
Smeliansky explains:

> Details ruled here too: the actors prepared a salad in the kitchen, cut up
> cold potatoes, shelled eggs etc. but it was a theatrical game in which the
> real-life minutiae were necessary in order to recall time past 'in detail'.
>
> (1999: 191–192)

Whilst the trappings of psychological naturalism may be evident here, the
overall perspective is a distanced one, facilitated by a playful (or ludic) atti-

tude to the subject matter. During the Glasgow masterclass Vasiliev explained that his aim with this project was to inject the spirit of jazz into the scripted production, to invite his actor-soloists to improvise away from the dominant theme or tune before being subsumed back into the ensemble.

Slavkin was also the author of the first Vasiliev play to tour Britain. After beginning life at the Taganka in 1985, *Cerceau* came to the BITE festival in London in 1987, playing at the Riverside. Monika Koch describes the style of the production:

> I thought it was like dance theatre. I saw it like movement, like dance, with a lot of blues music. And of course it had games in it [but] at the same time it is a very spiritual play. It gave the audience something to uplift them at the end of the play: a sense of hope without being kitsch.[21]

Koch's description indicates that Vasiliev's work in the late 1980s exhibited many of the hallmarks of the Russian tradition: a sense of musicality, a movement language as fluid as dance and a strong quality of ensemble.

In 1991 the pivotal production of *Six Characters in Search of an Author* came to Britain, leading Vasiliev into the development of his ludo system:

> When I started working on . . . Pirandello, I was never interested in the least in the psychological state of the character, I was interested in the consciousness of the characters and at that moment I started constructing the life of the actor not depending on the past of the characters but dependent on the future of that character . . . people are then thinking 'future', they are living not in themselves.
>
> (Vasiliev 1999)

Thus, the meta-theatricality of Pirandello took Vasiliev closer to the model of Platonic theatre proposed above, to an acting technique based not on introverted sense-perception but on prospective awareness.

As Vasiliev's interest in this ludic theatre has developed, the explicit physical theatricality of *Cerceau* has given way to a far more abstracted form of theatre. His stunning, white theatre spaces on Sretenka Ulitsa in Moscow, designed by Vasiliev himself with his collaborator Igor Popov and based on church architecture, sign this shift away from the traditional illusionary arena. At the same time the bleached stages have echoes of both a clinical laboratory and of the Platonic space outside the Cave, dazzling its audience as Plato's prisoner is dazzled by the unaccustomed glare of the sun. The whiteness of the theatre also signifies spiritual purity and the work Vasiliev puts on in this theatre increasingly resembles the proceedings of a Russian Orthodox church more than it does the repertoire of a theatre.

In *Joseph and his Brothers* hymns are sung by the cast and the stage space itself is reserved exclusively for chanted readings from the Bible, estranging the actors' dialogue in the way illustrated above. The scenes from the Bible are edited so that just two actors are in constant opposition, delivering their characters' lines in a functional, distanced manner. Any interaction between them is avoided. The props are limited to just two chairs and the gestural language of the cast to 'a few repetitive, stylized motions of the fingers, hands and arms' (Freedman 1993: 20). The naturalism of *Vassa* and the physical theatricality of *Cerceau* have clearly given way to a 'poor' minimalism on stage. But what is remarkable in this pared-down form of theatre is the layering of text: readings from Genesis continue throughout the presentation, added to which are the scenes from *Joseph* and, at a third level, the voices of Vasiliev's singers, topping the rest of the proceedings with a selection of hymns.

In *The Lamentations of Jeremiah* the Uranus building assumes 'the feeling of a Russian Cathedral' (Smeliansky 1999: 201), whilst a church choir, the Ensemble of Ancient Russian Ecclesiastical Music, takes centre stage. 'This is vertical theatre', remarks Anatoly Smeliansky in response, which leaves the soul 'in a state of peace and tranquillity' (1999: 201–202). The observation is striking in the current context. Smeliansky is describing the Uranus theatre and its vertical emphasis – the floors having been removed to reveal the ornate ceiling. But the notion of a vertical theatre also speaks to the training Vasiliev's actors have received and to the plane of action the Russian director is now pursuing – a spiritual plane in which the audience's minds are taken up and away from material concerns. Indeed, the choices made to accompany this 'theatrical prayer' (Smeliansky 1999: 202) seem designed to facilitate such an upward vision, fusing Christian imagery with that of Plato: white doves swoop and coo as the choir sings its sacred music. Arches like those in a cathedral are cut out of the white stage flats (once again directing our attention heavenward) whilst hundreds of candles flicker in the hands of the singers. In a gesture of symbolism which may owe more to Plato than to Russian Orthodoxy, the choir too are drawn into the ritual experience, changing their cloaks at first from black to white and then to sky blue – a further homage, it might be argued, to the Platonic hierarchy of realms.

But perhaps the clearest indication of Vasiliev's attempt to theatricalise the discipline of philosophy is in the staging of *The Republic* itself. Taking his form from Plato, Vasiliev's production is a series of 'dialogues' between the philosopher Socrates (bedecked in white, again) and his interlocutor. Smeliansky defines the aims of the piece: 'Five performers juggled with abstract ideas ... attempt[ing] to understand how human thought works and how these thoughts can be expressed theatrically' (1999: 199). As thought (*dianoia*) becomes paramount, upgraded from the third place position Aristotle accords it, behind plot (*muthos*) and character (*ethos*), so the driving force of the play is shifted from action to words – Vasiliev's 'word movement'. This move towards abstraction leads to the kind of stark minimalism we have suggested Plato's theatre might invite, in this case in the gestural language of the players. It also results in a heavy reliance on the audience's capacity for thought. At the same time, in this restricted theatricality one can identify a distance between character and player already highlighted in the training: 'The performing artist perched upon the person he was playing like a statue on a plinth. He did not just play a part, but play with the part' (Smeliansky 1999: 199). The metaphor indicates the quality of stasis in the production as well as the ludic attitude to character Vasiliev is encouraging in his students – the location of the actor outside of the character and the freedom to survey that character from without with a playful detachment.

John Freedman is less supportive of this development:

> Frequently, when two actors are carrying on a dialogue, other actors sit by silently, laughing and grinning among themselves or, more rarely, turning to the spectators to draw them into the process. It is not uncommon for the young actors to slip out of character (or at least pretend to) and laugh heartily at some moment in the text or the action which they find apparently amusing ... Meanwhile, actors left out of the action for extended periods are capable of slipping into their own world and staring blankly in to space.
>
> (1997: 133)

The playfulness of the actors comes through in this description very clearly but there is also a strong sense of exclusivity, generated by the sense of the audience being extrinsic to the proceedings – not understanding the in-jokes – or simply cut off by the introspection of the non-performing actors. Recalling Caillois, the audience seem able to detect the sense of *paidia* in the actor's performance but are not apprised of the rules (*ludus*) underlying this play. As such, it is a one-sided game and liable, therefore, to be shorn of its pleasure.

The other aspect that comes through clearly in this review of Vasiliev's *Republic* is the devaluing of character – at once a postmodern and a Platonic characteristic. Glaucon, whose role in Plato's original is at best as a mechanistic sounding board, is reduced to a 'computer' in Vasiliev's version, only able to respond with 'yes' or 'no'. Socrates too, who exhibits moments of ironic three-dimensionality in *The Republic*, simply 'channelled the flow of thought on stage' as Smeliansky puts it, conspicuously without 'psychology, or even the dregs of psychology' (1999: 199).

What is evident in both Vasiliev's staging of *The Republic* and in *The Lamentations of Jeremiah* is a bold attempt to reject the Newtonian framework of motivation we have argued is central to Stanislavskian practice. 'Action-reaction' is no longer the key conflicting dynamic in the work. Instead, and at best, the performance shifts to a different level of interaction, thought and counter-thought, perhaps – but where all the characters' thoughts are essentially travelling in the same (vertical) direction. Where the problems with this approach emerge is in the actor–audience relationship. A vertical theatre, in which the performer's energies are channelled directly upwards, runs the risk of missing its audience entirely – like heat in a draughty house.

Nor is it guaranteed to train confident actors, irrespective of its claims to liberate the actor. Critics have pointed consistently to the nervousness and instability of Vasiliev's ludo-trained actors. Even with a previous training, they often look ill at ease on stage, an outcome which may derive from their lack of autonomy within the training process. Whilst Vasiliev's method of rehearsal seems to give great scope to his actors, the apparent freedom this gives does not always find expression in self-confidence for an actor on stage. Both Freedman and Smeliansky refer to the lack of individuality in his casts and to the uncanny phenomenon of hero-worship for their director, measured by the actors' adoption of the 'Vasiliev look'. Smeliansky goes further: 'Vasilyev's theatre is, above all, him. He is all for actors as co-authors, but can only tolerate pupils and followers' (1999: 198).

It is this underlying dynamic which seems to manifest itself in certain performances of the School of Dramatic Art, a point crystallised by one theatrical choice in Vasiliev's production of *Joseph and his Brothers*: Vasiliev's own shadow, cast by a spotlight behind the director, stretches across the length of the stage for the entire first half of the play, dwarfing his actors and demanding (perhaps unwittingly) that they gaze on the Platonic symbol of illusion, not of intelligence. Such theatrical moments offer compelling evidence that Vasiliev's Platonic journey may ultimately be a personal one and that the philosophical development needed to leave the cave behind is his alone.

The balance of laboratory, school and theatre

In conclusion, the question of the laboratory and specifically the interplay of experimental workshop (or lab), school and stage needs revisiting. This relationship offers us an enlightening measure of a practitioner's theatrical methodology. Meyerhold's laboratory, for example, captured the productive energy of the Revolution, Chekhov's, a Romantic solitude. Lee Strasberg's Actors Studio had echoes of a psychoanalyst's couch, set up rather uncomfortably in the public domain.

Vasiliev's laboratory theatre is different again. He picks up on the strand of Stanislavskian thinking which culminated in the 1935 studio. Indeed, Vasiliev's earliest method of actor training was based on his own experiments with the Method of Physical Actions, the technique evolved by Stanislavsky at the Opera-Dramatic Studio. His developments in the ludo system are, moreover, predicated on an actor's understanding of the Stanislavsky System. But where Stanislavsky looked to his young actors and actresses to revivify his model of approach whilst simultaneously developing their own talents in a forum outside that of the Opera-Dramatic Studio, Vasiliev favours an older intake of students who contribute exclusively to the work of the School of Dramatic Art. A great deal of emphasis is placed on the interplay between school – the forum for the ludo system to be taught – and workshop, where Vasiliev offers his critical observations. But the final side to the triangular relationship appears at present to be of less value for Vasiliev.[22] In effect he has redefined the laboratory once again – in this case as a protective place for the construction of a new system based on his range of metaphysical influences: from Plato to Russian orthodoxy. One might call it a sanctuary.

Vasiliev's spiritual introspection has nothing to do with fear of critics; it is one response to the instability of the post-*perestroika* era. He has found security behind the protective walls of his laboratory, a stability working with his actors which he feels is compromised by public performance. In a sense his retreat echoes Plato's own direction: the stable, immutable realm is that which is furthest removed from the material conditions of life – a realm of abstraction and ideal form. The laboratory, at least for Vasiliev himself, is the environment which best facilitates such a remove into pure philosophy.

The School of Dramatic Art stands out as a model of a bygone age of state-supported, experimental work, bound not by the demands of audience revenue but by the exacting vision of its Artistic Director. Vasiliev and his non-accountable experimental research are bucking the trend, perhaps because his particular *perestroika* is both ancient and modern: ancient, in that it draws from a pre-Aristotelian theory of theatre; modern, because it is taking on the tradition of Stanislavsky and developing it further, responding in its own way to the two major forces to be reckoned with in the Moscow of this new century – capitalism and the Church.

Epilogue

Genetic modification and the backbone of tradition

Speaking to the *Moscow Times* theatre critic in 1998, Kama Ginkas, one of Anatoly Vasiliev's contemporaries and part of the post-*perestroika* burgeoning of directorial talent in Moscow, was asked the following question: 'Do you feel you exist within a tradition that comes from somewhere and goes somewhere?' Ginkas' response speaks very clearly to the sense of lineage expressed in this book:

> Without a doubt . . . I wasted enormous amounts of energy battling with the schooling I received. I'm still doing it today. I do everything possible to exceed its limits. But your schooling sits deeply in you. It's genetics. It's your backbone . . . I always feel I will never fall. Because my backbone is built. I may have strayed very far in what is superficial but not in what is essential.
>
> (1998: 10)

Based at the Young Spectator Theatre in Moscow since 1988, Ginkas in many ways is the antithesis of Vasiliev – his is a determinedly physical theatre, often base and explicit but always deeply engaging for an audience. But the two men do have two things in common: a fascination with Dostoyevsky – Ginkas is one of the foremost contemporary Muscovites to plough a *psychological* furrow in adapting Dostoyevsky – and a shared understanding of what constitutes 'tradition'.

A tradition, as Ginkas suggests, must not remain unquestioned. It must be challenged, battled against, 'reconstructed', as Vasiliev might have it, for without such a dynamic relationship with one's teaching the tradition may become stale, unmoving, or orthodox. At the same time, a tradition provides an important reference point, a compensating stability – something 'essential', as Ginkas sees it. He is speaking of his teacher, Georgy Tovstonogov, and the training he received at the Leningrad Institute of Theatre, Film and Cinema in the early 1960s[1] but it might just as well be Meyerhold talking, or Boleslavsky, or Ginkas' contemporary Mark Rozofsky at the Nikitska Gate Theatre.

For Ginkas' metaphor of the backbone is an enduring one. We might recall that Stanislavsky's System, as it evolved and grew up, has consistently been organised around a 'spine' – the progression from the conscious to the superconscious. This biological fulcrum, modelled in the many diagrammatic representations analysed in this book, bisects the inner and outer preparatory work of the performer at the same time as defining the actor's perspective on the role. Boleslavsky exported the same language – the 'spine of the role' – to America and it has remained a key terminological reference point in Strasberg's Actors Studio (Hirsch 1984: 203). For Meyerhold, the backbone of the actor's craft is to be found in physical dexterity. Responsiveness, rhythm, balance and precision all play a key role in the system of biomechanics. He preferred algebraic formulations, not biological models, to describe the task of acting, but nevertheless perceived his actors as symmetrical beings, equally gifted on left or right. Even Vasiliev's ludo system, in its verticality, has vestiges of the Stanislavskian spinal model, although it is founded on a very different set of philosophical premises.

But what is most revealing about Ginkas' appreciation of the Russian tradition of actor training is the tension inherent in the metaphor itself. The backbone is constantly under strain, keeping the upper-body supported and working against the force of gravity. At the same time it is the vehicle for receiving and sending messages both to and from the brain and hence, at its most fundamental, the spine is a 'psycho-physical' structure. This is one reason, perhaps, why it is so central to the Stanislavskian model.

As a stable structure, constantly under pressure from external forces, the backbone provides a fitting concluding image for this book for it expresses the creative dynamic between the progressive evolution of an acting tradition and the contemporary forces which influence and affect that progression. Each one of the practitioners encountered in this discussion has a distinct and identifiable line back to Stanislavsky – their genetic inheritance, one might say, is clear. But each one of them has also sought to defy their theatrical genes and develop an alternative system of acting.

These respective resistances, from Meyerhold's first rejection of Stanislavskian theory in 1905, to Vasiliev's calculated reconstruction today, map on to another set of ideas in balance – the mechanistic paradigm of Newtonian theory set alongside the organic holism of Goethe's Romantic science. They are the first two tributaries to emerge from the endemic tension in Stanislavsky's own thinking.

The signs are that this process will carry on as the System continues to be appropriated and reinvented. The focus here, on the practical training of an actor, is intended to reveal a pattern that is markedy different from a simple reading of Stanislavsky and his disciples 'through' scientific theory. Instead, the attempt has been to open up the theatre laboratory, to analyse the processes which go on inside and thus to demystify as well as celebrate the startling responsiveness of Russian theatre.

It is clear that what emerges from this opening up of the doors of the laboratory is an evolutionary form of life. The Stanislavsky tradition is manifestly healthy and alive – in Rozofsky's Nikitska Gate, in Vasiliev's School of Dramatic Art, even in Kama Ginkas' resistant homage to Tovstonogov at the Young Spectator Theatre. It will continue to evolve, to bifurcate further, gaining in complexity as it is modified to reflect new concerns. At the same time, if the dedication to tradition persists in the Russian school, as Ginkas promises, these evolutionary lines of development may still be traced, analysed and discussed in future books.

But the pressures of postmodernity and technology may well upset this delicate balance of past traditions and present influences. Science is fragmenting, yielding disciplines which are so specialised that debate and the exchange of practices may be hindered. As it stands, there are few signs of this fragmentation in the Russian tradition of actor training – Ginkas is not alone in celebrating a past teacher's contribution to present creative activities.[2] But if the theatrical diversity evidenced in this tradition should continue to flourish without a loss of potency, it is clear that genetics and the environment must both be respected.

Notes

Introduction: Science and Stanislavsky – the evolution of a tradition

1 There is much dispute as to the correct presentation of Stanislavsky's term 'System' (*systema*). Benedetti in *Stanislavsky and the Actor* warns that the capitalised term should never be used as it 'suggested a closed and rigid theory' (1998: x). Carnicke in her two recent publications on Stanislavsky (1998 and 2000) retains the form 'System' without question. Here, the capitalised form will be used, not to sign the System's rigidity, but to indicate its formative position in actor training: the System of systems.

2 Fyodor Kommissarzhevsky was the first to release material concerning the System in 1916. Following this, Michael Chekhov (in 1919) and Valentin Smishlayev (in 1921), 'a Proletkult theatre expert who came from the Moscow Art Theatre' (Mally 1990: 127) used the Proletkult's wide distributory facility to publish Stanislavsky's ideas before they were formally allowed out. Cf. Benedetti 1990: 248–249.

3 Cf. George (1989); Vanden Heuvel (1993); Nellhaus (1993); Grant (1993); Hancock (1995).

4 David E. George (1989) and William W. Demastes (1994), for example.

1 A System for the world?

1 For a full analysis of the history around these textual difficulties, see Benedetti 1990b and Carnicke 1984, 1993 and 1998. A very helpful glossary of established Stanislavskian terminology, complete with Russian terms, is included in the latter publication (168–182).

2 Aristotle believed that there were two different kinds of motion, Natural (i.e. vertical motion) and Unnatural (i.e. horizontal motion). Natural motion occurred when the object moved towards its natural place – a stone towards earth, steam rising to reach fire.

3 Cf. Hall 1981: 120: 'The *Principles* was a triumph of fantastic imagination which happens, unfortunately, never once to have hit upon a correct explanation.'

4 Consider Galileo's famous statement in *The Assayer* (1623): 'Philosophy is written in this grand book, the universe, which stands continually open to our gaze. But the book cannot be understood unless one learns to comprehend the language and read the letters in which it is composed. It is written in the language of mathematics.' Cf. Galileo 1957: 237–238.

5 Cf. Roach 1993: 62–63 for additional commentary on this relationship.

6 By Fritjof Capra, for example. Cf. Capra 1996: 38.

7 For Descartes, the soul created an idea of the emotion, be it wonder, love, hatred

desire, joy or sadness — the six primary passions — 'triggering the release of animal spirits to the appropriate organs'. Cf. Roach 1993: 64. Thus, feelings emerge from the soul (or cause) and are then manifest in bodily expression (effect). Emotions, then, are at the interface between ghost and machine.

8 From the BBC programme *Whiteheat*, 19 September 1994.

9 The introduction of Fordist/Taylorist principles in England, for example, was met with deep distrust for 'what appeared to be an American willingness to put greed and a lust for power before any humane values'. Cf. Pursell 1994: 107.

10 *Naucnaja organizacija truda* or Scientific Organisation of Work.

11 In fact his preferences may have lain with America more than with his own Soviet Union. Advocating 'Soviet Americanism', he went as far as to say that he wanted to see Russia transformed in to a 'new flowering America'. Cf. Bailes 1977: 385.

12 Gilbreth's investigations into photography as a tool for motion study began around 1912 and ended when he died in 1924. Gastev's researches began in 1911 and his institute was founded in 1920, receiving national status a year later and being named the Central Institute of Labour (CIT).

13 Toporkov's work is translated by Christine Edwards and is available under the title *Stanislavsky in Rehearsal* (1979). Novitskaya's work is interpreted, rather than translated, by Benedetti, forming the main body of *Stanislavsky and the Actor* (1998) and Maria Knebel's work with Stanislavsky is recorded by Sharon Carnicke in both her *Stanislavsky in Focus* (1998) and 'Stanislavsky's System', in Hodge (2000). Knebel's contribution also forms part of Bella Merlin's investigation (2003).

14 Cf. Crohn-Schmitt 1990: 97 and 148 (n. 23).

15 NATD Conference 'Signs, Gestes and Affects: Rationality and Feeling in the Work of Stanislavsky and Brecht', Sheffield Centre, Sheffield, 21 January 1995. At the time of writing, Benedetti's 'new' translations have still not been released.

16 From my notebook of the masterclass: 'Stanislavsky's Method of Physical Actions', at the Nikitska Gate Theatre, 13 June 1994.

17 Carnicke makes this fusion more explicit in her chapter on active analysis: 'Each camp's set of *"tasks"* were chosen to *conflict* with those of the other camp' (my emphasis). Cf. Carnicke 1998: 160.

18 From my notebook of the masterclass: 'Stanislavsky's Method of Physical Actions', at the Nikitska Gate Theatre, 13 June 1994.

19 A term used by Benedetti in *Stanislavsky and the Actor* to mean 'the thoughts that are going through our minds while we are speaking dialogue, or listening to others'. Cf. Benedetti 1998: 153.

20 From my notebook of Rozofsky's Stanislavsky class at the Nikitska Gate Theatre, 9 June 1994.

21 The spine is the American term for the through-action of the play or the character, transmitted by Boleslavsky in the early 1920s. Cf. Carnicke 1998: 181. It is also a term used by the Stanislavsky-inspired British director Mike Alfreds: 'We are establishing the spine on which we will build the flesh and muscles and blood of the play.' Cf. Allen 2000: 197.

22 Indeed, questions were being asked of Gastev's version of Taylorism as early as 1924: Gastev's 'use of the stop watch as the sole means of determining work norms was an especially exploitative and uncritical application of Taylorism to Soviet industry', according to the Group of Communists headed by Pavel Kerzhentsev. Cf. Bailes 1977: 389.

23 This is not to say that before Stalin there was not the same repressive culture. Richard Pipes quotes one of Lenin's commissars from 1920 using revealing language in the current context: 'Terror is a *system* . . . a legalised plan of the regime

for the purpose of mass intimidation, mass compulsion, mass extermination.' Cf. Pipes 1990: 793.

24 Joravsky calls this synthesis 'a tragicomic scandal' so forced as to be synthetic only in the sense of 'phony' [*sic*]. Cf. Joravsky 1978: 128.

25 Cf. Carnicke 1998: 153. 'That his system be perceived as universally applicable became an obsession in his last four years.'

2 The theatricality reflex

1 Meyerhold was one of only five people who attended (out of a possible one hundred and twenty). He was accompanied by Alexandr Blok and Vladimir Mayakovsky. Cf. Braun 1995: 152–153.

2 The high point of the science of 'psychotechnics' may be measured by Moscow's hosting of the Seventh International Psychotechnical Congress in September 1931. By the mid-1930s, psychotechnics was seen as having bourgeois tendencies and along with Gastev's biomechanics was abolished from all scientific journals. Cf. Joravsky 1978: 272, n. 50. Interestingly, this fall from grace for psychotechnics did not deter Stanislavsky from using the associated term psycho-technique in relation to his System as late as 1938.

3 See also Misler (1991).

4 GITIS was the State Institute of Theatre Art and GVYRM was the State Higher Director's Workshop. For a fuller discussion of Meyerhold's model of the theatre laboratory see Chapter 5.

5 From my own log of Alexei Levinsky's Cardiff workshop: Friday, 20 October 1995.

6 Ivan Sechenov is often described as the father of Russian physiology and was a great influence on Pavlov. Some sixty years before Pavlov's *Conditioned Reflexes*, Sechenov was arguing that psychical processes in humans and animals were only to be understood as responses to external stimuli and that physiology, not psychology, was the true science to examine human behaviour.

7 **tropism**: the response of an organism, esp. a plant, to an external stimulus by growth in a direction determined by the stimulus.
   taxis: the movement of a cell or organism in a particular direction in response to an external stimulus (*Collins English Dictionary*).

8 Talia Theatre Co., based in Manchester, has been collaborating with Bogdanov for a number of years, most recently (2004) touring a production of Chekhov's vaudevilles directed by Bogdanov. Cf. www.taliatheatre.com.

9 Officially, Meyerhold's work began to be rehabilitated in 1955 but Levinsky talked to me of a climate of secrecy surrounding the training he had as late as 1975. For details of the slow release of his ideas in print see Leach 1989: 173–174.

10 Strasberg, Clurman and Martin's responses are collated in the Documents' chapter of Law and Gordon (1996). For Carter's, van Gyseghem's, Macleod's and Houghton's descriptions of Meyerhold and his work see *The New Spirit in the Russian Theatre: 1917–1928* (1929), *Theatre in Soviet Russia* (1943), *The New Soviet Theatre* (3rd impression 1945) and *Moscow Rehearsals* (1938) respectively.

11 The observations that follow come in part from my work in two week-long masterclasses: with Levinsky 14–22 October 1995 (Centre for Performance Research) and with Bogdanov 30 August–4 September 1998 (International Workshop Festival), both of which have been documented by Peter Hulton's Arts Archive in Exeter.

12 Cf. Gordon (1995: 94–95).

13 Levinsky describes this as an abstract gesture but I have called it ducking here to evoke the overall pattern of actions.

14 Levinsky's interpreter for the Arts Archive videos, Rebecca Edgington, uses the term 'refusal' (*otkaz*) in the breakdown of the étude Throwing the Stone. In this instance, however, it is to describe a whole action within the étude, thus the Refusal (before the throw) is made up of an *otkaz*, *posil'* and *tochka*, or an *otkaz* within an *otkaz*. It is clear how confusions can occur! Cf. Levinsky 1997.

15 Meyerhold renamed Griboedov's play, whose original title was *Woe from Wit*.

16 For the full list see Kleberg in Russell and Barratt 1990: 191, n. 20. See also Stourac and McCreery 1986: 20, for an alternative translation.

17 Foregger, a colleague of Meyerhold's at GITIS, devised his own movement training called TePhyTrenage, and, following Alexei Gastev's lead, created what Fulop-Miller colourfully calls 'machine dances' in which 'priests and priestesses' danced to the 'New God of the Machine', transforming the discipline of dance 'into a mere expression of the mechanical'. Cf. Fulop-Miller 1927: 182.

3 The System, psychology and the US

1 Orlenev was, however, aware of Stanislavsky's work. Laurence Senelick records his 'admiration of Stanislavsky's taste and ideals' in his article 'The American Tour of Orlenev and Nazimova, 1905–1906'. Cf. Senelick 1992: 9.

2 This is partly due to the fact that Nazimova only played extra roles at the MAT but some critics have pointed to contemporary reports of her *insincerity* as an actress. Cf. Senelick 1992: 15, n. 21.

3 The classes with the established actors would not have included psycho-technique exercises at this time as these were only being performed by Stanislavsky – in the first instance on himself.

4 Cf. Allen 1999: 73: 'Stanislavsky's notion of the subconscious had nothing to do with Freud ... he argued that he was using terms such as "subconscious" and "intuition" in their "simplest, everyday connotation" and not in any philosophical or psychoanalytical sense.'

5 Vakhtangov defines his term thus:

> in the theater there should be neither naturalism nor realism, but fantastic realism. Rightly found theatrical methods impart genuine life upon the stage. The methods can be learned, but the form must be created. It has to be convinced by one's fantasy. That is why I call it fantastic realism.

For a full discussion, cf. Cole and Chinoy 1970: 185–191.

6 For details, cf. Roberts 1981: 97–109.

7 Roberts argues the same from a theatrical perspective:

> One consequence of Boleslavsky's gradual change of emphasis in the system was perhaps inevitable: among his students there sprang up two schools of thought. The majority of the Lab-trained actors embraced dramatic action as the fundamental core of the system as Boleslavsky and Ouspenskaya presented it, while a minority endorsed emotional memory as the key to the actor's art.

Cf. Roberts 1981: 171.

8 Freud arrived in America on 6 September 1909 whilst Boleslavsky opened in *A Month in the Country* on 9 December 1909.

9 Cf. Hale, 1971: 455: 'By 1917 Freud's theories had achieved perhaps a wider currency amongst physicians in America than those in any other country. See also his second volume on Freud, specifically Chapter 4, 'Culture and Rebellion': 'both groups [the intellectuals and the psychoanalysts] shared a deep faith in science, freed from its "narrow" 19th century limitations. They believed Freud had created a science of the emotions, close to the realities of daily life.' Cf. Hale 1995: 59.

10 O'Neill himself had psychoanalysis (in 1927). Cf. Bigsby 1982: 111: 'The vogue for Freudian theories in the Greenwich Village of the post-war period [i.e. after 1918] is hard to imagine today.'

11 Carl Lange (1834–1900) came to an almost identical theory of emotion entirely separately from James, thus the hybrid term 'James–Lange' indicates a theoretical rather than a professional affinity.

12 Cf. Gregory 1987: 808:

> Give me a dozen healthy infants ... and my own specified world to bring them up and I'll guarantee to take any one at random and train him to become any type of specialist I might select – doctor, lawyer, artist, merchant-chief and yes, even beggar-man and thief.

13 *The Ego and the Id* was translated into English four years later in 1927.

14 Within the membership of the Group Theatre, discussions of the Method have been published by Robert Lewis, *Method – or Madness* (1960); Harold Clurman, *The Fervent Years* (1957/1983); and Cheryl Crawford, *One Naked Individual: My Fifty Years in the Theatre* (1977).

15 By a freak coincidence these two quotations are on the same pages too!

16 Had Strasberg gone directly to the primary source of Stanislavsky himself, he would have realised that practical exercises for the exploration of emission and absorption abound in *An Actor Prepares*, under the heading Communion (1980a: 193–222).

17 Magarshack's book also collates a student's notes on Stanislavsky's lectures to the Moscow Bolshoi Theatre under the title *The System and Methods of Creative Art*.

18 The lectures in *On the Art of the Stage* were delivered by Stanislavsky between 1918 and 1922. *My Life in Art* was first published in 1924.

19 Later, Strasberg does acknowledge the right side of Stanislavsky's system, referring to the literal translation 'An Actor's Work on Himself'. He follows Magarshack, though, in suggesting that this book 'is better known in English as *An Actor Prepares*' (1988: 83) and there is no mention of the principles described in *Building a Character* – tempo-rhythm, plasticity of motion, diction and singing, for example.

20 Strasberg's notebooks cited in the book conflict with this testimony and indicate a study period of one year from 13 January 1924 to 30 January 1925. Cf. Strasberg 1988: 65.

21 The story is told in many sources on Strasberg. Here the source is Group Theatre actress Phoebe Brand, interviewed for the BBC programme *Reputations: Lee Strasberg: Method Man*, 1997.

22 This psychological perspective on relaxation is also reflected in the writing of Donald Freed, specifically in *Freud and Stanislavsky* (1981). There is not space within this chapter to deal fully with the problems of this approach but a sample of Freed on relaxation will exemplify:

> Inhibition is our great enemy. That's the negative of what we know in the Stanislavsky system as relaxation. Stanislavsky was virtually obsessed with relaxation. He didn't mean merely physical relaxation either. Unless you are relaxed, you cannot recreate; but you cannot be relaxed if you are inhibited. In this company, the accent has shifted ... Instead of just working for relaxation we are working against inhibition. We know more; and our frame of reference is such that the word 'inhibition' means more to us, is more understandable, than the word 'relaxation'.
>
> (88–89)

Freed's belief in the power of Freudian terminology is such that a complex psycho-sexual term is substituted for an uncomplicated term in the interest of 'clarity'.

23 In the light of this more explicit Freudian line from Strasberg, it is enlightening to note that he often asked his actors to seek psychoanalytical help to support the work he was doing with them. Most famously this is the approach he took with Marilyn Monroe, securing an analyst to work with his protégé who was practising in the same apartment block. Specialist psychoanalysis was thus viewed by Strasberg as a significant complement to his own pseudo-psychoanalysis. Cf. *Reputations* 1997 and Leaming 1998: 161.
24 From *Reputations* 1997.
25 From *Reputations* 1997.
26 Durham trained with Strasberg between 1954 and the late 1960s and has remained a member of the Actors Studio since.
27 Letter to the author, 9 December 1996.
28 Letter to the author, 9 December 1996.
29 The prompt copy of Stanislavsky's production, as interpreted by M Stroeva, is translated in Jackson 1967.
30 In addition to the founding Group Theatre members, Clurman, Adler and Stras-berg, Meisner does admit the influence of Michael Chekhov, who, he states, 'made me realize that truth, as in naturalism, was far from the whole truth'. Cf. Meisner and Longwell 1987: 10.
31 The Repetition Exercise forms the centrepiece of Scott Williams's workshop on Meisner, documented by Arts Archives. Williams was Meisner's assistant for many years and offers a good practical guide to the basics of the technique. Interestingly, he leaves out Boleslavsky from his introduction on the roots of the Method in America. Cf. Williams 2000.

4 A delicate empiricism

1 The book is housed in the Dartington Hall Archive, Dartington, Devon.
2 Compare Friedrich's *Wanderer above the Sea of Fog* (1818) with Goethe's statement of the solitary man, astride a rock 'enclasped' by nature.
3 Cf. Grotowski 1975: 153: 'Do not think of the vocal instrument itself, do not think of the words, but react – react with the body.'
4 Theosophy's founder Helena Blavatsky (1831–1891) influenced many artists in the twentieth century including Wassily Kandinsky and W.B. Yeats. Cf. Kandinsky 1977: 13 and Martin 1989: 81. Steiner, having joined the theosophists in 1902, split with them in 1913 to form the Anthroposophical Society.
5 I am indebted to Andrei Kirillov for providing this detail of Chekhov's biography.
6 Cf. Dartington Archive, Box 1, File E.
7 Young's own account does seem to suggest that Chekhov met with Steiner around 1934: 'Shortly before Beatrice burst in on [Chekhov's] dressing room [in 1934] he had asked Steiner whether he should give up the theatre and become a monk.' Given that Steiner died in 1925, this is clearly impossible. Cf. Young, 1982: 231.
8 Boxes IX and X.
9 The autobiography was translated by the maths teacher at Dartington at the time, Boris Uvarov. Chekhov obviously brought the Russian version with him to Dartington. Whilst at the time of writing it remains unpublished in English there are plans for it to be published in the near future, by Routledge. Cf. Dartington Archive: Box IV, File A.
10 Recently discovered in the archive and housed in Box T Estate 7a, folder D2, there is correspondence and a full Estimate for the work (dated September 1935, Professor Walter Gropius, Dr Ing, Adams, Thompson and Fry, Architects, 58,

Victoria Street) for the Proposed Additions to the Rear Stage of the Theatre at Dartington Hall. I am very grateful to Angie St John Palmer for this information.

11 Dartington Archive, 24 March 1937.

12 Martin was appointed in 1934 and immediately asked the question: 'Is the Arts Department to be primarily a professional undertaking . . . or primarily amateur and dilettante?' (Young 1982: 227). With Jooss, Laban and Chekhov all on board, the answer was clear.

13 Cf. Box I, Dartington Archive.

14 Box I, File C, Dartington Archive.

15 Meyer, born in 1896, hardly fits into the German Romantic period but, as an art historian, became associated with the movement of Romanticism. Cf. Chekhov 1991: 8.

16 Merlin was citing from materials held in the Dartington Archive.

17 Mala Powers is an actress and teacher who worked with Chekhov in America for the last years of his life and who continues to teach his technique today. She is also an Anthroposophist.

18 Zinder cites a host of names in his recent book including Peter Frye, Joe Chaikin, Bruce Meyers, Eugenio Barba and Odin Theatre as well as an international 'cabal' of Chekhov teachers amongst whom are listed Joanna Merlin, Jack Colvin, Mala Powers, Andrei Kirillov, Sarah Kane and Graham Dixon. Cf. Zinder 2002: 25–26.

19 The workshop materials and comments cited in this chapter are taken from my records of a Centre for Performance Research workshop with David Zinder in February 1999 in Aberystwyth.

20 Chekhov echoes this trinity in *On the Technique of Acting*, offering his own brief summary of Steiner's threefold human being: the head is the realm of thoughts and ideas (spirit), the chest the area of feelings (the inner life) and the legs the domain of the will. Cf. Chekhov 1991: 52–53.

21 Mala Powers cites Chekhov's nervous lighting of his pipe in Hitchcock's *Spellbound* (1945) as an exemplary 'little piece of art', a tiny moment of artistic dexterity revealing another side of his character and with a clear sense of the whole. Cf. Chekhov 1991: 166.

22 Chekhov himself lists twenty gestures and sixteen qualities in *On the Technique of Acting*. Cf. Chekhov 1991: 41. Rather like the biomechanical études being whittled down to five essential études, Chekhov's archetypal gestures are now, it seems, reduced to a minimum.

23 Chekhov's Qualities of Action and his notion of Atmosphere both point to the question of distance between the actor and his/her emotions. For a detailed analysis of how this is true for the latter, see Pitches and Shrubsall, 1999.

24 This idea has resonances with the practice of Rudolph Laban, of course and the two were at Dartington at the same time. But it also points to the Eurythmic principle of 'taking the gesture back into the word' (Chamberlain 2000: 94) – a fascinating fusion, one might say, of Rudolph Laban and Rudolf Steiner.

25 In a telephone interview, William Elmhirst told me that his mother, Dorothy, was so taken with Chekhov – she attended all his classes – that she may well have embraced anthroposophy were it not for Leonard's scepticism (14 April 1999).

26 Leach cites Talma in his article on Meyerhold and Chekhov as an exemplar of the Romantic school where the actor 'enters deeply into the emotions' and yields 'himself to the spontaneous flashes of his sensibility' (1997: 68). Talma himself, though, provides a counterpoint to this view. He does admit to rekindling the feelings of historical characters 'which I force into myself and feel in my very bowels' but later in the same passage acknowledges a level of critical reflection: 'I take stock of my acting almost as I play.' Cf. Collins 1964: 282.

5 The laboratory as sanctuary

1 I have kept the term 'ludo' when it reflects Vasiliev's particular use of the word as in 'ludo system' and in verbatim quotations. At other times, for grammatical sense I have used the adjective 'ludic', a word which Vasiliev's interpreter, Martin Dewhirst, did not use.

2 At the invitation of the IWF, Vasiliev has run masterclasses on three occasions in this country: in 1991 in London, in 1996 in Glasgow and in 1999 in London again.

3 Benedetti lists the studio's genesis in his biography of Stanislavsky. Cf. Benedetti 1990a: 207–208.

4 They are now published in Benedetti's translation/adaptation of Irina Novit-skaya's eye-witness account of the sessions entitled *Stanislavsky and the Actor* (1998).

5 As Roberts points out, though, Boleslavsky did not wholly reject the commercial stage. He was committed to selling the fruits of his experiments to commercial producers. Cf. Roberts 1981: 114.

6 All references to Vasiliev's work are to unpublished transcripts of his workshops or speeches. Roman numerals denote the section (I–V) of the 1996 transcript followed by the page number within the section. I am indebted to Dick McCaw the ex-artistic director of the International Workshop Festival for supplementing my own notes of the 1996 workshop with a written transcript of Vasiliev's words.

7 Also translated as *The Gentle Spirit*. *The Meek One*, however, captures the biblical reference: 'Blessed are the Meek', St Matthew Ch. 5, V. 3.

8 Socrates is credited with developing a method of examination, based on dialectic exchange between people, designed to pursue truth through detailed analysis.

9 Having been raised in a strictly Orthodox household, Dostoyevsky slowly rejected religion under the influence of V.I. Belinsky, only to return to it later in life. Irrespective of these fluctuations of faith, he nevertheless 'remained devoted to the figure of Christ' throughout his career. Cf. Gibson 1973: 12.

10 In theory, a third possibility would be possible – a physical reading of the text – but as the ensuing discussion will reveal, Vasiliev's practice in Glasgow simply did not embrace such a material level of investigation.

11 That Vasiliev doesn't cite Brecht amongst these texts is perhaps as much to retain the theoretical ground for himself as it is to claim a different purpose.

12 The unreferenced quotes and the following diagrams are all taken from my note-book of the workshop in 1996.

13 In the terminological minefield of Stanislavsky translation Events (sometimes known as Episodes) are large bits of the play and Facts small bits of the play as it is broken down for analysis, (although he did use the word Event for both large and small at times!) By Sub-events Vasiliev may mean Facts which in the Stanislavsky studio involve separate Actions for the actor to carry out, or the larger Event/Episode which has a Task for the actor to complete. Cf. Benedetti 1998: 150–151.

14 Koch trained extensively in Germany in *Tanztheater* before a year's postgraduate work at the Laban Centre in London. Following further Grotowski-based training, she saw Vasiliev's *Cerceau* at the Riverside in 1987 and resolved to work with him. She worked with Vasiliev at first in summer schools between 1990 and 1992 and then for two years from 1994–1996 at his School of Dramatic Art in Moscow. She is now a freelance choreographer and has taught at Coventry University Performing Arts department.

15 Personal interview, 31 May 2001.

16 Although it is important to note that the psychological plane does not disappear entirely:

> The action develops along two planes: the horizontal and the vertical . . . So we are working with both of them . . . We have to understand it [i.e. the Pawnbroker's monologue] in its horizontal aspect and in its vertical aspect. We saw that at one and the same time the hero experien[ces] different emotions: fear in his heart, that's a psychological factor, and rapture in his soul, that's a conceptual factor.

Cf. Vasiliev 1996: III, 14.

17 Cf. Freedman on the ludic vocal technique: 'Actors may dip into a whisper . . . or rise into a hysterical guttural yell. But in all cases, the basic rhythm remained the same' (1997: 133).

18 This throne is occupied by God (*Nous*) who, unlike the fluid perceptions of humankind, is immutable. Whilst this God is part of a pantheistic not monotheistic structure of belief, Plato does imagine Him as the Sun and, as the One, thus placing him at the pinnacle of his philosophical hierarchy.

19 For the genesis of the Stanislavsky Drama Theatre, cf. Marshall 1977: 185.

20 Details of these productions may be found in Smeliansky 1999: 188–192 and Freedman 1997: 132.

21 Personal Interview, 31 May 2001.

22 There are signs that this is changing. John Freedman, in his second volume of Moscow theatre reviews (1998), suggests that Vasiliev's *Lamentations of Jeremiah* was a 'coming-out for the theatre and the director who had become best known in Russia for being inaccessible'. Cf. Freedman 1998: xvi. In this decade there have been performances of Pushkin's *Mozart and Salieri* (2000) and Heiner Muller's *Medea Material* (2001) in the main theatre and several laboratory presentations. In his *Moscow Times* review of the former piece, Freedman admits that Vasiliev's predilection for seclusion may be changing: '*Mozart and Salieri* is the most recent and . . . the most fully realized of Vasilyev's experiments in recreating the art of theater . . . Vasilyev in the 1990s basically retreated into the shadows of his laboratory at the School of Dramatic Art. He allowed only limited public access to what he was doing; he lately has softened that policy.' Cf. *Moscow Times*, 10 March 2000.

Epilogue: genetic modification and the backbone of tradition

1 Ginkas (1941–) met his wife, Geta Yanovskaya (another scientist turned theatre director), at the Leningrad Institute in 1962 and graduated from the course in directing in 1967.

2 Lev Dodin, in an interview with Robin Thornber, declared in similar terms to Ginkas: 'One of my teachers was directly connected with Stanislavsky and another with Meyerhold. Probably, therefore, I absorbed from the milk of my theatre-parents this idea that theatre is not only an important part of life, but life itself.' Cf. Delgado and Heritage 1996: 72.

Bibliography

Adler, Stella (1999) *On Ibsen, Strindberg and Chekhov*, ed. Barry Paris, New York: Alfred A. Knopf.

Allen, David (1999) *Stanislavski for Beginners*, London: Writers and Readers Ltd.

—— (2000) *Performing Chekhov*, London: Routledge.

Aristotle (1961) *Physics*, trans. Richard Hope, Lincoln: University of Nebraska Press.

—— (1999) *Poetics*, trans. Kenneth McLeish, London: Nick Hern Books.

Babkin, B.P. (1949) *Pavlov: a Biography*, Chicago: University of Chicago Press.

Bailes, Kendall E. (1977) 'Alexei Gastev and the Soviet Controversy over Taylorism, 1918–1924', *Soviet Studies*, Vol. XXIX, No. 3, July, 373–394.

Baldwin, Jane (1995) 'Meyerhold's Theatrical Biomechanics: An Acting Technique for Today', *Theatre Topics*, Vol. 5, No. 2, 181–201.

Bann, Stephen (ed.) (1974) *The Tradition of Constructivism*, New York: DaCapo.

Barba, Eugenio and Savarese, Nicola (1991) *A Dictionary of Theatre Anthropology: The Secret Art of the Performer*, trans. Richard Fowler, London: Routledge.

—— and Raüke, Ralf (1995) *Meyerhold's Throwing the Stone*, Exeter: Arts Documentation Unit (Video).

Bekhterev, Vladimir Michailovitch (1933) *General Principles of Human Reflexology*, trans. Emma and William Murphy, London: Jarrolds.

Bell, Arthur, E. (1961) *Newtonian Science*, London: Edward Arnold.

Benedetti, Jean (1989) *Stanislavski: An Introduction*, London: Methuen.

—— (1990a) *Stanislavski: A Biography*, London: Methuen.

—— (1990b) 'A History of Stanislavski in Translation', *New Theatre Quarterly*, Vol. VI, No. 23, August, 266–278.

—— (ed.) (1991) *The Moscow Art Theatre Letters*, London: Methuen.

—— (1998) *Stanislavski and the Actor*, London: Methuen.

Bentley, Eric (ed.) (1976) *The Theory of the Modern Stage*, London: Penguin.

Bigsby, C.W.E. (1982) *A Critical Introduction to Twentieth Century American Drama, Volume One, 1900–1940*, Cambridge: Cambridge University Press.

Black, Lendley C. (1987) *Michael Chekhov as Actor, Teacher and Director*, Michigan: U.M.I. Research Press.

Bogdanov, Gennadi (1999) *Meyerhold's Biomechanics and Rhythm* (6 volumes), Exeter: Arts Documentation Unit (Video).

Boleslavsky, Richard (1949) *Acting: The First Six Lessons*, New York: Theatre Arts Books.

Bonham-Carter, Victor (1970) *Dartington Hall 1925–1957*, Dulverton: The Exmoor Press.

Bortoft, Henri (1996) *The Wholeness of Nature: Goethe's Way of Science*, Edinburgh: Floris Books.

Bradbury Malcolm and McFarlane, James (1991) *Modernism*, London: Penguin.

Braun, Edward (1995) *A Revolution in Theatre*, London: Methuen.

Bridgemont, Peter (1992) *Liberation of the Actor*, London: Temple Lodge.

Caillois, Roger (1962) *Man, Play and Games*, trans. Meyer Barash, London: Thames and Hudson.

Capra, Fritjof, (1983) *The Turning Point*, London: Flamingo.

—— (1996) *The Web of Life*, London: HarperCollins.

Carnicke, Sharon Marie (1984) 'An Actor Prepares/Rabota aktera nad soboi, Chast' I: A Comparison of the English with the Russian Stanislavsky', in *Theater Journal*, December, 481–494.

—— (1993) 'Stanislavsky Uncensored and Unabridged', in *The Drama Review*, T137, 22–37.

—— (1998) *Stanislavsky in Focus*, London: Harwood Academic.

—— (2000) 'Stanislavsky's System: Pathways for the Actor', in *Twentieth Century Actor Training*, ed. Alison Hodge, London: Routledge.

Carter, Huntly (1929) *The New Spirit in the Russian Theatre 1917–1928*, New York: Brentano's Ltd.

Chamberlain, Franc (2000) 'Michael Chekhov on the Technique of Acting: Was Don Quixote True to Life?', in *Twentieth Century Actor Training*, ed. Alison Hodge, London: Routledge.

—— (2004) *Michael Chekhov*, London: Routledge.

Chekhov, Anton (1980) *Five Plays*, trans. Ronald Hingley, Oxford: Oxford University Press.

—— (1994) *Uncle Vanya*, in *The Plays of Chekhov*, Moscow: Nikitska Gate Workshop Text.

Chekhov, Michael (1936a) *The Path of the Actor*, trans. Boris Uvarov, Dartington: Dartington Hall Archive.

—— (1936b) *Theatre School Policy*, Dartington: Dartington Hall Archive.

—— (1937) *Colour and Light: Mr Chekhov's Criticism of March 15th*, Dartington: Dartington Hall Archive.

—— (1942) *To the Actor: Some New Ideas about Acting (with Exercises)*, Dartington: Dartington Hall Archive.

—— (1953) *To the Actor: On the Technique of Acting*, London: Harper and Row.

—— (1985) *Lessons to the Professional Actor*, New York: Performing Arts Journal Publications.

—— (1991) *On the Technique of Acting*, London: HarperPerennial.

—— (1992) *On the Theatre and the Art of Acting: A Guide to Discovery with Exercises*, ed. Mala Powers, New York: Applause.

—— (2002) *To the Actor on the Technique of Acting*, London, Routledge.

Childs, Gilbert (1995) *Rudolph Steiner: His Life and Work*, Edinburgh: Floris Books.

Clurman, Harold (1983) *The Fervent Years: The Group Theatre and the Thirties*, New York: Da Capo.

Cole, Toby (ed.) (1955) *Acting*, New York: Crown Publishers.

—— (1961) *Playwrights on Playwriting*, New York: Hill and Wang.

—— (1970) *Actors on Acting*, New York: Crown Publishers.

—— and Chinoy, Helen Krich (1970) *Directors on Directing: The Emergence of the Modern Theatre*, London: Peter Owen.

Collins, Herbert F. (1964) *Talma*, London: Faber and Faber.

Crawford, Cheryl (1977) *One Naked Individual: My Fifty Years in the Theatre*, New York: Bobbs-Merrill.

Crohn-Schmitt, Natalie (1986) 'Stanislavski, Creativity and the Unconscious', *New Theatre Quarterly*, Vol. II, No. 8, November, 345–351.

—— (1990) *Actors and Onlookers: Theatre and Twentieth Century Views of Nature*, Illinois: Northwestern University Press.

Day, Aidan (1996) *Romanticism*, London: Routledge.

Delgado, Maria and Heritage, Paul (eds) (1996) *In Contact with the Gods: Director's Talk Theatre*, Manchester: Manchester University Press.

Demastes, William W. (1994) 'Re-inspecting the Crack in the Chimney: Chaos Theory from Ibsen to Stoppard', *New Theatre Quarterly*, Vol. X, No. 39, 242–254.

Descartes, René (1968) *Discourse on Method and the Meditations*, trans. F.E. Sutcliffe, London: Penguin.

Dostyoyevsky, Fyodor (1955) *The Idiot*, trans. David Magarshack, London: Penguin.

—— (1995) *A Gentle Creature*, trans. Alan Myers, Oxford: Oxford University Press.

—— (1996) *The Gentle Spirit*, trans. David McDuff, London: Penguin.

Drama Review, The (1983) Vol. 27, No. 3, Fall (Michael Chekhov Edition).

du Prey, Deirdre Hurst (1979) 'The Training Sessions of Michael Chekhov', in *Dartington Theatre Papers*, Third Series, 1979/80, No. 9, Totnes: Department of Theatre, Dartington College of Arts.

Eaton, Katherine Bliss (1985) *The Theatre of Meyerhold and Brecht*, Connecticut: Greenwood Press.

Edwards, Christine (1965) *The Stanislavsky Heritage*, London: Peter Owen.

Eisenstein, Sergei (1988) *Writings: Vol. 1, 1922–1934*, trans. and ed. Richard Taylor, London: British Film Institute.

Fergusson, Francis (1949) *The Idea of a Theater*, Garden City: Double Day and Co.

Fink, Karl J. (1991) *Goethe's History of Science*, Cambridge: Cambridge University Press.

Fitzpatrick, Sheila (1970) *The Commissariat of the Enlightenment: Soviet Organization of Education and the Arts under Lunacharsky*, Cambridge: Cambridge University Press.

—— (1982) *The Russian Revolution 1917–1932*, Oxford: Oxford University Press.

—— (1992) *The Cultural Front: Power and Culture in Revolutionary Russia*, Ithaca: Cornell University Press.

Ford, Henry (1929) *My Philosophy of Industry*, New York: Coward-McCann.

Freed, Donald (1981) *Freud and Stanislavsky*, Michigan: Ann Arbor.

Freedman, John (1993) 'A Glimpse into Anatoly Vasilyev's School of Dramatic Art', in *Slavic and East European Performance*, Vol. 13, No. 2, Summer, 19–22.

—— (1997) *Moscow Performances: The New Russian Theatre 1991–1996*, London: Harwood Academic Publishers.

—— (1998) *Moscow Performances II: The 1996–7 Season*, London: Harwood Academic Publishers.

—— (2000) 'The Changing Space of Russian Theatre', in *Theatre Forum*, No. 17, Summer/Fall, 3–11.

Freud, Sigmund (1985) *Art and Literature*, trans. James Strachey, London: Penguin.

—— (1986) *The Essentials of Psychoanalysis*, trans. James Strachey, London: Penguin.

—— (1995) *Five Lectures on Psychoanalysis*, London: Penguin.

Frome, Shelley (2001) *The Actors Studio: A History*, Jefferson: McFarland.

Fulop-Miller, René (1927) *The Mind and Face of Bolshevism*, trans. F.S. Flint and D.F. Tait, London: G.P. Putnam's Sons.

Galileo (1957) *Discoveries and Opinions of Galileo*, trans. Stillman Drake, New York: Double Day.

Gash, Anthony (2000) 'Plato's Theatre of the Mind', in *Theatre Theories from Plato to Virtual Reality*, ed. Anthony Frost, Norwich: Pen and Inc.

George, David E.R. (1989) 'Quantum Theatre – Potential Theatre: a New Paradigm?', *New Theatre Quarterly*, Vol. V, No. 18, 171–179.

Gibson, A. Boyce (1973) *The Religion of Dostoevsky*, Philadelphia: Westminster Press.

Ginkas, Kama (1998) 'Russian Theatre is not a Time Killer: John Freedman Interviews Kama Ginkas', *Theatre Forum* No. 12, Winter/Spring, 4–13.

Gladkov, Aleksandr (1997) *Meyerhold Speaks, Meyerhold Rehearses*, trans. Alma Law, London: Harwood Academic Publishers.

Goethe, Johann Wolfgang (1946) *Goethe's Botany: The Metamorphosis of Plants and Tobler's Ode to Nature*, trans. Agnes Arber, Chronica Botanica, Vol. 10, No. 2, 63–126.

—— (1967) *Theory of Colours*, trans. Charles Eastlake, London: Frank Cass and Co.

—— (1996) *Goethe on Science*, ed. Jeremy Naydler, Edinburgh: Floris Books.

Gogol, Nikolai (1997) *The Government Inspector*, trans. Steven Mulrine, London: Nick Hern Books.

Gorchakov, Nikolai M. (1994) *Stanislavsky Directs*, trans. Miriam Goldina, New York: Limelight.

Gordon, Mel (1974) 'Meyerhold's Biomechanics', *The Drama Review*, Vol. 18, No. 3, 73–88.

—— (1984) 'Reconstructing the Russians', in *The Drama Review*, Vol. 28, No. 3, 11–16.

—— (1987) *The Stanislavsky Technique: Russia*, New York: Applause.

—— (1995) 'Meyerhold's Biomechanics', in *Acting (Re)Considered*, ed. Philip Zarrilli, London: Routledge.

Gottlieb, Vera (1984) *Chekhov in Performance in Russia and Soviet Russia*, Cambridge: Chadwyck Healey.

Grant, Gary (1993) 'Shifting the Paradigm: Shephard, Myth and the Transformation of Consciousness', *Modern Drama*, Vol. 36, 120–130.

Gray, Camilla (1986) *The Russian Experiment in Art*, London: Thames and Hudson.

Green, Michael (ed.) (1986) *Russian Symbolist Theatre*, Ann Arbor: Ardis.

Gregory, Richard (ed.) (1987) *The Oxford Companion to the Mind*, Oxford: Oxford University Press.

Gribbin, John (1984) *In Search of Schrödinger's Cat: Quantum Physics and Reality*, London: Wildwood House.

Grotowski, Jerzy (1975) *Towards a Poor Theatre*, London: Methuen.

Haber, Samuel (1964) *Efficiency and Uplift: Scientific Management in the Progressive Era*, Chicago: University of Chicago Press.

Hale, Nathan G. Jr. (1971) *Freud and the Americans, Volume 1: The Beginnings of Psychoanalysis in the United States 1876–1917*, Oxford: Oxford University Press.

—— (1995) *Freud and the Americans, Volume 2: The Rise and Crisis of Psychoanalysis in the United States*, Oxford: Oxford University Press.

Hall, A. Rupert (1981) *From Galileo to Newton*, New York: Dover.

Halliwell, Martin (1999) *Romantic Science and the Experience of the Self*, Aldershot: Ashgate.

Hammer, Mark (2000) 'The Stella Adler Conservatory', in *Method Acting Reconsidered: Theory, Practice, Future*, ed. David Krasner, London: Macmillan.

Hancock, Alan (1995) 'Chaos in Drama: Metaphors of Chaos Theory as a Way of Understanding Drama Process', *Drama*, Vol. 3, No. 3, Summer, 2–7.

Heisenberg, Werner (1958) *Physics and Philosophy*, London: George Allen and Unwin Ltd.

Hirsch, Foster (1984) *A Method to their Madness: the History of the Actors Studio*, New York: Da Capo.

Hodge, Alison (ed.) (2000) *Twentieth Century Actor Training*, London: Routledge.

Honderich, Ted (ed.) (1995) *The Oxford Companion to Philosophy*, Oxford: Oxford University Press.

Hoover, Marjorie L. (1974) *Meyerhold: the Art of Conscious Theater*, Amherst: University of Massachusetts Press.

Houghton, Norris (1975) *Moscow Rehearsals*, New York: Octagon Books.

Hoyningen-Huene, Paul (1993) *Reconstructing Scientific Revolutions: Thomas S. Kuhn's Philosophy of Science*, Chicago: University of Chicago Press.

Huizinga, Johan (1970) *Homo Ludens: A Study of the Play Element in Culture*, London: Maurice Temple Smith.

Jackson, Robert (ed.) (1967) *Chekhov: a Collection of Critical Essays*, Englewood Cliffs, NJ: Prentice-Hall.

James, William (1950) *The Principles of Psychology: Vol. II*, New York: Dover.

—— (1977) 'What is an Emotion?', *Dartington Theatre Papers*, First Series, 1977/78, No. 5, Totnes: Department of Theatre, Dartington College of Arts.

Johansson, Kurt (1983) *Aleksej Gastev: Proletarian Bard of the Machine Age*, Stockholm: Almqvist and Wiksell.

Johnstone, Keith (1981) *Impro*, London: Methuen.

Joravsky, David (1978) 'The Construction of the Stalinist Psyche', in *Cultural Revolution in Russia: 1928–1931*, ed. Sheila Fitzpatrick, Bloomington: Indiana University Press.

—— (1989) *Russian Psychology*, Oxford: Basil Blackwell.

Kandinsky, Wassily (1977) *Concerning the Spiritual in Art*, trans. M.T.H Sadler, New York: Dover.

Kleberg, Lars (1990) 'The Nature of the Soviet Audience: Theatrical Ideology and Audience Research in the 1920s', *Russian Theatre in the Age of Modernism*, eds Robert Russell and Andrew Barratt, London: Macmillan.

—— (1993) *Theatre as Action*, London: Macmillan.

Krasner, David (ed.) (2000a) *Method Acting Reconsidered: Theory, Practice, Future*, London: Macmillan.

—— (2000b) 'Strasberg, Adler and Meisner: Method Acting', in *Twentieth Century Actor Training*, ed. Alison Hodge, London: Routledge.

Kuhn, Thomas. S (1970) *The Structure of Scientific Revolutions: 2nd Ed*, Chicago: University of Chicago Press.

Law, Alma and Gordon, Mel (1996) *Meyerhold, Eisenstein and Biomechanics*, London: McFarland.

Lawton, Lancelot (1924) *The Russian Revolution*, London: Macmillan and Co.

Leach, Robert (1989) *Vsevolod Meyerhold*, Cambridge: Cambridge University Press.

—— (1994) *Revolutionary Theatre*, London: Routledge.

—— (1997) 'When he Touches Your Heart: The Revolutionary Theatre of Vsevolod Meyerhold and the Development of Michael Chekhov', *Contemporary Theatre Review*, Vol. 7, Part 1, 65–83.

Leach, Robert (2000) 'Meyerhold and Biomechanics', in *Twentieth Century Actor Training*, ed. Alison Hodge, London: Routledge.

—— and Borovsky, Victor (eds) (1999) *A History of Russian Theatre*, Cambridge: Cambridge University Press.

Leaming, Barbara (1998) *Marilyn Monroe*, London: Orion.

Leonard, Charles (1984) *Michael Chekhov's To the Director and Playwright*, New York: Limelight.

Levinsky, Alexei (1997) *Meyerhold's Biomechanics: A Workshop*, Exeter: Arts Documentation Unit (Video).

Lewis, Robert (1960) *Method – or Madness*, London: Heinemann.

Ling, Peter J. (1990) *America and the Automobile: Technology, Reform and Social Change, 1893–1923*, Manchester: Manchester University Press.

Loren, Graham (1993) *Science in Russia and the Soviet Union: A Short History*, Cambridge: Cambridge University Press.

Macleod, Joseph (1943) *The New Soviet Theatre*, London: George Allen and Unwin Ltd.

Magarshack, David (1967) *Stanislavsky on the Art of the Stage*, London: Faber.

—— (1986) *Stanislavsky: A Life*, London: Faber.

Mally, Lynn, (1990) *Culture of the Future: The Proletkult Movement in Revolutionary Russia*, Berkeley: University of California Press.

Marshall, Herbert (1977) *The Pictorial History of the Russian Theatre*, New York: Crown Publishers.

Martin, Stoddard (1989) *Orthodox Heresy*, London: Macmillan.

Mason, Felicity (1993) *The Training Sessions of Michael Chekhov*, Exeter: Arts Documentation Unit (Video).

Medvedev, Zhores A. (1978) *Soviet Science*, New York: W.W. Norton and Co.

Meisner, Sanford and Longwell, Dennis (1987) *On Acting*, New York: Vintage.

Merlin, Bella (2003) *Konstantin Stanislavsky*, London: Routledge.

Merlin, Joanna (2000) *Michael Chekhov's Psychological Gesture*, Exeter: Arts Documentation Unit (Video).

Meyer, Michael (1992) *Ibsen*, London: Cardinal.

Meyerhold, Vsevolod (1991) *Meyerhold on Theatre*, trans. Edward Braun, London: Methuen.

Misler, Nicoletta (1991) 'Designing Gestures in the Laboratory of Dance', *Theatre in Revolution: Russian Stage Design, 1913–1915*, ed. Nancy Van Norman Baer, London: Thames and Hudson, 157–158.

Murdoch, Iris (1977) *The Fire and the Sun: Why Plato Banished the Artists*, Oxford: Oxford University Press.

Naydler, Jeremy (ed.) (1996) *Goethe on Science*, Edinburgh: Floris Books.

Nellhaus, Tobin (1993) 'Science, History, Theatre: Theorizing in Two Alternatives to Positivism', *Theatre Journal*, Vol. 45, 505–527.

Newton, Isaac (1966) *Principia: Vols 1 and 2*, trans. Andrew Motte, revised by Florian Cajori, Berkeley and Los Angeles: University of California Press.

—— (1952) *Opticks*, New York: Dover.

Padegimas, Gytas (1994) *The Time is Not Out of Joint: On Certain Aspects of Michael Chekhov's Pedagogy*, unpublished article for Chekhov International Workshop, Emerson College, Sussex.

Pavlov, Ivan (1927) *Conditioned Reflexes: An Investigation of the Physiological Activity of the Cerebral Cortex*, trans. G.V. Anrep, New York: Dover Publications.

—— (1932) 'The Reply of a Physiologist to Psychologists', trans. Dr R.S. Lyman, in *The Psychological Review*, Vol. 39, No. 2, March, 91–127.

—— (1955) *Selected Works*, trans. S. Belsky, Moscow: Foreign Languages Publishing House.

Picon-Vallin, Béatrice (1990) *Meyerhold: Les Voies de la Création Théâtrale*, Vol. 17, Paris: Centre National de la Recherche Scientifique.

Pipes, Richard, (1990) *The Russian Revolution: 1899–1919*, London: HarperCollins.

Pirandello, Luigi (1985) *Six Characters in Search of an Author*, in *Three Plays*, trans. John Linstrum, London: Methuen.

Pitches, Jonathan (2000) 'Theatre, Science and the Spirit of the Time: Towards a Physics of Performance', in *Theatre Theories from Plato to Virtual Reality*, ed. Anthony Frost, Norwich: Pen and Inc.

—— (2003) *Vsevolod Meyerhold*, London: Routledge.

—— and Shrubsall, Anthony (1997) 'Two Perspectives on the Phenomenon of Biomechanics in Contemporary Performance: an Account of Gogol's *Government Inspector* in Production', *Studies in Theatre Production*, No. 16, 93–128.

—— (1999) 'Atmosphere, Space, Stasis: Staging Pinter's *A Kind of Alaska* and *Mountain Language* Using the Techniques of Michael Chekhov', *Studies in Theatre Production*, No. 19, 36–66.

Plato (1970) *The Laws*, trans. Trevor J. Saunders, London: Penguin.

—— (1971) *Timaeus and Critias*, trans. Desmond Lee, London: Penguin.

—— (1987) *The Republic*, trans. Desmond Lee, London: Penguin.

Polyakova, Elena (1977) *Stanislavsky*, trans. Liv Tudge, Moscow: Progress.

Poplawski, Thomas (1998) *Eurythmy: Rhythm, Dance and Soul*, Edinburgh: Floris Books.

Pursell, Caroll (1994) *Whiteheat*, London: BBC Books.

Rayfield, Donald (1998) 'Chekhov's Lasting Challenge', *The Times Higher Education Supplement*, 5 September, 24.

Reputations (1997) *Lee Strasberg: Method Man*, produced and directed by Clare Beavan: BBC.

Ribot, Théodule (1911) *The Psychology of the Emotions*, London: Walter Scott.

Roach, Joseph R. (1993) *The Player's Passion*, Michigan: University of Michigan Press.

Roberts, J.W. (1981) *Richard Boleslavski: His Life and Work in the Theatre*, Michigan: UMI Research Press.

Rudnitsky, Konstantin (1981) *Meyerhold The Director*, trans. George Petrov, Ann Arbor: Ardis.

—— (1988) *Russian and Soviet Theatre*, trans. Roxane Permar, London: Thames and Hudson.

Russell, Robert and Barratt, Andrew (eds) (1990) *Russian Theatre in the Age of Modernism*, London: Macmillan.

Sarlós, Robert Károly (1982) *Jig Cook and the Provincetown Players: Theatre in Ferment*, Amhurst: University of Massachusetts Press.

Sayler, Oliver M. (1923) *The Russian Theatre*, London: Brentano's Ltd.

Schmidt, Paul (ed.) (1996) *Meyerhold at Work*, New York: Applause.

Schuler, Catherine (1996) *Women in Russian Theatre: The Actress in the Silver Age*, London: Routledge.

Segel, Harold B. (1979/1993) *Twentieth Century Russian Drama*, Baltimore: Johns Hopkins University Press.

Senelick, Laurence (1981) 'Stanislavsky's Double "Life in Art"', in *Theatre Survey*, Vol. 22, No. 2, 201–211.

—— (ed.) (1992) *Wandering Stars: Russian Emigré Theatre 1905–1940*, Iowa: University of Iowa Press.

—— (1997) *The Chekhov Theatre: a Century of the Plays in Performance*, Cambridge: Cambridge University Press.

Sepper, Dennis L. (1988) *Goethe Contra Newton: Polemics and the Project for a New Science of Colour*, Cambridge: Cambridge University Press.

Shakespeare, William (1989) *Hamlet*, ed. Harold Jenkins, London: Methuen.

Shakh-Aziziova, Tatyana (1994) 'Chekhov in Chekhov's Year', unpublished lecture at the Nikitska Gate Theatre, 16 June.

Shepherd, A.P. (1983) *A Scientist of the Invisible*, Edinburgh: Floris Books.

Sherrington, Charles (1949) *Goethe on Nature and on Science*, Cambridge: Cambridge University Press.

Shklovsky, Viktor (1965) 'Art as Technique', in *Russian Formalist Criticism*, eds. Lee T. Lemon and Marion J. Reis, Lincoln: University of Nebraska Press.

Sievers, W. David (1955) *Freud on Broadway: A History of Psychoanalysis and the American Drama*, New York: Hermitage House.

Simonov, P.V. (1962) *The Method of K. S. Stanislavski and the Physiology of Emotion*, Moscow.

Slonim, Marc (1963) *Russian Theater from the Empire to the Soviets*, London: Methuen.

Smeliansky, Anatoly (1991) 'The Last Decade: Stanislavski and Stalinism', trans. Susan Larsen and Elise Thoran, *Theater*, Vol. 12, No. 2, 7–13.

—— (1993) *Is Comrade Bulgakov Dead?*, London: Methuen.

—— (1999) *The Russian Theatre After Stalin*, Cambridge: Cambridge University Press.

Stanislavsky, Constantin (1958) *Stanislavski's Legacy*, trans. Elizabeth Hapgood, London: Max Reinhardt.

—— (1967) *On the Art of the Stage*, trans. David Magarshack, London: Faber.

—— (1979) *Building a Character*, trans. Elizabeth Hapgood, London: Methuen.

—— (1980a) *An Actor Prepares*, trans. Elizabeth Hapgood, London: Methuen.

—— (1980b) *My Life in Art*, trans. J.J. Robbins, London: Methuen.

—— (1981) *Creating a Role*, trans. Elizabeth Hapgood, London: Methuen.

—— (1990) *An Actor's Handbook*, trans. Elizabeth Hapgood, London: Methuen.

Steiner, Rudolf (1928) *The New Art of Education*, London: Anthroposophical Publishing Co.

—— (1942) *Theosophy*, London: Rudolf Steiner Publishing Co.

—— (1959) *Speech and Drama*, trans. Mary Adams, London: Rudolf Steiner Press.

—— (1964) *Knowledge of the Higher Worlds and its Attainment*, California: Health Research.

—— (1973) *Goethe's Conception of the World*, New York: Haskell House.

—— (1984) *The Essential Steiner*, New York: Harper and Row.

—— (1992) *Colour*, trans. John Salter and Pauline Wehrle, Sussex: Rudolf Steiner Press.

—— (1994) *How to Know Higher Worlds*, trans. Christopher Bamford, New York: Anthroposophic Press.

Stevens, Anthony (1991) *On Jung*, London: Penguin.

Stourac, Richard and McCreery, Kathleen (1986) *Theatre as a Weapon: Workers' Theatre in the Soviet Union, Germany and Britain*, London: Routledge and Kegan Paul.

Strasberg, Lee (1988) *A Dream of Passion*, ed. Evangeline Morphos, London: Blooms-
bury.

—— (1991) *Strasberg at the Actors Studio: Tape Recorded Sessions*, ed. Robert H.
Hethmon, New York: Theatre Communications Group.

—— (2002) 'My Russian Notebook, 1934', in *Re:direction: A Theoretical and Practical Guide*, eds. Rebecca Schneider and Gabrielle Cody, London: Routledge.

Strindberg, August (1958) *Three Plays*, trans. Peter Watts, London: Penguin.

—— (1976) *Plays One*, trans. Michael Meyer, London: Methuen.

Stroeva, M.N. (1967) 'The Three Sisters in the Production of the Moscow Art
Theatre', *Chekhov a Collection of Critical Essays*, ed. Robert Jackson, New York:
Prentice Hall.

Styan, J.L. (1971) *Chekhov in Performance*, Cambridge: Cambridge University Press.

—— (1981) *Modern Drama in Theory and Practice 2: Symbolism, Surrealism and the
Absurd*: Cambridge: Cambridge University Press.

Symons, James M. (1971) *Meyerhold's Theatre of the Grotesque: Post Revolutionary Productions, 1920–1932*, Florida: University of Miami Press.

Taylor, Frederick Winslow (1947) *Scientific Management*, New York: Harper and Row.

Toporkov, Vasily Osopovich (1979) *Stanislavski in Rehearsal*, trans. Christine
Edwards, New York: Theatre Arts Books.

Turgenev, Ivan (1983) *A Month in the Country*, trans. Isaiah Berlin, London:
Penguin.

Van Gyseghem, André (1943) *Theatre in Soviet Russia*, London: Faber and Faber.

Van Norman Baer, Nancy (ed.) (1991) *Theatre in Revolution: Russian Stage Design
1913–1935*, London: Thames and Hudson.

Vanden Heuvel, Michael (1993) 'The Politics of the Paradigm: A Case Study in
Chaos Theory', *New Theatre Quarterly*, Vol. IX, No. 35.

Vasiliev, Anatoly (1991) 'In Search of a Method: Anatoly Vasiliev Works on the
Gambler by F.M Dostoyevsky', trans. Annelis Kuhlmann: unpublished transcript
of Masterclass, London, 11–22 September.

—— (1992) 'Theatre as Monastic Community: An Interview with Anatolij Vas-
siliev Conducted by Michael Haerdter', *Theaterschrift*, No. 1, 46–78.

—— (1996) Sections I, II, III, IV and V: unpublished transcripts of International
Workshop Festival Masterclass, trans. Martin Dewhurst, RSAMD, Glasgow,
23–27 September.

—— (1999) 'Directors Talk Shop', Centre for Performance Research, Cardiff, 9 September.

Vineberg, Steve (1991) *Method Actors: Three Generations of an American Acting Style*,
New York: Schirmer Books.

Vucinich, Alexander (1970) *Science in Russian Culture 1861–1917*, Stanford: Stanford
University Press.

Watson, J.B. (1924) *Behaviorism*, Chicago: University of Chicago Press.

Williams, Scott (2000) *Sanford Meisner: the Exercise of Repetition*, Exeter: Arts Documentation Unit (Video).

Wilson, Colin (1985) *Rudolf Steiner: The Man and his Vision*, Wellingborough:
Aquarian Press.

Woodworth, Robert S. and Sheehan, Mary R. (1964) *Contemporary Schools of Psychology*, London: Methuen.

Wordsworth, William and Coleridge, Samuel Taylor (1965) *Lyrical Ballads*, eds
R.L. Brett and A.R. Jones, London: Methuen.

Worrall, Nick (1972) 'Meyerhold directs Gogol's *Government Inspector*', *Theatre Quarterly* No. 2, 75-95.

—— (1996) *The Moscow Art Theatre*, London: Routledge.

Young, Michael (1982) *The Elmhirsts at Dartington: The Creation of an Utopian Community*, London: Routledge and Kegan Paul.

Zarrilli, Phillip (ed.) (1995) *Acting (Re)Considered*, London: Routledge.

Zeami (1984) *On the Art of the No Drama: the Major Treatises of Zeami*, trans. J. Thomas Rimer and Yamazaki Masakazu, Princeton: Princeton University Press.

Zhdanov, Andrei Alexsandrovich *et al.* (1935) *Problems of Soviet Literature: Reports and Speeches at the First Soviet Writer's Congress*, ed. H.G. Scott, London: Martin Lawrence Ltd.

—— (1950) *On Literature, Music and Philosophy*, trans. Eleanor Fox *et al.*, London: Lawrence and Wishart Ltd.

Zinder, David (2002) *Body Voice Imagination: A Training for the Actor*, London: Routledge.

Index

Lightning Source UK Ltd.
Milton Keynes UK
19 January 2011

165967UK00001B/36/P